Sylvia Pankhurst™

Sylvia Pankhurst
Sexual politics and political activism

Barbara Winslow

Foreword by Sheila Rowbotham

VERSO
London • New York

This edition first published by Verso 2021
First published by UCL Press 1996
Reprinted by Routledge 2003
© Barbara Winslow 1996, 2003, 2021
Foreword © Sheila Rowbotham 1996, 2003, 2021

1 3 5 7 9 10 8 6 4 2

Verso
UK: 6 Meard Street, London W1F 0EG
US: 20 Jay Street, Suite 1010, Brooklyn, NY 11201
versobooks.com

Verso is the imprint of New Left Books

ISBN-13: 978-1-83976-162-1
ISBN-13: 978-1-83976-164-5 (US EBK)
ISBN-13: 978-1-83976-163-8 (UK EBK)

British Library Cataloguing in Publication Data
A catalogue record for this book is available from the British Library

Library of Congress Cataloging-in-Publication Data
Names: Winslow, Barbara, 1945– author. | Rowbotham, Sheila, writer of
  introduction.
Title: Sylvia Pankhurst : sexual politics and political activism / Barbara
  Winslow, Medger Evers College, City University of New York ; foreword by
  Sheila Rowbotham.
Description: London ; Brooklyn, NY : Verso, 2021. | Series: Feminist
  classics | 'First published by UCL Press 1996' – Title page verso. |
  Includes bibliographical references and index. | Summary: 'In this
  illuminating political biography, historian Barbara Winslow recovers
  Sylvia Pankhurst's life and work for a new generation of socialists and
  feminists. From Pankhurst's organizing with immigrant and working women
  in London's East End to her revolutionary communism, growing
  internationalism, and committed anti-fascism, Winslow gives us the story
  of a brilliantly inspiring unorthodox feminist and unorthodox
  socialist' – Provided by publisher.
Identifiers: LCCN 2021009125 (print) | LCCN 2021009126 (ebook) | ISBN
  9781839761621 (paperback) | ISBN 9781839761645 (ebk)
Subjects: LCSH: Pankhurst, E. Sylvia (Estelle Sylvia), 1882–1960. |
  Suffragists – Great Britain – Biography. | Feminists – Great
  Britain – Biography.
Classification: LCC HQ1595.P34 W56 2021 (print) | LCC HQ1595.P34 (ebook)
  | DDC 305.42092 [B] – dc23
LC record available at https://lccn.loc.gov/2021009125
LC ebook record available at https://lccn.loc.gov/2021009126

Typeset in Sabon
Printed and bound by CPI Group (UK) Ltd, Croydon CR0 4YY

For Jessie and Samantha

Contents

↩

Foreword

Sheila Rowbotham

A political biography of Sylvia Pankhurst is long overdue. For a figure who made her mark on history first as a suffrage leader and then as a recalcitrant left-wing communist, she has received relatively little serious consideration as a political innovator. Part of the problem has been that the two Sylvia Pankhursts became lodged quite separately in the historical memory. Historians of feminism have focused on the suffrage movement; while labour historians have noted her role in the formation of the Communist Party and her famous dispute with Lenin, in which she was branded an ultra-leftist. Sliced in two, like the lady in the conjurer's box, the whole Sylvia has proved elusive.

Barbara Winslow's biographical examination of her politics, in contrast, spans both periods of Pankhurst's activism and describes in depth the anti-war organizing that connects the two. She tackles head on the paradox in Pankhurst's politics: the shift from the agitation for the vote to a socialist and anti-imperialist commitment, in which gender hardly features. Her account reveals continuities of approach as well as the manner in which force of circumstance was to wrench apart interconnections between socialism and feminism. This study of Sylvia Pankhurst illuminates wider questions, which were to become buried, about how gender and class were being articulated by radicals in the early years of the twentieth century.

Sylvia Pankhurst rejected the feminism that, in the course of the struggle for the vote, her sister Christabel and her mother Emmeline came to adopt. This was a form of feminism that subordinated all other kinds of social oppression to the unequal relationship between men and women. Instead, Sylvia Pankhurst sought to connect the emancipation of women with the emancipation of the working class and the colonial peoples subjected to imperialism. In attempting to combine socialism and feminism, she developed demands that took account of the specific needs of working-class women, which she recognized as distinct from the middle-class women of her own circles who predominated in the suffrage movement. Barbara Winslow demonstrates how Sylvia Pankhurst was to act as the catalyst for the gendered class politics that began to emerge from grass-roots mobilization in London's East End, among women whom most middle-class social reformers assumed were incapable of self-organization.

This divergence from the narrower view of feminism that prevailed in the organization formed by herself, her sister and her mother – the Women's Social and Political Union (WSPU) – was not easy. Not only did it entail a break with her family, it also meant being excluded from the organization for which she had sacrificed her artistic career, her health and her youth. Yet, when Sylvia Pankhurst looked out at the shabby streets around the Old Ford Road, she simply did not see the world in Christabel's Manichaean terms – a world of masculine evil and female victimization. The working-class men who supported the suffrage movement were oppressed too and there were socialist men prepared to struggle for women's rights. Her refusal to break with the labour movement aroused Christabel's fury and led to her expulsion from the WSPU.

There is always an element of mystery in the factors that bring individuals of broadly similar backgrounds to make very different political and personal choices. Barbara Winslow notes Sylvia's admiration for her father, Richard Pankhurst, and her close and loving relationship with Keir Hardie, as well as her political collaboration with George Lansbury in East London.

Sylvia Pankhurst, as a member of the formidable Pankhurst family, was in a high-profile position, but she was not, of course, entirely alone. Many other women struggled to connect feminism and socialism. The emergence of a militant suffrage movement before the First World War created a tactical and theoretical turmoil among socialists of all species. They had to decide whether to go for the limited measure of votes for women on the same terms as men or the wider demand for adult suffrage, which, although more democratic, was arguably unrealistic. This choice between the possible and the principle created numerous splits and disputes in socialist groupings, ranging from Fabians on the right to the Marxist sect of the Socialist Labour Party on the left. The suffrage movement also provoked arguments that went beyond "women's issues": raising the conflicting claims of individual rights and collectivist concepts of society as an organism; the significance of Parliament or of workplace emancipation; and the extent to which political organizations could have a line on all issues and aspects of personal experience.

It was to be the Independent Labour Party (ILP), however, the group to which the Pankhurst family was so closely linked, that was to be most deeply affected by the challenge presented by the women's movement. It was not just the split between the ILP and the WSPU but the impact of feminism within the ILP itself; for when the Pankhursts left some women continued to work from within. Among them were Isabella Ford, a middle-class feminist and socialist ILPer in Leeds who gravitated towards the constitutionalists in the National Union of Women's Suffrage Societies (NUWSS) and worked for a labour suffrage alliance when Christabel was denouncing the labour movement.

The choices were not easy; individual women can be seen oscillating between strategies and between loyalties in the pre-war period. For working-class women the lived experience of class and gender made organizational options more complex. For instance, Selina Cooper, a Lancashire working woman and socialist, was involved with the NUWSS but aware of the class gulf between her and its middle-class leaders. Hannah Mitchell, a working-class housewife, grew impatient with socialist men who talked of equality and yet still waited imperiously for their teas to be made. She joined the Women's Social and Political Union, only to be disillusioned by the ruthless leadership style of Emmeline and Christabel. It was her socialism that gave her an alternative vision. The Independent Labour Party, which had shaped her politics, regarded the socialist cause not simply as about an external change in society but also as an inward change of heart that affected relationships between individuals.

In contrast, the militancy of the WSPU propelled it away from attempts to form alliances with the labour movement, and away from the ethical and utopian strands in the socialism of the ILP, which emphasized the transformation of daily life and human relationships. Two very different organizational models were at issue, and not simply feminism versus socialism. Christabel, contemptuous of sentiment, saw an organization as a weapon concentrated on a goal – not as a process of collective growth and individual development. Moreover, the increasing emphasis in the WSPU on the *interests* of women as a sex was very different from the mainstream ILP's organic approach to socialism as a vision of society that transcended particular interests.

The openness and pragmatism of the ILP meant that it was able to interact with conflicting political currents. Immediately before the First World War there were left-wingers who had become increasingly disillusioned with the power of Parliament and were ready to listen to some of the syndicalist calls for direct action. The syndicalists stressed class conflict; they too presented a view of politics as a clash of clear-cut interests. Unlike Christabel, however, they saw class, not gender, as the key. In practice, too, their belief that the workplace was the main site of struggle tended to emphasize the better-organized male-dominated forms of employment. Nonetheless, despite the apparent divorce, feminism and syndicalism had an impact on each other. For there was, in this syndicalist-influenced Left, a respect for militant action and an idea that learning came from doing. This was the point of contact between syndicalism and left-feminists who were caught between an unresponsive political establishment and a militant feminism that dismissed class. This shared rebellion makes Sylvia Pankhurst's political trajectory more comprehensible.

Sylvia Pankhurst, as Barbara Winslow shows, had shifted towards a socialism committed to direct action by 1914. However, far from endorsing a pure syndicalism, she still retained a recognition of a need to negotiate with the state in order to secure legislation and resources. She also hangs on to a utopianism that is rooted in the ILP and the earlier Socialist League of William Morris. She wanted not only a redistribution of wealth but to transform the circumstances of work and daily life in communities.

Barbara Winslow shows how in the difficult years of the First World War Sylvia struggled with these diverse political influences to create a unique form of local community organizing. It becomes apparent reading her account that the very differing influences all contribute to the extraordinary political creativity of the socialist suffrage movement in East London. Sylvia Pankhurst sought to mobilize at the grass roots and to influence Parliament to pass laws to meet the practical problems faced by East London working-class women. Always aware of immediate needs, she pitted herself against the top-down welfare that Liberals and some sections of the labour movement endorsed as part of the war effort. She tried to institute her own democratic alternatives of workplace and community control over basic needs such as food, housing and the conditions of mothering; becoming embroiled, as Barbara Winslow points out, in those messy details that so frequently thwart utopian islands in the world-as-it-is – lack of money and human venality. These meant, however, that hers was not simply a politics of opposition, which was a strong tendency in the syndicalist Left. She kept a vision of what-might-be in her prefigurative communal projects.

Her attempt to short-circuit the state occurred moreover when a tremendous division appeared within the socialist movement about how to approach the state because of the First World War. Opposition ranged from ethical socialists and religious groups such as the Quakers, who were anti-militarist on moral grounds, to revolutionary leftists like Sylvia who opposed the capitalist war. Those sections of the labour movement that went along with the war, including women trade union organizers, were to be increasingly incorporated with the new machinery of consultation and regulation that Lloyd George established. In contrast, the isolated minority who opposed the war were very wary of the coercive aspects of the state's intervention that they could see happening around them. The wartime government evicted shop stewards from their workplaces and set up a web of intelligence agents and provocateurs who tracked down feminist pacifists and munitions workers alike. The authorities established military curfews, raided houses on suspicion of prostitution, arrested couples who were making love in parks. To those who were against the war such as Sylvia Pankhurst, welfare seemed merely to be a sop to soften the Leviathan powers of a capitalist state. On the other hand, Sylvia was all too aware of the bad conditions of women at work, which required regulation, or of the needs of soldiers' dependants for state allowances. Her political demands consequently reveal a constant tension between the working-class women's needs for state resources and her political abhorrence of the extension of control into daily life that was being justified by the wartime coalition.

Sylvia Pankhurst tried to overcome the dichotomies of class and gender, direct grass-roots action and representative democracy, statism and anti-statism not as a theorist but as an activist. She was forced to think on her feet, responding as issues arose, and she had to move quickly because new circumstances were coming at her all the time. Caught in the political and social maelstrom of the First World War and its aftermath, she was unable to work through many of the insights that came tumbling in from practical human needs she confronted and from the overpowering inspiration of the Russian Revolution. Aware of the necessity to control food prices and the distribution of provision because of wartime inflation and scarcities, she could also see the limits of the emphasis upon the workplace in the soviets. Her idea of social soviets, as Barbara Winslow explains, was an attempt to extend direct forms of democracy into communities to include women and others who were not in paid employment.

She was not alone in the realization that the direct democracy of the workplace soviets excluded people in the community. There was unease in the shop stewards' movement about this. Indeed, it soon inclined many of the leaders of the shop stewards to Lenin's theories and the Communist Party, which appeared to have overcome the limits of syndicalism. The cost was to be the subordination of the direct expression of democracy to the authority of the single party and the suppression of individual rights through the invocation of a collective, the party or the soviet state.

Barbara Winslow shows how Sylvia Pankhurst's attempts to socialize the basic necessities of consumption were part of the wider libertarian impulse in socialism, which was tragically defeated. In this lost political strand, both an insistence on democracy and an effort to extend class consciousness can be seen. Rosa Luxemburg, inspired by the mass strikes that appeared in several European cities before and during the First World War, struggled to theorize an alternative to Lenin's view of the party. These communal uprisings united workers and women in the working-class neighbourhoods; rebellion was not only about the conditions of work but also about consumption. Women came out onto the streets and met in the market place and the courts of apartment blocks. They operated a particular kind of women's movement, which Temma Kaplan has described as "female consciousness" – demanding not political equality with men but access to resources as women in the working class. Similarly in the United States, Canada and Mexico in the same period, inflation provoked a series of rebellions of poor women over the price of food and housing.

Sylvia Pankhurst's community action and the rent strikes in Glasgow and other British towns were thus part of a wider pattern of resistance that was linking work and community in the early twentieth century and in which women played a prominent part. Unlike feminism, which claimed individual rights, these movements based their demands on collective social needs.

The struggle for the social wage did not entirely disappear between the wars – it did however go into somewhat different channels. Barbara Winslow points out that several of the women who had been active with Sylvia Pankhurst in this kind of gendered class politics became involved in the historic battle in local government to get the richer boroughs in London to help pay for poor relief in working-class areas. The focus turns to the state and politics to legitimate redistribution. Access to social resources was not just a woman's issue but it had gendered class significance because of the role of working-class women in the family. The impetus of this important movement among labour women between the wars was, however, for reform within existing society not for the revolutionary transformation in which Sylvia Pankhurst believed. However, her conflict with the leaders of the new Communist Party meant she was to be at odds with the organized revolutionary Left as well. Isolated and ostracized, Sylvia Pankhurst's particular contribution, the linking of class and gender through a vision of democratic community, faltered in the 1920s. Confined to narrow paths, she retained her political purity but lost the breadth and complexity of her more hopeful years. Barbara Winslow shows nonetheless that Sylvia Pankhurst's politics opens up a series of possibilities, which were valuable even though they were not realized in practice.

This political biography spreads beyond one country for Sylvia Pankhurst was an internationalist long before the dramatic events in Russia made her a world figure. Ideas passed between countries, and forms of action were taken over and transplanted. For instance, Barbara Winslow shows that Sylvia Pankhurst investigated radical experiments in local government in the United States as well as Hull House in Chicago formed by Jane Addams. Hull House had in turn drawn on the East London settlement, Toynbee Hall, formed by Leonard Montefiore after a visit to nineteenth-century utopian communities in the United States. The interconnecting forms of social action in communities are paralleled by the crossing over of ideas of social unionism before the First World War. Elizabeth Gurley Flynn and Margaret Sanger's work with women and children during the Lawrence textile strike in Massachusetts is comparable to the attempt to rescue strikers' children during the Dublin lockout. There was also of course the dockers' strike of 1910 in Britain when Jewish anarchists in the East End had provided homes and sustenance for the children of the dockers, who were often suspicious and prejudiced against the Jewish immigrants fleeing from the pogroms. In these strikes the boundaries of class, gender and ethnicity were to be transcended through solidarity.

Barbara Winslow demonstrates that Sylvia Pankhurst's links with Ireland through James Connolly, the leader of the Easter Rising of 1916, were of crucial significance. It was James Connolly's execution by the British that hardened the division between the revolutionary left-wing opposition and the wartime coalition government. This connection also makes Sylvia Pankhurst's intransigence towards the Labour Party more understandable.

During the First World War Sylvia Pankhurst also found herself in an uneasy alliance with constitutionalists in the suffrage movement who had once been her formal rivals because of their stand against the war. She was thus to be involved in the internationalist, feminist, pacifist and anti-war campaigns that were a vital part of the opposition to the war. Characteristically, she was aligned with the move to democratize foreign diplomacy, which brought together radicals and Liberals in the First World War. Her internationalism led her to be more aware of racism and anti-imperialism than her contemporaries on the British Left. Barbara Winslow describes how the Caribbean poet, Claude McKay, who was part of the Harlem Renaissance in the United States, pays tribute to her in his autobiography.

Sylvia Pankhurst was thus both an innovator at the micro-level of local politics and a figure capable of taking on the big issues of foreign policy and imperial rule. She emerges from this study as a politician of extraordinary scope.

However, this is not a political biography about tidy philosophical concepts, but an account of a woman whose ideas were expressed through action. Sylvia Pankhurst continued to pursue the revolutionary vision of 1917. She was one of those optimists of the will who continue to sell their version of the truth on cold street corners while the world passes by about its business. Inevitably the call to rebel tends to grow strident from ceaseless and futile repetition and the very refusal to accommodate is in danger of stiffening into a crusty eccentricity. Sylvia Pankhurst did not escape these perils of a commitment to an unrealized political ideal. There are signs too in later life of the Pankhurst hauteur turning into an inner arrogance of spirit that drove even sympathizers away from her. Great democrats can be personally overbearing and principles of equality can be propounded in a stiff-necked and authoritarian manner.

Barbara Winslow tells her story, however, not as a personal tragedy but as a vital legacy for the contemporary endeavour to create a feminism that connects gender to the oppressions of class, race and ethnicity. The politics of Sylvia Pankhurst also intimates a socialism yet to be realized, a socialism in which the rights of the individual and a combination of direct and representative democracy are inseparable from the struggle against exploitation and all forms of social injustice.

Preface

On trial in November 1920 for publishing seditious articles in her newspaper, *Workers' Dreadnought,* Sylvia Pankhurst defended herself:

> Because I had been a suffragette and had fought for the cause of women, the women came to me and asked me to help them. I had dying babies brought to me. I had to start clinics and find accommodations for people whose fathers were fighting for the capitalists' government of the country. I used to sit up all night writing, begging for money for these people. We had good families of people coming to my house without a penny and with six or seven children, and I opened two penny restaurants where you could get two penny meals. These expenses used to pass through my hands; I used to spend a hundred and fifty pounds a week on that. But I know it is all palliatives; it will not do any good really; I want to change the system; I am going to fight it if it kills me.[1]

The magistrate, Sir Alfred Newton, was not impressed and sentenced her to five months' hard labour. This was by no means the first time she had stood trial for her politics. Between 1906 and 1914 she had been arrested and jailed nine times for her militant suffrage activities.

Throughout her life Sylvia Pankhurst was a feminist, an internationalist, a socialist and a champion of the oppressed. Her international socialist stature was such that she could challenge even Lenin's vision of communism. She constantly fought the British government, opposing imperialism and particularly supporting the struggles for

African and Indian independence.

Though Sylvia Pankhurst's role in the suffrage movement is well known, her significance as an organizational innovator who created political connections between gender and class and struggled to foster the grass roots of socialist democracy has been neglected by historians.[2] Sylvia Pankhurst did more than just play a significant role in the suffrage and communist movements. She put both socialist and feminist theory into practice by building a working women's suffrage and community organization. From 1912 to 1924 she lived and worked in the East End of London. Her East London Federation of the Suffragettes (ELFS) demanded far more than votes for women: it fought for day-care centres, better housing, the socialization of housework, inexpensive but good public restaurants, decent medical care, free milk for children, unionization of women workers, and equal pay for equal work.

Sylvia Pankhurst saw her organizations – the ELFS, the Workers' Suffrage Federation (WSF) and the Workers' Socialist Federation (WSF) – in contrast to the other women's suffrage organizations, as part of the labour and socialist movements. In this respect, her work challenged the feminism of many of the other organizers for women's suffrage. Pankhurst and the East London Federation fought not just for one political reform on behalf of a select group of women but for full social, political and economic emancipation.

It is difficult to write about Sylvia Pankhurst. She was exciting, courageous, dogmatic, unpredictable, demanding, inconsistent and complicated. She does not fit neatly into a particular feminist or socialist apostolic succession. Her life, her work and her role in the socialist, labour and feminist movements are not only historically fascinating but very relevant today. Pankhurst built two different types of organization: one, a feminist organization rooted in the working-class district of London's East End; the other, a revolutionary socialist organization open to men and women but led by women. Many of the women of the ELFS and WSF, like Pankhurst, remained active in and leaders of the future struggles of the socialists, unemployed, trade unionists and anti-fascists. Pamkhurst was a woman battling not only the injustices of capitalism, but often the male chauvinism and elitism of her comrades. She grappled with problems of theory, tactics and direction that today's women's movement also faces: How and in what ways may a women's movement be divided along class lines?

What is the relationship between feminism and peace? How can the struggle for women's liberation and socialism be reconciled?

Sylvia Pankhurst is a link between the socialist movement of the late nineteenth century – the world of Friedrich Engels, Edward Carpenter, Eleanor Marx, Louise Michel, William Morris – and the twentieth-century working-class politics of Alexandra Kollontai, Lenin, James Connolly, Rosa Luxemburg, Nicholai Bukharin, and Antonio Gramsci. Sylvia was also a pioneer in connecting feminism and socialism – in particular with her discussion of the social soviets. She exposed the narrow class bias of the middle-class suffrage organizations, thus questioning their concept of feminism. She was equally a challenge to the male chauvinism of the socialist Left, which dismissed or ignored women's struggles, whether for the vote, equal pay or sexual freedom. Perhaps because her theory was expressed through activity rather than writing, she paid the price of being neglected by both socialist and feminist historians. Recognition of her contribution to socialist and feminist theory and action is long overdue.

Acknowledgements

It has taken me 25 years to write this book. I began work on it when I was a student at the University of Washington in Seattle. I was taking a course on twentieth-century Britain from Dr Giovanni Costigan and one of our required readings was George Dangerfield's *The strange death of liberal England*. As an activist in the women's liberation movement, I fell in love with the Pankhurst family and in particular with Sylvia. She was a militant, radical woman who organized working-class women, opposed the First World War, turned pubs into day-care centres, and debated with Lenin on communism. I had to learn more. While a graduate student of E. P. Thompson's at the Centre for the Study of Social History at the University of Warwick, I did an MA thesis on the East London Federation of the Suffragettes and then at the University of Washington in Seattle I completed a PhD dissertation on Sylvia Pankhurst's political work in the East End of London.

Subsequent events in my life such as full-time motherhood, full-time politics and full-time work kept me from finishing my book on Sylvia. But constant pressure, prodding and reassurance from family and friends enabled me finally to complete it.

Five people were instrumental in the evolution of this book: Stephanie Golden, an extraordinary writer, editor and friend, turned my first dissertation draft into a coherent manuscript; Lucia Jones and I were students together at Warwick, she too wrote an MA thesis on Pankhurst. We travelled together to Amsterdam to read the Pankhurst Papers at the International Institute for Social History. We shared not only cramped quarters but ideas as well. For 25 years

Sheila Rowbotham gently prodded me to finish the book – she gave me much needed editorial and political suggestions, pointing out all the various "connections" of Sylvia's radicalism to other activists and thinkers, and she reminded me of my occasional sectarian lapses. Wilhelmena Schreuder at the International Institute for Social History in Amsterdam helped me go through the Pankhurst Papers on several occasions. She also corrected sections of my manuscript. Finally, the book could not have been completed without the help of Joan Smith. For many years, I was unable to work out my own ideas about Pankhurst's political contributions to socialist–feminist theory. Joan's friendship and collaboration enabled me to develop and deepen this work.

Thanks are due to the librarians at the British Library of Political and Economic Sciences, London, the British Museum, the Fawcett Library, the International Institute for Social History, Amsterdam, the London Museum, the Marx Memorial Library, the National Library, Dublin, and the National Library of Scotland, to Elspeth King, to The People's Palace, Glasgow, and to the Trades Union Congress House, London, and the Williams College Library, Williamstown, Massachusetts.

I would like to thank Paul Avrich, Roz Baxandall, Alden Bell, Carol Berkin, Eileen Boris, Ian Bullock, Dina Copelman, Jill Craigie, Anna Davin, Candace Falk, Deborah Gardner, June Hannam, Dorothy Helly, Sandra Holton, Jill Liddington, Temma Kaplan, Jane Marcus, Richard Pankhurst, Barry Pateman, Kirsty Reid, Carolyn Stevens, Dorothy Thompson, E. P. Thompson and Ken Weller for all the comments, criticisms and assistance they gave me over the years. Alex Burgo translated Italian into English.

Certain people lent me their homes: Penny McCallum in Glasgow, Judith Condon, Laurie Flynn and Claire and Roland Muldoon in London. Bette Craig and Chuck Portz gave me their beautiful farmhouse in Williamstown, Massachusetts, where I was able to finish one draft of the manuscript.

I also wish to thank my family, Eugenia Ames, Deborah Larkin, Luella LaMer Slaner and Alfred Slaner for all their support and encouragement.

Michelle Aluqdah, Darcy Cobb, Glenn King, Lisa Miller and Verne Moberg, gave invaluable technical assistance to me, for I am a technical Luddite! Cate MacPherson at UCL Press and Liz Paton helped me with the final technical corrections and changes. Finally, I owe thanks to my extended family – my friends who bore with me as I agonized and enthused over the book and encouraged me at every page and endnote of the way: Jacalyn Barnett, Marjorie Fine, Roberta Faulstick, Paula Gellman, Judith Kaufer, Jesse Lemisch, Molly Nolan, Ron Napal, Margit Reiner, Neil Smith and Tony Vigilante (who helped me with my footnotes).

Barbara Winslow

List of organizations

ASE Amalgamated Society of Engineers
BSP British Socialist Party
CGT Confederation Generale des Travailleurs (General Confederation of Laborers)
CLP Communist Labour Party
CP(BSTI) Communist Party – British section of the Third International
CPGB Communist Party of Great Britain
ELFS East London Federation of the Suffragettes
ELFS/WSPU East London Federation of the Suffragettes/Women's Social and Political Union
ETU Electrical Trade Union
ILP Independent Labour Party
ISEL Industrial Syndicalist Education League
IWW Industrial Workers of the World
KAPD Kommunistische Arbeiterpartei Deutschlands (Communist Workers' Party of Germany)
KPD Kommunistische Partei Deutschlands (Communist Party of Germany)
LCC London County Council
LRC Labour Representation Committee
LWC London Workers' Committee
MNSWS Manchester National Society for Women's Suffrage
NCF No-Conscription Fellowship
NSWS National Society for Women's Suffrage

NESWS	North of England Society of Women's Suffrage
NFDDSS	National Federation of Discharged and Demobilised Soldiers and Sailors
NFWW	National Federation of Women Workers
NTWF	National Transport Workers' Federation
NUR	National Union of Railwaymen
NUWCM	National Unemployment Workers' Committee Movement
NUWSS	National Union of Women's Suffrage Societies
NUX	National Union of Ex-Servicemen
PRIB	People's Russian Information Bureau
RTSSC	River Thames Shipbuilders and Ship-Repairers' Committee
SDF	Social Democratic Federation
SLP	Socialist Labour Party
SSAU	Soldiers', Sailors', and Airmen's Union
SSWCM	Shop Stewards' and Workers' Committee Movement
SWSS	South Wales Socialist Society
TUC	Trades Union Congress
UWO	Unemployed Workers' Organisation
WEC	War Emergency Committee (War Emergency Workers' National Committee)
WLEWC	West London Engineers Workers' Committee
WFL	Women's Freedom League
WILPF	Women's International League for Peace and Freedom
WSF	Workers' Socialist Federation (1918–20)
WSF	Workers' Suffrage Federation (1916–18)
WSPU	Women's Social and Political Union

Chapter One

Early influences

The origins of Sylvia Pankhurst's socialist feminism are rooted in her family's activities in the Lancashire women's rights and suffrage movement as well as in the emerging socialist and labour movement.[1] Her father, Richard Pankhurst, and mother, Emmeline Goulden, had been political activists who were moving away from the Liberal Party and towards the socialism of the Independent Labour Party (ILP), which stood for, among many things, independent political activity of the working class. Both were supporters of women's rights and by the 1890s had grown impatient at the state of the women's suffrage movement and the refusal of the Liberal government to campaign for women's suffrage.

Pankhurst, born in 1882, her older sister Christabel, born in 1880, and her younger sister, Adela born in 1885, were expected to help their parents organize meetings or "salons". A brother, Harry, was born in 1889. In the 1890s the Pankhurst circle was reading *Fabian essays*, published by the newly formed Fabian society, as well as Edward Bellamey's *Looking backward*, Prince Kropotkin's *Fields, factories, and workshops,* and Robert Blatchford's *Merrie England.* This literature was fundamentally non-Marxist, anti-industrial, utopian and romantic. It nonetheless became the basis for Pankhurst's later communism.

The Pankhurst home became a meeting place for intellectuals and activists from around the world – socialists, anarchists, radicals, republicans, feminists, atheists and freethinkers. This political atmosphere also contributed to Pankhurst's later socialist–feminism. The revolutionary artist and founder of the Socialist League, William Morris, was a constant visitor and became one of Pankhurst's earliest heroes. Artistically, he exerted a great influence on her, as is evident in her later suffrage drawings and designs, and his political influence was reflected in her later visionary non-industrialized communalism. In her parents' home she also met Tom Mann, an internationally known trade union leader. Thirty years later they both would be founding members of different communist parties.

Pankhurst was also acquainted with the women political radicals of the day. She met Annie Besant, a leader of the London match girls' strike, freethinker, birth control advocate and sexual radical. Harriot Stanton Blatch, daughter of Elizabeth Cady Stanton, was also an ardent feminist, a member of the Women's Franchise League, and one of the Pankhurst's closest friends. Pankhurst was particularly fascinated with Louise Michel, an anarchist–feminist leader of the 1871 Paris Commune.

In the summer of 1898 Pankhurst was at her adored father's bedside when he died from a perforated ulcer. She was overcome with grief, and spent the rest of her life trying to live by one of his many admonitions: "If you do not work for others you will not have been worth the upbringing."[2]

After Richard Pankhurst's death, Emmeline took on part-time paid employment and continued her involvement with ILP politics. Christabel continued her education on the Continent. Pankhurst decided to become an artist. She won a prestigious scholarship to the Municipal School of Art in Manchester and then in 1901 was awarded the Lady Whitworth Scholarship for that year's best woman student. At 14 she had spent nine months in Venice to study mosaic and fresco painters. Her experiences in Italy only strengthened her early commitment to social equality. Her Italian sojourn clearly influenced her later decision to give up being an artist to become a political activist: "What I saw of the nobility, whose society my compatriot [a Miss Newitt] dearly prized, did but heighten my desire for a new social order, and for a better status for women."[3]

Pankhurst returned home to Manchester to help her mother run a business while Christabel started law school at Owens College, also in Manchester. Circumstances were changing in the Pankhurst family. In 1901, while attending a college lecture, Christabel met Eva Gore-Booth, the daughter of aristocratic Anglo-Irish landowners, and Esther Roper, a middle-class daughter of a manufacturing family. In 1897 both women founded the North of England Women's Suffrage

Society (NEWSS), which was one of the 16 affiliates of the National Union of Women's Suffrage Societies (NUWSS), the established women's suffrage organization founded in 1897 by Millicent Garrett Fawcett. The NEWSS differed from the NUWSS in that it sought membership primarily from working-class women. Gore-Booth and Roper were also involved in the trade union movement and in the ILP.

From 1901 to 1904 Christabel became a political protégé of Roper and Gore-Booth, speaking at public meetings, going to factories, collecting petitions and serving in numerous trade union organizations. Emmeline was becoming re-energized, although Pankhurst claims that her mother's jealousy over Christabel's personal friendships and political activities prompted a renewed interest in the campaign for women's suffrage.

By 1903 Emmeline and Christabel were moving away from the political ideals of Richard Pankhurst. In that year the ILP erected a building that was to be dedicated to Richard Pankhurst. While working on the decorations of the hall, Pankhurst discovered that women were not allowed to join this particular branch of the ILP because it was affiliated to a social club open to men who were not all members of the ILP. Women were not allowed in that social club and therefore not allowed in that ILP branch. The Pankhurst women were outraged that a hall dedicated to the man who had devoted his life to women's equality would be maintained by an organization that did not allow women to join.

Then, to add insult to already smarting injury, Phillip Snowden, then on the executive board of the ILP, announced at a meeting in Pankhurst Hall that he actively opposed women's suffrage. Christabel refused to speak to him; Emmeline openly declared she had wasted her time in the ILP and announced she wanted nothing more to do with labour representation until women's issues were taken seriously.[4]

It was in response to what Emmeline and Christabel perceived as indifferent and hostile attitudes by much of the male leadership of the socialist and labour movement that on 10 October 1903 half a dozen women members from the ILP met at the Pankhurst home to found a group initially called the Labour Representation Committee. Christabel thought the name too clumsy and, since it was already the name of a women's textile organization founded by Roper and Gore-Booth, she suggested the name be the Women's Social and Political Union (WSPU).

As Emmeline and Christabel began to devote themselves to the WSPU, Pankhurst realized they could manage without her. In 1904 she won a scholarship to the Royal College of Art in London. She helped found the Fulham branch of the WSPU in 1905, attended women's suffrage meetings in London, lobbied Parliament, and even gave an occasional speech.

While she was struggling with her art in London, the fledgling WSPU was looking for a new political direction. It held meetings, attracted some new women, most of whom were affiliated to the ILP, and asked prospective candidates for local office to state their attitudes on women's suffrage. In 1905 Pankhurst, along with her mother and other members of the WSPU, went to Parliament to see if a women's suf-frage bill allowing women to run for local elections would reach the floor of the House of Commons. Over 300 women were at first disappointed then furious while Members of Parliament laughed and cheered at anti-suffrage speeches. At the end of the parliamentary session Emmeline Pankhurst called upon the women to follow her outside to demonstrate and protest against the government. Emmeline Pankhurst believed that "[t]his was the first militant act of the WSPU".[5]

In the summer of 1905 Pankhurst left London to campaign for the WSPU in Lancashire. She was 22 years old and fully committed to the socialism of the ILP, to women's suffrage and to the issues of feminism. The early influences of her family and the political development in the north of England led Pankhurst to develop her unique commitment to working-class feminism.

Another factor that was instrumental in Sylvia Pankhurst's political development was her relationship with Keir Hardie.[6] Their friendship and later love affair developed Pankhurst's attitudes towards love, marriage and sexuality as well as her political commitment to socialism and feminism. The relationship with Hardie also affected Pankhurst's relationship with her mother and sister. To Pankhurst, Hardie was a friend, father figure and mentor, as well as a lover, and their relationship, which lasted from 1904 to 1913 or 1914, strengthened her political convictions and activism. It enabled her to stand up to her mother and Christabel as they not only broke from socialist politics but also turned on her.

James Keir Hardie played a central role in the creation of a politically independent labour movement in Britain. A founding member of the Independent Labour Party (ILP), he was the first Labour Party representative in Parliament.[7] Born in 1856, Keir Hardie was the illegitimate son of a working-class Scotswoman, Mary Keir, who later married an often-unemployed, drunken seaman named David Hardie. Poverty characterized his boyhood; at the age of 8 he went to work in the coal mines. As a young man, he was a union organizer and labour journalist.

Hardie became a close friend and political ally of Richard and Emmeline Pankhurst as a result of their common political commitments to the ILP in the 1890s. After Richard Pankhurst's death, Hardie remained friendly with Mrs Pankhurst and stayed close until the schism between the WSPU and the ILP made the friendship impossible to sustain. Pankhurst also considered him a friend and looked forward to his visits to the Pankhurst home. He was one of the earliest and staunchest supporters of the WSPU.

Hardie had an unconventional marriage to Lily Wilson and had one daughter, Nan. He and his wife lived apart for most of their marriage, and when Hardie was elected to Parliament in 1900, Lily did not move to London with him. Hardie claimed to be a strict teetotaller and Calvinist and led a very austere life while serving as an MP. But he did have a number of affairs with other women. Before becoming involved with Pankhurst, he had been intimate with a Welsh woman, Annie Hines. It was even rumoured in socialist circles that he was having an affair with Emmeline, when in fact he was beginning his relationship with Pankhurst.

In an unpublished short story of 1932, Pankhurst wrote about an older man – clearly Hardie – who had been duped into a loveless marriage with a woman who claimed to share his interests. Another woman – much younger and clearly Sylvia Pankhurst – falls in love with him, but refuses to become sexually involved until she is convinced his is a marriage in name only. The young woman's mother believes that the Hardie character is in love with *her* and becomes furious with her daughter when she finds out otherwise. This story is of course fiction, but its picture of sexual rivalry between mother and daughter is clearly one way in which Pankhurst dealt with her mother's later renunciation of her.[8]

Pankhurst renewed her friendship with Hardie in 1904 when she moved to London to become an art student. At some point it developed into an intimate relationship. Hardie may have been the first man with whom Pankhurst had sexual relations; certainly none of her writings gives any indication that she had other sexual encounters. She was not particularly straitlaced, coming as she did from a family of sexual radicals; she had read the literature of sexual radicalism and was especially influenced by the ideas of Walt Whitman and Edward Carpenter. She also had been moved by novels that dealt with the plight of young unmarried women who have affairs with married and older men.[9]

Her two closest friends in London were Keir Hardie and her brother Harry. Hardie took the two young Pankhursts under his wing, inviting them to his flat in Nevill's Court and taking them to lunch, dinner, or Parliament. He also began seeing Pankhurst alone. She wrote that the friendship began with "rambles in the weald of Kent" and visits to his apartment.[10] She was fascinated with every detail of his life, including his austere apartment, decorated with engravings of an 1867 franchise demonstration and portraits of Walt Whitman, Robert Burns and William Morris. Hardie kept a picture of Pankhurst over his mantle and two of her paintings on the wall. His taste in reading paralleled hers: Shelley, Byron, William Morris, Scott, Shakespeare and Walt Whitman, although Robert Burns was his favourite. Both read the "modern" writers, such as Ibsen, Anatole France, Galsworthy and Shaw.[11] The two became devoted companions, sharing secrets, for example, about their childhoods. Hardie confided to Pankhurst that he was illegitimate, something that pained him deeply;[12] while professing many radical ideas about love and marriage, Hardie himself was conventional in many respects, and illegitimacy was not conventional. He also knew that if such information became general knowledge it could hurt him politically: legitimacy, although perhaps not important to some socialists and sexual radicals, was very important to the working class.

Convention meant so much to Hardie that he never left his wife to marry Pankhurst. Although their affair was known in some circles, they were not public lovers. General knowledge of their affair would have hurt Hardie politically. If Pankhurst was saddened, disappointed or angered at Hardie's refusal to marry her, or to put her first in his affections publicly, she never mentioned it in her writings. Nor did she ever write about the complications and contradictions of having an affair with a married man.

Hardie helped all the Pankhursts launch the WSPU but worked most closely with Sylvia Pankhurst. Her relationship with him created friction between her and her mother and sister. Whether or not sexual jealousy was involved in this friction, there was at this time growing disagreement among the Pankhursts over the question of whether or not to work with the Labour Party and with men. With some justification, Christabel wrote in the *ILP News* (in August 1903) that socialists could not be counted on as allies in the struggle for women's rights. "Some day when they are in power, and have nothing better to do, they will give women votes as a finishing touch to their arrangements." She ended the article declaring, "Why are women expected to have such confidence in the men of the Labour Party? Working men are just as unjust to women as are those of other classes."[13] In 1906, the WSPU severed its ties with the ILP, and in 1907 both Christabel and Emmeline resigned from the organization.

As the suffragette campaign escalated after 1910, Emmeline and Christabel Pankhurst, well aware that the leadership of the Labour Party was indifferent, if not hostile, to the women's suffrage movement, came to see men – especially men in the Labour Party and working-class men – as the enemy. There may have been another underlying personal/sexual reason for conflict among the Pankhursts. In all probability both Christabel and Emmeline were involved in lesbian relationships, although there is little documentation on the subject.[14] Christabel possessed extraordinary charisma, and her followers all but worshipped her, throwing flowers at her feet when she spoke. According to Pankhurst, "Elizabeth Robins, the novelist, fell in love with her."[15] So did others. Emmeline Pethick-Lawrence was totally entranced by Christabel and spent many weekends alone with her at the Pethick-Lawrence country home – much to Emmeline Pankhurst's resentment.[16]

Emmeline Pankhurst and the composer Ethel Smythe shared a home together in the last years of suffragette militancy. Their mother's relationship with Smythe was something that both Pankhurst and Christabel wanted to play down, and they urged Smythe not to write about it. Yet, in her book, *Female pipings in Eden,* she not only hints at her own and Emmeline's homosexuality but also indicates that Pankhurst's heterosexuality might have been a reason for her estrangement from mother and sister. Smythe quotes a letter she wrote to Emmeline in 1913: "I couldn't help reminding [Christabel] that I always said . . . that Sylvia would never fall into line and would always be a difficulty given the fact that since C. is not on the spot.

Sylvia will never be an Amazon. If it isn't JKH it will be somebody else."[17] Here we can see how the political and personal can be closely linked; how the issue of sexual orientation and preference might have been a factor in the growing rift among the Pankhurst women. Not only was Hardie a male, but he was a socialist and a member of the ILP and the Labour Party. Furthermore, he wanted to bring suffrage militants and the labour movement together.

Emmeline and Christabel, for their part, wanted nothing to do with the treachery of men, especially men in the labour movement. They wanted a WSPU of women who were handpicked or aristocratic (in both the literal and figurative sense), believing, in fact, that suffragettes were aristocratic because of their militancy. The presence of men would be intrusive and divisive and would weaken the women's cause. Pankhurst's loyalty to her mother and to the WSPU was therefore always suspect.

The estrangement between Pankhurst and her mother, the loneliness she felt as a misunderstood and poverty-stricken art student, only made her need of and love for Hardie greater. As the young woman became more involved in work with the WSPU, she depended on him not only for love but also for political guidance. He introduced her to Emmeline and Frederick Pethick-Lawrence, who became leaders and financial backers of the WSPU, and who remained her lifelong friends. For suffrage meetings, he helped to arrange halls, speakers and contingents from the East End. Hardie introduced her to other socialist women who helped her in the early years of the London movement.

He also watched over her personally. Pankhurst had complained to him that women art students faced discrimination with regard to scholarships at the Royal College of Art. Hardie asked a parliamentary question on the subject, which exposed the fact that scholarships were awarded at a ratio of one woman to thirteen men.[18] When she moved to a small apartment on Cheyne Walk in the Chelsea section of London, "ill and lonely", with only 25 shillings to her name and a rent of 11 shillings, Hardie came to her rescue.[19] He took her out to dinner and also helped her to sell her paintings and textile designs and to get some of her suffragette articles published.

In 1906, they had a serious quarrel over politics – a quarrel that reflected the political differences between suffragettes and some members of the ILP. On 8 March, Hardie was a featured speaker at a WSPU meeting in Exeter Hall in London. He announced that, if a women's suffrage bill was not granted within two years, he would personally get involved in organizing a movement that would stop at nothing less than full adult suffrage. Uttering the words "adult suffrage" at a WSPU meeting was worse than waving the proverbial red cape in front of a bull. The WSPU slogans were most emphatically "Votes for Women" and "This Session". The leaders of the WSPU believed, and for very good reason, that the phrase *adult suffrage* had always been the code words used by Liberals and now Labour Party supporters to ask women not to agitate for the vote until or unless all men were enfranchised. *Adult suffrage* was also code for adult *manhood* suffrage.

At the end of the meeting Pankhurst approached Hardie and told him why his speech had aroused such fury. "In my sorrow I said that my friendship with him might even become a competitor with my loyalty to the suffrage cause."[20] This comment reflects her conflict: she was a socialist, a feminist, a suffragette and a Pankhurst. Were her loyalties to a male-dominated labour movement and Labour Party whose leadership was hostile and indifferent toward women's suffrage and feminism, or to her mother and sister's middle-class women's suffrage organization? Even though Hardie supported women's suffrage, the WSPU and Pankhurst, he was more committed to the Labour Party (which he had founded) and to adult suffrage. During their discussion, he pointed to a line of homeless men waiting to get into a nearby shelter. "Do you ask me to desert these?"[21] They left each other saddened. Despite this unresolved quarrel, their relationship continued.

But the tempo of political events affected Sylvia Pankhurst's relationship with the WSPU and with Hardie. On 13 October 1905, the issue of women's suffrage finally forced itself onto the national political agenda: Christabel and Annie Kenney, a Lancashire mill girl and new recruit to the WSPU, disrupted a Liberal Party meeting in the Free Trade Hall in Manchester. Christabel had intended to create a disturbance, even to the point of getting arrested and jailed. She stood up at the meeting and asked Sir Edward Grey, then a prospective candidate for Parliament, if the Liberal Party would introduce a bill enfranchising women. Grey refused to answer, but Christabel refused to be silent. The two young women unfurled a banner reading "Votes for Women" and scuffled with police trying to eject them. Determined to get arrested, Christabel spat at one of the arresting officers. She got her wish and spent the night in jail.[22]

Even though most of the publicity concerning Christabel and the WSPU was unfavourable, it brought the WSPU enthusiasm and new members. It also put the WSPU in the national spotlight and ended the press blackout on the issue of women's suffrage. Christabel's strategy was brilliant and immediately effective in terms of mobilizing women and public opinion. Instead of lobbying individual Members of Parliament to introduce a women's suffrage bill, the WSPU demanded that the party in power be responsible for enacting parliamentary legislation giving women the vote. The subsequent militant acts of the suffragettes generated publicity more than it furthered their cause.

Militancy took on different meanings as the suffrage campaign escalated. In the early years, militancy meant heckling politicians; suffragettes would be thrown out of political meetings and then sometimes arrested and jailed. It also meant confronting police and hostile male observers during countless demonstrations at Parliament or 10 Downing Street. After 1910, when the government began force-feeding suffragette hunger-strikers, militancy escalated into mass acts of property destruction such as window breaking and then, later, individual acts such as arson. It was militancy that created a new spirit among women. Martha Vicinus comments:

> The WSPU built upon [a] foundation of religious belief, military discipline, and the work community, but it tapped something deeper – an extraordinary idealism that found its fullest expression in the utter sacrifice of self for the cause. The fierce loyalty and strength of the movement sprang from spiritual self confidence that unleashed enormous energies not only for the vote, but also for a total reorganization of society.[23]

In 1906, Pankhurst's art scholarship ended. She was painfully aware that, amid all the excitement of suffrage militancy, the close-knit Pankhurst family ties were unravelling. Although she realized that Christabel had always been her mother's favourite, Pankhurst claimed that she loved Christabel too much to be jealous. In reality, Pankhurst's resentment and bitterness toward her sister are obvious throughout her writings. For example, when Christabel announced her break with Hardie and the Labour Party in June 1906, Pankhurst commented acidly that "what interest she had ever possessed in the Socialist movement, in which she had been reared, she had shed as readily as a garment".[24] But Pankhurst sorely missed her mother's affections:

In those closing days of the college session, so full of anxiety for me, and those of my fellows, who were also facing a precarious future, I expected a letter from my mother, if only of encouragement. None came. We were no longer a family: the movement was overshadowing all personal affections. I had written to her regularly every second day in all the years of my absences. Now, my last letter unanswered, I ceased to write at all, except on matters of importance. The world seemed lonely and cold.[25]

Once out of college, Pankhurst devoted herself to the WSPU. She refused any payment from her mother, eking out a living from the sale of pictures, designs and articles. She did not want to be on the WSPU payroll because she wanted to continue her career as an artist, she did not want to be financially dependent upon her mother and sister, and, finally, she was aware of developing political differences:

I was not wholly in agreement with the policies and ideals of my sister and others who were controlling the movement, and whilst I did not wish to disrupt the movement by urging other policies, I desired to preserve my independence and to remain as an unpaid worker for the cause. The decision to put first my artistic work and my personal career and comfort – or whether to put the suffragette movement first when I saw the opportunities to aid it, had frequently to be made. The decision was always the same: the movement always took first place when I believed I could really assist it by any sacrifice or effort I could make.

And she concluded:

I never consulted anyone. From childhood I had always found evasion of anything which appeared to me to be a duty too painful to be persevered in. I knew no peace of mind 'til I had done what appealed to me as the right thing.[26]

In October 1906, Sylvia Pankhurst went to prison for the first time. Charged with using abusive language, she was sentenced to 14 days in Holloway jail. This experience made a lasting impression on her, and she remained concerned about prison reform, especially as it related to women prisoners, for the rest of her life. She was horrified at the filth of the prison, the lack of sanitation, the solitary confinement, the meagre and unpleasant prison food, and the lack of exercise and privacy. She was convinced that the health of the imprisoned suffragettes as well as that of all other prisoners was seriously and permanently damaged by the experience. She wrote later:

The haste, the lack of privacy, the character of the food, the want of exercise, the solitary confinement, the airless condition of the cell told their tale on most prisoners, producing digestive and other disorders. In numbers of cases imprisonment as a suffragette proved the onset of an illness eventually necessitating a surgical operation. [27]

Christabel pleaded with her sister not to expose prison conditions – so as not to divert any attention away from the issue of votes for women. But Pankhurst ignored her, writing about her experiences in jail in articles published in the *Pall Mall Gazette*, which also published her sketches. She was besieged with interviews. "Probably even Christabel could now feel content that there was no danger of losing the Votes for Women train in the quagmire of prison reform", she wrote later. [28]

In the summer of 1907, after a second imprisonment, Pankhurst took time off from the WSPU and travelled throughout Scotland and England to paint and draw working women and men. She went first to Cradley Heath in the Black Country of Staffordshire and produced a number of watercolours and drawings. In Leicester she worked among women in the shoe factories, and in Wigan she studied "pit-brow girls", women who worked in the coal mines. She proceeded to Scarborough to study fisherwomen, returned to Staffordshire to draw potters, went on to Berwickshire in Scotland to study farm labourers, and came finally to Glasgow, where she sketched women toiling in the cotton mills. [29]

Pankhurst's paintings and drawings reflect her ongoing commitment to her father's socialism. With compassion, but not romanticism, she depicted the lives, work and struggles of ordinary working women. In two paintings of women working in Glasgow cotton mills, the women are painted in front of the machinery. They look at the viewer with a straightforward yet somewhat sad expression. In one of these paintings, entitled *Changing the bobbin,* one woman is barefoot. Pankhurst's work is traditional; it did not challenge existing portrayals of women – or of men for that matter. In terms of subject matter and use of colour, she was either not aware of or chose to ignore the more avant-garde artists of the nineteenth and early twentieth centuries. [30]

Although Pankhurst was happiest living in working-class communities where she could draw and paint, she could not escape the pull of the suffrage struggle. She was always torn between her desire to create art and her commitment to the movement. Her discomfort grew as the differences between herself and her mother and sister widened.

Although the WSPU had been formed by women members of the ILP, Christabel, Emmeline and others quickly renounced their allegiance to the party. Pankhurst never abandoned hers, even when challenged by her autocratic sister. In 1907, Pankhurst was called away from her painting in Wigan to meet Christabel at WSPU headquarters because a WSPU organizer had complained that during a by-election campaign Pankhurst had announced to the crowd that she was a socialist.

> Christabel interrogated me. . . . It had been necessary to convince the people we were not Conservatives. "You should have said we used to be Liberals," said Christabel with her engaging smile. "I do not agree," I answered. We knew each other's tenacity. The subject dropped.[31]

Pankhurst was also unlike her mother and sister in dress and temperament, which became even more apparent after 1912. Both Emmeline and Christabel were immaculately groomed, impeccably garbed and stylishly coiffed. Pankhurst, on the other hand, as art student (dressed in the sloppy bohemian style cultivated by most of them) and as suffragette, was often carelessly dressed in outmoded and borrowed clothing; her hair was always coming undone. Her coworker Helen Crawfurd, a Scottish suffragette and, later, peace activist and communist, described her as an intense creature, very unlike her sister Christabel:

> She was one of those people whom it was impossible to keep tidy; her hair was always tumbling down. One day I met her outside the hotel and noticed that she had her blouse on inside out. I got her behind some packing cases and helped her change it.[32]

Pankhurst also lacked the driving ambition of her mother and sister, and during the early years of militant suffrage agitation shied away from the limelight. Instead, she saw herself as a rank-and-file suffragette, attending and organizing meetings, heckling politicians and going to jail as well as using her talent to draw numerous posters and to design WSPU exhibitions, brooches, banners and medals.

Following her father's example, Pankhurst believed that tireless, uncomplaining hard work and sacrifice for the cause were worthwhile in themselves. However, this did not bring her mother any closer. Instead, as suffrage militancy increased, the disagreements became more pronounced, although for the sake of family and suffragette unity Pankhurst did not voice her opinions publicly until 1912. Her first book, *The suffragette* (1911), gives no hint of discord even though later, in her second book, *The suffragette movement* (1931), she wrote that she was already uneasy about the increasingly dictatorial leadership of the WSPU.[33]

Nor was she alone in this regard. In 1907, the Women's Freedom League, led by Charlotte Despard and Teresa Billington-Greig, was formed in protest at the lack of democracy within the WSPU.[34] In particular, Despard and Billington-Greig, two of the better-known WSPU leaders, objected to the fact that Emmeline and Christabel were proposing to abolish the constitution of the WSPU, disallowing its members the right to vote on policy. It seemed ludicrous to belong to a women's suffrage organization that denied its own members the vote.

In 1912, Emmeline and Frederick Pethick-Lawrence were expelled from the WPSU because they opposed its terrorist tactics. Pankhurst agreed with them that women's suffrage would be won not by isolated and individual acts of violence, but rather by mass actions ranging from deputations to Parliament to demonstrations to – on occasions – mass window breaking. However, she did not take any measures to oppose the expulsion, such as writing protest letters in *Votes for Women* or other suffragette publications; nor did she resign in protest.

Pankhurst also took issue with her mother and sister's increasingly extreme attitude toward men. In the early years, when the WSPU still identified with the ILP, men had not been considered the enemies of women's rights; the government in power had been. As the suffrage movement gained momentum, however, Emmeline and Christabel's attacks on men – particularly working-class men – became more pronounced. Pankhurst was horrified at having to campaign at a Bury St Edmunds election with a WSPU organizer who was "such a virulent feminist, she actually asserted that married women were 'contaminated' and should be segregated".[35]

Testifying in court in 1912, Emmeline pointed out the higher virtues of women:

> I found out that the kind of old women who came into the workhouse were in many ways superior to the kind of old men who came into the workhouse. They were more industrious; in fact it was quite touching to see their industry, to see their patience, and to see the way the old women over sixty or

seventy years of age did most of the work in the workhouse . . .
I found that the old men were different.[36]
Emmeline remarked bitterly that these men – who were not responsible to society – were allowed to vote, whereas respectable and socially responsible women like herself could not.[37] A popular suffrage poster, on display at the London Museum, suggests that certain categories of men should be disenfranchised: lunatics, proprietors of white slaves, those unfit for military service and drunkards.

In 1912, Christabel wrote a notorious pamphlet called *The great scourge,* claiming that 80 per cent of *all* Englishmen of all classes were carriers of venereal disease and were deliberately infecting Englishwomen. The pamphlet reflected a number of beliefs held by other contemporary feminists, who argued that the standards of sexual morality applied to women should also hold for men. Hence, the slogan: "Votes for Women and Chastity for Men!"[38] Ironically, conservatives – especially the Church of England, one of the most vehement opponents of women's suffrage and women's rights – enthusiastically endorsed Christabel's theories about the innate depravity of the English male.

Throughout the suffrage campaign, Emmeline reiterated her belief that "the horrible evils that are ravaging our civilization will never be removed until women get the vote", implying that men were responsible for these "evils".[39] In this way, the political justification for granting women's suffrage changed. Instead of reiterating the Liberal belief in natural rights, Emmeline now argued for class rights as a basis for citizenship.[40]

As the suffrage agitation continued, Christabel and Emmeline's attitude toward men hardened. They criticized Pankhurst for inviting men to speak on suffrage platforms and, worse, for accepting invitations from male socialists to speak at their meetings. Pankhurst opposed this growing separatist trend, having hoped the suffrage movement would work with the newly formed Labour Party. Increasingly, she saw the issue of women's suffrage and emancipation in class terms. Thus, she and her mother and sister were also at odds over who should be enfranchised.

The debate over enlarging the franchise had begun in 1832 when the British state had taken votes as well as property from women in extending the franchise to middle-class men. The radical wing within the Liberal Party argued for full adult suffrage – that is, adult male suffrage and, by implication, full adult female suffrage. This demand was taken on by the small socialist groups. These organizations, particularly the Social Democratic Federation (SDF), saw the demand for women's suffrage as part of the larger class question. When the Independent Labour Party was formed in 1893, it inherited traditional radical liberalism and some commitment to adult suffrage. The ILP became formally committed to adult suffrage. Although its leadership opposed the women's suffrage movement, its rank-and-file membership was supportive of and active in different women's suffrage organizations.[41]

The WSPU, like all the other women's suffrage organizations of the time, shared the traditional Liberal viewpoint regarding women's suffrage; it demanded votes for women on the same basis as votes for men. However, given that the majority of working-class men were unable to vote, the suffrage bill supported by the women's suffrage organizations would also deny the franchise to the majority of working-class women. Mary Macarthur, organizer for the Women's Trade Union League, commented:

> We have . . . a tremendous suffrage movement in England, but unfortunately the supporters of that movement are mainly middle-class, leisured women. They are asking for the suffrage on a limited basis, a basis that would not enfranchise the women we represent. If the bill were passed, not 5% of the women we represent – 200,000 women – would get the vote.[42]

Bertha Poole Wyle, a suffragist who did not belong to the WSPU, agreed that if its demands were met only middle-class women would win the vote. "The suffrage bill which all suffrage organisations are supporting", she wrote in 1909, "does not give the factory girl the vote and naturally she is not interested in its passage. But this bill does enfranchise a large number of self supporting women."[43]

Pankhurst's disagreements with her mother and sister reflected this difference over who was to be enfranchised. She was torn between her political sympathies for the ILP and for the WSPU. In spite of her growing unease with the political direction that the WSPU was taking, Pankhurst continued to work for it. Her last major contributions to the organization – of which she was very proud – were artistic. She designed the WSPU emblem: an angel standing on her toes blowing a horn and holding a banner inscribed "Freedom"; in the background are prison bars and the letters "WSPU". She also designed another emblem in which a woman sowing seeds is encircled with the words "Votes for Women" and "WSPU". A third emblem shows a young woman in flowing Grecian robes striding out of a prison over broken chains. She carries a swirling banner that bears the slogan "Votes for Women".

Pankhurst also designed the WSPU calendar. It contains a winged angel holding a lamp and guiding a young woman who is dressed in prison attire and carrying a banner that says "Votes for Women". The rest of the calendar is embellished with an intricate border of leaves and grapes, showing the unmistakable influence of William Morris. Pankhurst's greatest artistic work for the WSPU was the decorations for a major WSPU exhibit at the Prince's Skating Rink in Knightsbridge, London, in 1909. She had less than three months to design canvases for a hall measuring over 250 feet by 150 feet. Her creation is filled with symbolism and generously uses the WSPU colours of purple, green and white. The central piece contains a 13 foot high figure of a young female sower surrounded by flowers (representing hope) and by thistles (representing adversity). Over the sower's head are three doves of peace. On another panel a young woman bearing a sheaf of grain is surrounded by angels on tiptoe carrying stringed instruments. Over everything arch stylized grapes and leaves, reminiscent of her earlier suffrage designs and, as always, showing the clear influence of Morris and Walter Crane. Throughout her life, Pankhurst spoke of her excitement in producing these and other murals.[44]

These images are even more traditional, more rooted in nineteenth-century, Pre-Raphaelite socialist symbolism than are Pankhurst's other paintings and drawings of working-class women. In this respect, her art did not completely mirror her life. Although she saw herself as a radical who challenged the status quo, her paintings – especially her artwork for the suffragette cause – show little of the drama, rebellion and challenge to male authority that she and her suffrage comrades demonstrated.[45]

From 1909 to 1911, after she had moved into the East End of London, Pankhurst continued to paint. She did a portrait of Keir Hardie that now hangs in the National Portrait Gallery in London; depicting him as a kindly, expressive person, it clearly show her love and admiration. She produced as well her only self-portrait, which also hangs in the National Portrait Gallery. It is different from most of the existing photographs of her, mainly because she looks almost ethe-really happy. In this self-portrait, she wears a head scarf (common to working-class women).

In the summer of 1909, suffrage militancy and government obsti-nacy escalated. Marian Wallace Dunlop became the first suffragette to go on a hunger strike in protest at being refused political status during her imprisonment.[46] Suffragettes proceeded to raise the ante by breaking windows and, once in prison, going on more hunger strikes. The government became more obdurately opposed to granting votes for women and responded brutally by force-feeding the hunger-striking suffragettes.

Christabel was quick to realize the importance of window smashing and hunger striking. These tactics not only escalated the protest but also reinforced the suffragettes' commitment to the cause. Their sorority grew ever tighter, more closely bound together by the combi-nation of illegal actions and common suffering. For its part, the Liberal government reacted more illiberally – and irrationally – to each new suffragette exploit.

In *The suffragette movement,* Sylvia Pankhurst wrote that she had misgivings about the window smashing, believing that appeals to the masses – and by this Pankhurst meant the working class – had not yet been fully exhausted. "I believed then and always that the movement required, not more serious militancy by the few, but a stronger appeal to the great masses to join the struggle," she explained. "Yet," she con-tinued, "it was not in me to criticize or expostulate."

> I would rather have died at the stake than say one word against the actions of those who were in the throes of the fight. I knew but too surely that the militant women would be made to suffer renewed hardships for each act of more serious damage. Yet, in the spate of that impetuous movement, they would rush enthu-siastically to their martyrdom, and bless, as their truest saviours, the leaders who summoned them to each new ordeal.

She concluded: "Posterity, I knew, would see the heroism of the mili-tants and forget their damage, but in the present, they would pay severely."[47]

By 1911, Pankhurst was unable to adopt the despotism of her mother and sister and objected to the political direction of the WSPU, to its hostility toward the labour movement, and to the blind loyalty demanded from each of its members. She decided that she wanted to act upon her own socialist and feminist convictions. However, she was not yet ready to make a formal, open break with her mother and sister; she wished rather to strike out on her own in the hope that she could make some small contribution to working women and to the cause of women's suffrage.[48]

In 1911 and 1912, Pankhurst made two trips to the United States to raise money for the suffragette cause, to generate support for the WSPU and to find new ways to earn money as a journalist. These trips marked another important stage in her political development. For the first time ever she was on her own, and far away from her family and Hardie: writing, speaking, making new friends and political acquaintances. She proved herself to be resourceful and daring, going to places that few would visit. For the most part, she was well received by the press, and the contacts she made in the publishing industry helped her to earn a meagre living. All of this must have infused Sylvia Pankhurst with a strong sense of self-worth and independence. It was most likely this experience that enabled her, when she went back to England, to embark upon political work that was not dictated by her mother and sister but that she thought important.

Her separate itineraries on both trips are confusing because, without ever explaining why, Pankhurst compressed them into one in all her writings.[49] A possible explanation might be that Pankhurst and her sister were involved in some sort of clandestine activity in the United States in 1912. Christabel may have travelled from her hideout in Paris, where she was escaping from arrest in Britain, to New York. On 22 April 1912, the *New York Times* ran an article headlined "Why is Christabel hiding?" which reported that a police officer had recognized her on the ship *Mauretania*. He claimed that Christabel was hiding in New York and being helped by Pankhurst.[50] Nellie Rathbone, who was Pankhurst's secretary at the time, also claimed that Christabel had gone to America when Pankhurst was there.[51] Perhaps the sisters were going to meet in America for WSPU business; perhaps one was going to America in the hope of countering the political work of the other. Neither woman ever wrote in her later works about whether or not Christabel went to America. Perhaps the *Times* and Nellie Rathbone were mistaken.

Pankhurst first arrived in New York City on a bitterly cold January day in 1911. She was met at the boat by her old family friend Harriot Stanton Blatch and a corps of newspaper reporters. Pankhurst was not impressed with American reporters. "Don't you take notes?" she scolded, demanding accurate reports. "We are not stenographers," came the indignant reply. Sending for notebooks and pencils, Pankhurst dictated both the questions and the answers.[52] The results pleased her, for soon she was besieged with requests for speeches.

In New York, she became immediately involved in a laundry workers' strike. Elizabeth Gurley Flynn, the famous International Workers of the World "rebel girl", recalled speaking with Pankhurst at one of the rallies for the strikers. Margaret Sanger, another socialist feminist and pioneer of women's rights and birth control, was also there.[53] Pankhurst made a short speech of support to the picketers, calling on them to "remember the hundreds of British women who have suffered violence in the cause of their enfranchisement".[54]

Pankhurst was immediately struck by the racial and ethnic divisions within the American working class. She was impressed that, despite this diversity, ethnic groups worked together. At the picket-line rally she attended, speeches were made by one young Italian in his native tongue and by the young black picket-line captain.[55] Throughout her trips, she was always aware of and sensitive to racial and ethnic issues.

In New York, she met the well-known socialist feminist Crystal Eastman, her equally famous brother Max Eastman (the editor of the radical magazine *The Masses*) and the Lewisohn sisters, well known for their work at the Henry Street Settlement.[56] She spoke to eight hundred people in the Flatbush area of Brooklyn.[57] The *New York Times,* referred to her as a "rosy cheeked slip of an English girl", even though she was 29 years old, and praised her for being an effective and attractive suffragette.

Other newspapers were also enamoured of Pankhurst, though they covered her in a patronizing manner, commenting on her appearance as much as on the political content of her speeches. The *Albany Evening Journal* described her as a "frail English girl"; the *Denver Post* commented that she was "frail" and "homely" and wore plain clothing; and the *Denver Express* said that she was "the soul of unpretentiousness, a synonym of simplicity and a compendium of information on all that pertains to the progress of women", adding that she looked young and unsophisticated.[58] Not all journalists thought Pankhurst homely. The *Columbus Citizen* called her "the expert on plain and fancy suffragetting" and a "charmer" and claimed that "she is heralded here, the militant suffragette. Militant is she? You bet she is – but in the way women have been militant even long before Venus de Milo made such a hit with the men, that they stood for her as a goddess."[59] The *Lawrence Daily Journal World* also reported on her activities favourably, but was somewhat scandalized to note that Pankhurst did not wear a corset.[60]

Not all the newspapers were favourable. The *Chicago Daily News*, angered that Pankhurst spent little time with its reporters, wrote a series of articles about her, complete with unflattering caricatures of her as some sort of ruffian.[61] The *New York Times* was less favourable to Pankhurst on the second trip than it had been on the first. The *Times* reporter was obviously annoyed at her response to a question about the chivalry of the men on board the doomed *Titanic*. Pankhurst was quoted as saying that their chivalry was just an archaic formality in comparison with the way in which men really treated women. The reporter editorialized that Pankhurst "wants to vote, she wants a voice in public affairs, she wants to hold public office, but she also wants a safe place in a lifeboat at the expense of a useful man's life if she happens to be in a wreck".[62]

Pankhurst travelled extensively across the United States and Canada, going as far north as New Brunswick, as far west as California and as far south as Tennessee. She spoke on the average of two times a day in Albany, Baltimore, Boston, Cincinnati, Columbus, Indianapolis, Kansas City, Minneapolis, New York and Pittsburgh. She spoke to a Social Problems class at Oberlin College and to the Senate and the House of Representatives in Des Moines, the only woman to do so since Susan B. Anthony. She also spoke to state legislatures in Albany, New York and Lansing, Michigan, and to the state judiciary committees in Illinois and New York.[63]

Pankhurst helped to organize a women's suffrage group in Fargo, North Dakota. One afternoon, she met a group of men and women, "many of them socialists", who told her there was no women's suffrage society in all of North Dakota. That evening, a group of women met Pankhurst and organized the Votes for Women League of North Dakota, and decided to oppose the anti-suffragists who were running for the state legislature. Pankhurst suggested to the new group that men be admitted as associate members but not be given voting rights.[64]

Pankhurst made a special point of visiting prisons and was appalled by the horrendous conditions of the Harrison Street Jail in Chicago, as well as by the barbaric treatment of prisoners in cages in Tennessee. She also visited "model" prisons in Bedford, New York and Framingham, Massachussetts, where she was more favourably impressed.[65] Throughout her travels Pankhurst was aware of the extent of the racial discrimination in the USA. Horrified by racism, she made attempts to get to know black Americans. She opposed racism publicly and spoke to black audiences, even though she was attacked by the press as well as by sister suffragettes for speaking at a black college in Tennessee.[66] Speaking to African-American audiences, Pankhurst was unique among suffrage activists in both Britain and the United States.[67]

Pankhurst was also disturbed by the treatment of the native population in America. Speaking at an Indian college in Arkansas, she commented that whites manipulated Indians on a reservation she had visited in New Mexico. She was unhappy to learn that the Indians had abandoned their native craft work in favour of making cheap toys and dolls for white children.[68] To the modern reader, much of the language Pankhurst used in commenting on race relations in the United States seems itself a kind of patronizing racism. For example, in one passage in *The suffragette movement*, Pankhurst described a prisoner she visited in Tennessee as a "pale Negress, with a face of beautiful despair, [who] recalled wonderful Lydia Yavorska in Maxim Gorky's *Lower Depths*".[69] However, in the context of the period, she showed an amazing sensitivity and openness not found in many English people at the time.

In Tennessee, she also met the Cumberland Socialist Society and, in the town of Lebanon, spoke about women's suffrage at a pencil factory. At this meeting, the men got a glimpse of Pankhurst's ability to handle hecklers and questioners deftly and with an engaging sense of humour. During the question-and-answer period, an old man stood up and asked, "If we give you women the vote *will you go out and work on the roads?*" The men roared their approval. At that time, in order for men to vote in Tennessee, they were required to spend a certain amount of time building public roads.

Pankhurst responded by asking "every man voter in the audience who had ever worked on the road to hold up his hand". The men, who understood that she was exposing the class bias of the voting laws, showed their approval by clapping, whistling and yelling. The voting law was designed to guarantee cheap labour for public works. Poor men worked on the roads in order to vote, but the wealthy were exempt. Pankhurst continued by reminding her audience that the "rule which said that every voter must work a certain length of the road was not a law of God, but had merely been set up by men law-makers, as a provision suited to themselves". She concluded: "If women had been enfranchised they might have decided that every voter must be able to cook a dinner, make a suit of clothes or manage a household."[70]

Pankhurst made two special trips to Milwaukee because it had a socialist mayor, and she wanted to see "municipal socialism" in action. Although she was pleased with much of the progress made, she nonetheless had her criticisms. The administration was "careful and conscientious", but she saw "few really radical changes affecting the wages and well being of the Councils' employees and the poorer members of the community".[71] Concerned that City Council meetings were not open to the general public, she urged the mayor that at "all meetings of the Council and its committees, both Press and Public [should] be present to hear the debates ... [O]nly thus can the busy populace be kept closely informed as to the doings of their city government and induced to take a vital and constant interest in them."[72]

Pankhurst advocated a form of workers' control of the city government, arguing that the scrubwomen and the garbage collectors should control their own departments. She also anticipated automation, adding, "if these have not been emancipated by mechanical inventions and opportunities of a more genial employment".[73] In general she believed that the Milwaukee city administration placed too much power in the hands of the mayor and was too dominated by business interests. "The Bureau of Economics and Efficiency was too heavily weighted with accountants, businessmen and university professors, who had no practical knowledge of the hardship, toil and struggle of poorer working lives."[74]

Pankhurst argued with the mayor about women's suffrage, feminism and socialism. "I was anxious to make him feel that even under socialism it would not be satisfactory to women to leave everything to be managed by men." She further pointed out that it was "strange how few even of the best of men can quite see that we need the power to work out our own salvation as much as they do". The argument became more heated; Pankhurst's voice rose and her cheeks grew hot. Finally, after debating the plight of working women, the mayor admitted that the working man's wife was "the slave of the slave".[75]

Pankhurst's observations of the Milwaukee socialist administration were very much in tune with her general vision of socialism and women's liberation. It is clear that her socialism was not the top-down state or municipal socialism advocated by the Fabians and Progressives, where middle-class intellectuals and technicians made the world "better" for the poor or working class, but socialism from the bottom up, with workers controlling both industry and government. Similarly, her vision of women's emancipation came from the power of working women themselves, organizing and rebuilding their workplaces, homes and communities on their own terms.

Pankhurst saw America as a land "with harsh, rude extremes, rough and unfinished, yet with scope and opportunity for young people and with more receptivity to new ideas than is found in the old country".[76] She even thought she might become an American citizen – but she never returned to the United States.

During both her trips to America, Pankhurst corresponded with Hardie, writing him many lengthy and sometimes maudlin love letters. For the most part, the correspondence is that of any lonely separated couple. They address each other as "My dearie". She asks, "How is my darling?" and cries, "I am homesick for the want of you."[77] He calls her "little sweetheart".[78] She constantly complains that he doesn't write enough and that his letters never arrive in time at the intended destination. At one point Pankhurst wrote, "My darling I am longing to be in your arms, away from it all."[79]

She wrote Hardie love poems from America:

> Last night when all was quiet you came to me.
> I felt in the darkness by my side
> Waiting to feel your kisses on my mouth.
> The clasping of your arms and your dear lips
> Pressing on me 'till my breath comes short.
> All I know so well of you, each touch
> Every caress, your breaking under your voice.[80]

Aside from this subject, Pankhurst's letters covered a wide range of topics, including detailed impressions of her trip as well as her ideas on sexuality. The letters do show that Hardie and Pankhurst were close friends and political confidants as well as lovers.

However, after Pankhurst's second return from the United States in 1912, their relationship continued for only a brief period. On the back of a personal letter to Hardie written when she began her work in the East End is the word "Advent".[81] Pankhurst never explained its meaning. Perhaps it meant the end of her affair with Hardie and the beginning of another relationship. Romero speculates that perhaps Pankhurst was pregnant.[82] If she was, she either miscarried or aborted. But there is nothing in her later writings that indicates a pregnancy at this time.

The affair with Hardie ebbed after Pankhurst began work in the East End. Why it ended can only be guessed at. Her work consumed all her time and passion and perhaps there was no longer room in her life for such a relationship. There might have been other reasons as well. Pankhurst's trip to America gave her a tremendous amount of self-confidence as well as a tiny income from her lectures and published writings that enabled her to remain independent of her mother and sister. She was striking out on her own, and within a very short time she became as prominent in the news as they – if not more so. Not only was she no longer the lonely, somewhat jealous and neglected daughter and sister; she developed new, intense relationships with a close-knit group of women in the East End – especially the American Zelie Emerson. Perhaps the need for an intense relationship with the older Hardie was not as pressing as it had been when she was a young art student. Hardie's health began to fail after 1913. Perhaps he, too, did not have the strength to maintain such an intense friendship with a woman, one just approaching her thirties. Nevertheless, they remained close friends throughout the rest of the militant suffrage campaign, and Pankhurst never wavered in her adoration and admiration of him.

Chapter Two

᪷

The East End

Sylvia Pankhurst returned from her trip to America resolved to live in the East End of London and take up among the "people of the abyss".[1] Her goals were ambitious:

I regarded the rousing of the East End as of utmost importance. My aim was not merely to make some members and establish some branches, but the larger task of bringing the district as a whole into a mass movement, from which only a minority would stand aside.[2]

It was a daunting task. She described the area in which she had made her home in an account of a walk she took in 1917 through Poplar, down the East India Dock Road, where one side was the long blank wall of the dock into which the prisonlike dock gates were set. Here, besides habitual dockers, unemployed men from all sections of industry came seeking, too often in vain, a casual job. Meetings were held at these great gates. They were also the site of many riots by industrial workers and the unemployed.

The dock gates were the front door into Poplar. Away from the main road were meaner and dingier streets where people were herded together in hideously dilapidated houses. In the side streets, as densely populated as rabbit warrens, the little two-storey houses vied with each other in their decay. They had little yards behind broken fences, with sunken paving stones where pools of water collected and a row of toilets with their doors often half broken.

In the High Street, shop after shop stood empty owing in part to vandalism by children and in part due to high rents. Here and there stood a dignified house with an imposing door. In one small closed-in court were the Hanbury Buildings. One entered through a narrow stone staircase, with damp slimy walls. At the top of the staircase were the open doors of three toilets, all of which were out of order. To the left was the small washhouse, with a water tap and a copper pot for boiling clothes. Seven families shared the washer and toilets, and the women took turns each week cleaning them. The two small rooms occupied by each family opened on to each other, for they shared a front door. Rent varied from 4s. 6d. to 6s. 6d. a week. There was no water in the apartments, light was dim, the staircase wet and muddy. The washhouse was filled with smoke because the boiler was broken and dangerous, wrecked by children who had nowhere to play.

A woman got off her knees, putting aside her pail and scrubbing brush. She had two children and was expecting a third. She worked at Marston's Biscuit and Preserving factory because her husband's wage was too small to keep the family together. When she came home from work, she cooked, cleaned and washed. The older child went to school, and she had to pay a woman to care for the youngest. Her tiny rooms were beautifully clean and decorated for the Christmas season. This was one of the East End's more fortunate women.[3]

Pankhurst was particularly horrified by the conditions of women and children: "Some of the children are barefooted, many have broken boots, their clothes are old and shabby – but that is nothing – it is terrible that so large a population is dwarfed and stunted by blinding poverty."[4] She described one woman who "still in her thirties, but already beginning to look old, stands at her door holding her pale wasted little baby; one of her children recently died of a heart complaint, another is in a hospital with a tubercular hip".[5]

The East End was dominated by the docks. The Royal Victoria and Albert, Millwall, St Katherine's, and East and West India docks contained all the contradictions of the British Empire. Here, the riches of the world passed through the hands of England's poorest and most degraded people. The ebb and flow of employment at the Port of London determined to a great extent the quality of life in the East End, for everyone who lived there was related in some way to a dockworker.

In 1890, about 100,000 people had been employed at the docks in various jobs, but the numbers were decreasing.[6] It was difficult to ascertain exactly how many worked on the docks, for the majority were casual workers and therefore not counted as dock labourers. The casuals' wages did not adequately cover their living expenses, and the largest group of applicants for poor law relief in the East End were dockers.[7]

Although most male workers in the East End were casual dock labourers, there were other industries, including the gas works and heavy engineering and chemical industries. Workers in these industries, like the dockers, suffered from low wages and job insecurity. Some areas had basically one industry. Limehouse, for example, had four large breweries, which made the adjoining borough of Stepney one of the centres of alcoholism in London.[8] These conditions of male employment had consequences for women in the East End. The family could not survive without the combined wage labour of all.[9] For the unskilled, it was impossible to survive without female labour.

In the East End, 35 per cent of the female workforce was employed in skilled domestic service, a particularly hated profession. Between 1911 and 1921, domestic service declined about 20 per cent as an occupation. In this same period, 14 per cent of women worked in the clothing trade, 12 per cent were clerical workers, 8 per cent worked in commerce and finance, and 6½ per cent in nursing and teaching.[10] Thousands of women and children, along with some men, were employed in the sweated trades by subcontractors to make artificial flowers, beadwork, matches, sacks, nails and clothing of various types – all for a pittance and under intolerable working conditions. Charles Booth, writing in *Darkest England*, explained how his "blood boiled with impotent rage" over the conditions of those who suffered from sweating:

> These firms which reduce sweating to a fine art, who systematically and deliberately defraud the workman of his pay, and grind the faces of the poor, who rob the widow and the orphan, and who for a pretence make great professions of public spirit and philanthropy, these men nowadays are sent to Parliament to make laws for the people.

"The old prophets sent them to hell," Booth raged. "But we have changed all that. They send their victims to Hell and are rewarded by all that wealth can do to make their lives comfortable."[11]

Women outnumbered men two to one in the sweated industries.[12] Women worked alone or with help from their children, although child labour was often a hindrance and held up the mother's work.[13] Many of the women in the sweated trades were married to dockers; in West Ham, for example, this was true of over half the women.[14]

These women often worked only when their husbands were laid off, although many worked full time.

The 1909 Trades Boards Act fixed minimum rates in the low-paid industries, but these were often evaded. Writing in 1912 for the *Daily Herald,* a socialist newspaper, Sylvia Pankhurst commented:

> When at one of the meetings, I referred to the fact that the Trades Board has set up a minimum wage of 6d an hour for all the men in the trade, and a minimum wage of only 3¼d an hour for only 80% of what are called "ordinary" women workers, the Board refused to define the term "ordinary". A woman interrupted me to say that the outworkers are finding the regulation minimum wage is evaded by employers with impunity, and that garments are given out to the women who make 3¼d, which they find take not an hour, but three hours to finish.[15]

The women of the East End suffered not only from the misery of their work but also because they had even less chance to escape it than did their husbands. R. Sinclair, a sociologist, best describes their plight:

> For women, the normal opportunities of employment were far less, but the penury of their men drove women and children to work at home. The art of making match boxes with artificial flowers flourished in the family home, which often consisted of one room. The career of domestic service which the Victorian century offered to women provided little escape from East London. The best domestic positions to which the rough mannered children of the slums could aspire were in the East London homes of the poorest tradesmen or ambitious artisans which yielded no training, no written references of any value, and with the slums' suspicion of formalities, the girls generally left without notice.[16]

Along with underemployment went high rates of alcoholism (higher for women than for men) high rates of illegitimate births, and a high infant mortality rate. Edwardian society placed women on the altar of virtue, obedience and perfection, yet prostitution flourished before the averted eyes of police and employers in East London.[17]

It was important to Sylvia Pankhurst's organizing efforts that there had been a history of working-class and feminist agitation. In the East End, women and men – dockers, laundresses, gasworkers, sweated workers and ladies' maids – were united in the common disenfranchisement of poverty. The connection between the suffrage campaign and other forms of social injustice was there from the start. When the WSPU began suffrage campaigning in London in February 1905, a number of members organized and led a procession of working women to urge passage of the Unemployed Workmen's Bill, legislation dealing with the employment of unemployed workers in farm colonies. Dora Montefiore, a socialist and WSPU organizer for London, marched alongside East End socialist George Lansbury, Will Crooks (who had been elected the first working-class mayor of Poplar in 1901) and 1,000 working women. Pankhurst had been commissioned by Keir Hardie to design the posters.[18]

The active involvement of the WSPU with East End women began a few months later when it sent Annie Kenney to "rouse London". She went to see Dora Montefiore, who introduced her to the women who had taken part in the movement to support the Unemployed Workmen's Bill.[19] Kenney convinced these women that it was necessary to fight for the vote; a few days later a number of them went with her to ask questions of Liberal politicians at the Albert Hall.

In 1906, the WSPU decided to concentrate its efforts on campaigning in London, the centre of political power. Kenney and Sylvia Pankhurst, then a student at the Royal College of Art, agreed that they should "follow all the other popular movements by holding a meeting in Trafalgar Square, and a procession of the East End women in the unemployed movement at the opening of Parliament".[20]

The two women worked hard to publicize this procession. Legally, Trafalgar Square could not be used, so Keir Hardie rented Caxton Hall for them. George Lansbury and Will Crooks promised to help. Pankhurst and Kenney received unexpected support from a number of women such as Flora Drummond, who had recently joined the WSPU, and on 16 February 1906 over 300 women from the East End marched to Caxton Hall to participate in the first "Women's Parliament". Upon hearing that the Liberal Party was not including votes for women as part of its parliamentary legislative programme, the women from Caxton Hall marched to Parliament and lobbied their MPs.

In that year, the Canning Town branch of the WSPU was formed. Again, the initiative was taken by a group of women who had been involved in the unemployed agitation and also in the ILP.[21] The Canning Town WSPU was the first East End working women's suffrage organization and it was, for the most part, at odds with the WSPU leadership, in particular Christabel and Emmeline Pankhurst. Most members of the East London group were members of or sympathetic to the ILP at a time when the WSPU leadership was moving away from socialism. In contrast to the official policy of the WSPU, the Canning Town branch demanded votes for all working women.[22] In fact, the estrangement between the Canning Town local and Clements Inn (the new London headquarters of the WSPU) was so great that Mrs Knight, the Canning Town branch secretary, resigned as early as January 1907, complaining that headquarters "were not keeping their promises to the working woman".[23]

Mrs Knight had correctly appraised the WSPU position on working-class women. In 1906, Christabel put it very succinctly:

> Surveying the London work as I found it, I considered that in one sense it was too exclusively dependent for the demonstrations upon the women of the East End. The East End women are more used to coming out in large numbers, for many of them had done so in connection with labour demonstrations and at the beginning of our campaign it was natural for organisers to rely mainly on them. It was, however, the right and duty of women more fortunately placed to do their share, and the larger share in the fight for the vote which might be, whatever our hopes to the contrary, long and hard. Besides, critical murmurs of "stage army" were being unjustly made by Members of Parliament about the East End contingents and it was evident that the House of Commons, and, even its Labour members, were more impressed by the feminine bourgeoisie than the feminine proletariat.[24]

The WSPU began to abandon the East End just at the time when branches were forming in Bow and Bromley. The Poplar WSPU branch had 30 to 40 members and met regularly, often with the Canning Town WSPU.[25]

From 1907 until 1912, the WSPU paid little attention to the East End. But there was continued suffragette activity there. The Actresses Franchise League performed suffragette plays and held meetings in the East End.[26] Lucy Baldock, a WSPU member who was active in the East End agitation from the very beginning, received letters from working women asking for help and advice. "Dear Madame", wrote one laundry worker:

I am writing to ask whether or not you could help us laundry girls of West Ham to obtain more money and fairness to all. Most of the girls are willing to do something, but are unable to because they have no leader or anyone else to speak for them.[27]

Other suffragettes were invited to speak at women's trade union meetings. During the 1912 strike involving the London tailors, machinists and dressers, Charlotte Despard, the militant socialist suffragette, was invited to speak on the vote and working women.[28] All this activity underscored Sylvia Pankhurst's belief in the interconnection between labour issues and women's suffrage.

Finally, and ironically, another place where the suffragettes met and interacted with women of the East End was Holloway prison. Many imprisoned suffragettes worked with other "non-political" prisoners to win a few prison reforms. They helped some of the poorer women to get their sentences reduced. Pankhurst describes a shabbily dressed woman who, in the middle of a suffragette meeting, rose to have her say:

I want to speak for the suffragettes for what they've done in Holloway. Before they came, we had wooden spoons and tin pint pots and only a stool to sit on, now we have proper spoons with mugs and chairs. And we have garters now instead of our stockings all falling down at exercise. And we have a clean cell and everything decent as it should be.[29]

The women of the East End remembered this. "I have seen the suffragettes in Holloway," shouted one woman at an East End rally. "They have made things better there!"[30] The sharing of prison experiences and fighting together for prison reform helped to create a bond between some suffragettes and the women of the East End.

Thus, Sylvia Pankhurst chose the East End for her organizing campaign for specific political reasons: the East End was the greatest homogeneous working-class area accessible to the House of Commons by popular demonstrations. The creation of a women's movement in that "great abyss of poverty" would be a call and a rallying cry to the rise of similar movements in all parts of the country. Pankhurst's goal was clearly to build a socialist women's movement:

I was anxious too, to fortify the position of the working woman when the vote should actually be given; the existence of a strong self-reliant movement amongst working women would be the greatest aid in safeguarding their rights in the day of settlement.

Moreover, I was looking to the future; I wanted these women of the submerged mass to be, not merely the argument of more fortunate people, but to be fighters on their own account, despising mere platitudes and catchcries, revolting against the hideous conditions about them, and demanding for themselves and their families a full share of the benefits of civilisation and progress.[31]

Pankhurst began her campaign with her close friend, the American Zelie Emerson, a young woman whom Pankhurst had met in Chicago. From a wealthy Michigan family, Emerson had been involved with the settlement house movement in Chicago.[32] She followed Pankhurst to London, and there they worked together very closely. Their friendship was very intense, possibly even sexual. After a quarrel in 1914, Emerson wrote an apology professing that "nothing that has happened or may happen between us can ever alter my feelings toward you", and hoping that after the war "I can be of some service to you and the cause for that is, after all, the only thing that matters". She concluded the letter by telling Pankhurst she was keeping a lock of her hair.[33]

During the suffragette activity in the East End, Emerson proved to be as courageous as Pankhurst, risking hunger, thirst and sleep strikes in prison. The police fractured the American woman's skull on two different occasion in 1914, and while in jail she had appendicitis. Once when the prison ordeal overwhelmed her and she attempted suicide, Pankhurst was allowed to go into Emerson's cell and comfort her.[34] When war broke out in 1914, Emerson was deported back to the USA, where she continued to work in Hull House and eventually moved to Florida.[35]

Pankhurst and Emerson began the East End campaign by walking down the Bow Road looking for a space to set up a shopfront WSPU office. Once they had found a place, they began to organize meetings. It was not an easy or pleasant task because, although many women attended the meetings, more often than not young boys would show up at the outdoor gatherings and throw garbage, dead fish and newspapers soaked in urine. On one occasion a group of rowdy boys tried to overturn a cart that was being used as a platform. Some East Londoners came to Pankhurst's rescue, and two of them – Elsa Dalglish, a landscape painter, and Melvina Walker, a former ladies' maid and docker's wife – joined the WSPU. They became close friends andsupporters of Pankhurst throughout her experiences in the East End.

In November 1912, the East London constituency of Bow and Bromley became the centre of attention for the suffragette movement, and this agitation and organization was the beginning of the East London Federation of the Suffragettes (ELFS). The renewed interest began when George Lansbury, the Labour MP for the constituency, a well-known champion of the women's cause and a hardened socialist campaigner, confronted the Liberal prime minister, Herbert Asquith, with the question of forced feeding and the suffragettes' treatment in prison. During a question-and-answer session in the House of Commons, Asquith claimed that the women could leave prison at any time if they co-operated with the authorities. Quivering with rage, Lansbury shook his fist at Asquith, exclaiming, "You know they cannot. You will go down in history as the man who tortured women."[36] Lansbury was ordered to leave the House of Commons.

He received letters of congratulation and support for this action, including some from individuals and organizations in the East End. Ellen Spencer wrote, "As an East End woman, I thank you from my heart for your brave and splendid conduct on behalf of women in the House of Commons yesterday."[37] The Poplar Trades Council passed a resolution that "heartily congratulates Mr. George Lansbury, MP, in his protest in the House of Commons on behalf of the women prisoners".[38]

W. Andrade, writing for the Millwall East Branch of the National Union of Gasworkers and General Labourers, also praised Lansbury:

> I should consider that I was not doing my duty if I neglected writing you to congratulate you on the noble action you took in the House yesterday. . . . I am doubly glad that there are such men as you who are prepared to rouse the rights of the people.[39]

Deciding to stake his political future on women's suffrage, Lansbury resigned his seat in Parliament in November 1912 and ran again on the single issue of votes for women. He received no support from the official Labour Party or the ILP but was helped by the women's suffrage movement – militants and non-militants alike.

The Lansbury election campaign during November generated a great deal of excitement in the East End, putting the impoverished area of London for once in the national spotlight. The WSPU, the National Union of Women's Suffrage Societies (NUWSS, the leading non-militant or constitutional wing of the suffrage movement, led by Millicent Garrett Fawcett), the Women's Freedom League (WFL), the Men's League for Women's Suffrage and the New Constitution Society set up offices in his district to help Lansbury win.[40]

Leading trade union and socialist speakers also came to the East End. Ben Tillett (leader of the dockers), Will Thorne (leader of the gasworkers), Stella Cobden-Sanderson (daughter of radical Richard Cobden) and Victor Grayson (socialist MP for the Colne Valley) all spoke at meetings for Lansbury. Emmeline Pankhurst, by then one of England's greatest orators, made numerous speeches.[41] At first, the WSPU put all its resources into getting Lansbury elected. The *Daily Herald*, which Lansbury edited, commented:

> One point in connection with the WSPU is worth noting. It is that they are out for all they are worth to return Mr. Lansbury, thus taking a very different attitude from that taken at previous elections. This time it is not a case of keeping someone out, so much as to send Mr. Lansbury in. To this end, they will be working persistently and incessantly day and night until the end.[42]

The *Suffragette*, the official newspaper of the WSPU, echoed the *Herald*:

> The election in Bow and Bromley marks a turning point in the movement for Votes for Women. It is the beginning of the end of the politician's resistance to the enfranchisement of women. Those whose political fate is at stake in this contest have now to see that Mr. Lansbury is triumphantly re-elected, that he is returned to Parliament empowered and authorised by his constituents to fight this government and anti-suffragists.[43]

The WSPU's active endorsement did not last long, however, and after the initial burst of enthusiasm, it did little to support Lansbury. It was during this election campaign that the differences between Pankhurst and Christabel surfaced – differences that would eventually result in a formal split in the WSPU in 1914.

Since Pankhurst had set up a Votes for Women office in a Bow Road baker's, in an area she knew and loved, it would have been most sensible to put her in charge of the WSPU's Lansbury campaign. Instead, the WSPU sent in an inexperienced organizer. Worse than her inexperience and general incompetence, however, was her hostility to the labour movement and to men in general. Pankhurst complained:

> The WSPU organiser was mainly concerned to uphold the superiority of her organisation. She had no sympathy with the Labour movement. She was supremely unaware of the long hard struggle

and sacrificing effort on the part of poor earnest volunteers.[44]
The organizer also refused to involve WSPU members in the more
mundane though crucial election work, such as door-to-door canvass-
ing and the registration of voters.

Others in the Bow constituency realized that the WSPU would not
support socialist and trade union issues, or the politics that Lansbury
represented. One constituent, G. Saunders Jacobs, warned Lansbury:

> You cannot rely on all the workers of the women's organisa-
> tions. Their cause is righteous but it does not help when some of
> their canvassers go around saying that they do not agree with
> your socialism, but they are supporting you on the suffrage
> question – in fact, frankly that they are using you as a tool. My
> wife and I soon found out a lot of that when we were canvassing
> for you.[45]

The hostility between the WSPU and the local labour organizations
no doubt contributed to Lansbury's defeat. The WSPU and Lansbury's
local Labour Party supporters refused to work with each other. The
height of this ridiculous sectarianism occurred on election day, when
the Labour Party would not send the voting lists (which contained the
names and addresses of eligible voters) to the WSPU, and, in return,
the WSPU would not allow men to use its cars. "Mrs. Pankhurst would
never allow the Union to work under the men!" declared the WSPU
organizer.[46] That evening, Lansbury went to Sylvia Pankhurst, asking her to get a group of women together to persuade voters to turn
out. "I gathered what workers I could, but time was short," wrote
Pankhurst.[47]

In spite of this last-ditch effort, Lansbury lost the election by 4,042
to 3,291. In 1910, he had been sent to Parliament by a vote of 4,315 to
3,452.[48] Pankhurst had thought his defeat "inevitable" because the
East End was politically more backward than areas such as the industrial North. Furthermore, she was aware that many of the Labourites
blamed the suffragettes for Lansbury's having given up his seat in the
first place.[49]

The *Daily Herald* also blamed the defeat on the inability of many
working-class men to vote. "The register was 18 months old and
removals were many," explained one editorial.[50] The loss did not necessarily mean that the district was anti-Lansbury or even against
women's suffrage. The majority of Lansbury's supporters were ineligible to vote. There had been huge demonstrations for Lansbury in

the East End; one in Victoria Park attracted fifty thousand people.[51] The number of letters Lansbury received from constituents and the encouragement of local East End labour and radical groups indicate that popular support for Lansbury was greater than the election vote would suggest.

The Lansbury election campaign helped to build the East End branches of the WSPU:

> Votes for Women Shops in the East End are at 198 Bow Road, 34 Green Street, Bethnal Green; at 174 East India Dock Road, Poplar and Commercial Road in Limehouse. An open-air campaign of special meetings each day is being organised in each of these districts and also a series of large outdoor meetings.[52]

However, neither Christabel nor Emmeline was impressed. Clements Inn, the WSPU headquarters in London, decided that the organization would leave the East End in order to concentrate on other, more "important" areas.

Pankhurst was able to persuade her mother not to leave the East End immediately after the Lansbury loss, which would have meant conceding defeat. She urged that the WSPU organize a large deputation of East End working women to meet the government – in particular Lloyd George, a member of the Cabinet. Emmeline Pankhurst agreed. Drummond, Pankhurst and other WSPU organizers worked ceaselessly to organize the demonstration. According to the *Daily Herald*, their efforts paid off:

> In Stepney, the greatest interest and enthusiasm was shown at the open air meeting on January 1, and several women offered to join the demonstration. . . . In Bethnal Green ground is gained day by day. . . . In Limehouse the meetings held by the WSPU are attracting tremendous attention and most helpful sympathy. Strangers come forward and offer help in various ways and everything points to the great response that will be made for this part of East London. Bethnal Green, Poplar, Camberwell and Bermondsey are all hearing of Mrs. Drummond's deputation.[53]

On 20 January 1913, over 1,000 women marched to Parliament, and Lloyd George met 12 of them. He promised that the Liberal government would not back down from supporting a women's suffrage bill and assured the deputation he would meet them again. Four hours later, the government announced that no women's suffrage bill would be introduced in Parliament. Sylvia Pankhurst and other suffragettes on the deputation, enraged at this deceit, threw rocks at the House of Commons.

After this latest trick by the government, the WSPU, as promised, formally moved all its offices out of the East End. Sylvia Pankhurst and her supporters decided to go it alone and remain there, continuing the work that they had begun.

⚜

Chapter Three

The East London Federation
of the Suffragettes

The East London Federation of the Suffragettes (ELFS) was from its inception a radical, militant, working-class, feminist organization. It was not solely concerned with votes for women, although suffrage was the primary focus of its activities. It was a community organization that admitted men, but it was always led by women. Its main purpose was to expose the exploitation and oppression of women in all aspects of life. "Our cue", wrote Sylvia Pankhurst, "was to fan the flame of popular enthusiasm and to broaden our movement to take in even greater numbers and new sections." Moreover, "it was necessary to rouse the poor women of London, the downtrodden mothers whose lot is one dull grind of hardship in order that they may go in their thousands to demonstrate before the seats of the Almighty".[1]

The ELFS used militant tactics and regarded itself as part of the labour movement, for it saw the achievement of equality and emancipation as inseparable from a socialist organization of society. Most important, Pankhurst interpreted socialism as working-class self-emancipation and applied this to the working-class women who joined: "We must get members to work for themselves and let them feel they are working for their own emancipation," she said.[2]

Pankhurst also believed that building organizations of working women to fight for women's rights was part of the working-class struggle for socialism. Writing to Captain White, a friend and supporter, in 1914, she explained:

> I am a socialist and want to see the conditions under which our people live entirely revolutionised, but because I believe nothing will be accomplished without the help of women, I feel that my first work must be to do what I can to secure for women the

entrance into the political scheme, without which they can never play anything but a subordinate part in the social recon-struction.[3]

Following the formal withdrawal of the WSPU leadership from the East End, Pankhurst was determined to build branches there, even if it meant organizing without the help of the national WSPU office.

On 7 February 1913, Pankhurst and Emerson set off down Roman Road to look for an available space. Both women were invigorated by the area – it was a tiny road but "seething with life", crowded with people, shops and stalls. They found an office at number 321, a small place with an apartment above the shop, consisting of a parlour, a tiny kitchen and three small upstairs rooms. The rent was 14s. 6d. a week. Pankhurst lived in this apartment. This time, their organizing was much easier than when they had set up the shop in Bow Road, for they started with more sympathy.

The immediate tactical objective of the federation, like that of the WSPU, was to force the Liberal government to draft a bill enfranchis-ing women and to maintain a rigorous campaign against the govern-ment until this was achieved. ELFS/WSPU members heckled Liberal politicians at meetings, held public debates, and organized demon-strations and mass marches. When imprisoned, they went on hunger strikes and were force-fed along with the rest of their suffragette sisters.

However, even though the ELFS was still formally a part of the WSPU, there were substantial tactical differences between the two. The federation would not attack the Labour Party, even Labour candi-dates not sympathetic to women's suffrage or those who would con-sider woman's suffrage only in the context of full adult suffrage. This policy was necessary to maintain support among political activists in the East End. Pankhurst made her position clear about working with men when she wrote a Mr Lapworth, an East End friend:

> It is so hard to induce working women to come out and make speeches and really take a prominent part in political move-ments that we must, even apart from the vote, be constantly lay-ing emphasis on the woman's side of things; but nothing is further from my wish than to be bitter and disagreeable towards the men and especially the men down here who have stood by us so splendidly.[4]

The ELFS/WSPU also opposed the WSPU's advocacy of individual acts of arson and destruction of property, believing that mass action was more effective than individual and dramatic acts of terror, however daring or newsworthy.

Pankhurst, Emerson and Dalglish knew that militant tactics would be necessary to establish the ELFS and to create sufficient publicity to enlist more women into its ranks. On the evening of 14 February the ELFS held its first public meeting at Bromley Public Hall on Bow Road. Afterward those attending marched to the local bank and police station, where they broke some windows. Emerson and Pankhurst were arrested and imprisoned. Their fines were paid anonymously by Mrs Pankhurst, and they were quickly back in action.[5] Another demonstration was organized for 17 February, and this time an undertaker's parlour, the Public Hall in Bromley and the local Liberal Club ended up with broken windows. Pankhurst, Emerson, Mrs Watkins (a local dressmaker), Alice Moore, and Annie and Willie Lansbury (the son and daughter of George Lansbury) were arrested.

The next day at the Thames Police Court, Willie Lansbury, Emerson and Pankhurst were sentenced to two months' hard labour; no fines were offered as options. The others were given one month's service. The sentences illustrate the government's response to suffragette activity, for they were unusually harsh for the crime of window breaking.[6] However, they served their purpose for the federation. These sentences, as well as the brutal treatment accorded the ELFS/WSPU prisoners in Holloway, evoked sympathy and support from East End people, who organized more processions and demonstrations to Holloway and Brixton prisons.

The East End men and women sentenced to jail for the suffragette cause were making sacrifices far greater than those the suffragettes of the respectable West End had to make. Jobs were lost, and children, husbands and other relatives had to be cared for by relations or friends or had to look after themselves. The ELFS/WSPU raised money and organized child-care facilities to help alleviate this problem. In addition, the treatment of working-class suffragettes in the prison was harsher than that meted out to the wealthy and influential.

The brutal treatment of the suffragettes by the Liberal government has been well documented. In particular, forced feeding had an added dimension of a sexual assault, a violent intrusion akin to rape. A woman who refused to eat would be held down by four to six male and female prison officials. A feeding tube would be inserted through her nose, and a gruel – often laced with brandy – would be fed into it. The prisoner usually struggled, screamed, fainted and, after the ordeal, vomited. Suffragettes afterward spoke of the pain and the inner rage at the humiliation endured, emotions very similar to those of rape victims.[7]

When Sylvia Pankhurst was imprisoned in February 1913, she immediately went on a hunger strike and this time decided to fight when the wardens tried to force-feed her. In an article for the *Suffragette* entitled "They tortured me," Pankhurst described how she hid in a corner of her cell, clutching her prison comb, brush, shoes and basket. She intended to throw them at the warders when they entered, but at the moment they walked in, she couldn't do it.

It took six warders and two doctors to hold her down and force the tube through her nasal passages. After the feeding was over, she vomited, then fainted. This torture went on twice a day for a month. In this period she lost 35 pounds, dropping from 132 to 97 pounds. Her eyes, she said, looked "like cups of blood," and the experience was so painful that she could hardly sleep.[8] Pankhurst felt that her name and prominence in the suffrage movement resulted in her being treated with unusual viciousness. She was locked in solitary confinement and not allowed to exercise with the other prisoners.

In order to assure the suffragettes outside that she was resisting, she smuggled a letter, via Zelie Emerson, out of the prison to her mother:

Dearest Mother,

I am fighting, fighting, fighting, I have four, five and six wardresses every day as well as two doctors. I am fed by a stomach tube twice a day. They prise open my teeth with a steel gag pressing it in where there is a gap in my teeth. I resist all the time. My gums are always bleeding. The night before I vomited my last meal and was ill all night, and was sick after both meals yesterday.

I am afraid they may be saying we don't resist. Yet my shoulders are bruised with struggling whilst they hold the tube into my throat. I used to feel I should go mad at first and be pretty near it, as I think they feared, but I have gotten over that.[9]

Emmeline managed to get her daughter's letter published in the *Daily Mail,* and a renewed outcry against forced feeding resulted. However, nothing was done to remedy the situation. Pankhurst and Emerson resumed their protest by beginning what the *Suffragette* called a "new and terrible form of protest", the hunger and thirst strike.[10] They were brutally force-fed. Pankhurst also began pacing up and down in her cell day and night – adding a sleep strike to the hunger and thirst strike. After she collapsed unconscious, the doctors ordered her release. She had been imprisoned for five weeks.

Sylvia Pankhurst was subjected – or perhaps subjected herself – to more hunger strikes and forced feedings than most suffragettes. Christabel, by contrast, never went on a hunger strike and escaped to Paris when forced feeding was introduced. Emmeline, who did hunger-strike when jailed, was never force-fed. No doubt the Liberal government feared an even greater escalation of suffragette violence if Mrs Pankhurst was hurt.

There are a number of possible reasons for Pankhurst's willingness to endure repeated torture. She had never been healthy, even as a child, and she was aware that hunger, thirst and sleep strikes, combined with forced feeding, would only damage her already frail health. She clearly had a flair for being a martyr, a trait that continued in her later struggles. Possibly she needed to make it clear that she was the most self-sacrificing Pankhurst, and one of the most self-sacrificing suffragettes, all but giving her life to the cause. It also could be argued that her constant arrests, hunger strikes and then forced feedings were but a desperate way of getting attention from her mother, who clearly favoured Christabel.

The ELFS/WSPU organized its first major demonstration on the following 25 May, Mothering Sunday, which the federation renamed Women's May Day. It was intended as a working-class feminist celebration, in the way that May Day was celebrated by socialist, trade union and other working-class organizations. The Bow, Bromley and Poplar branches spent weeks preparing for this demonstration, and their hard work resulted in a tremendously successful march. According to the *Daily Herald*, "thousands and thousands of women were drawn into the streets" carrying almond branches, waving purple, green and white banners – the colours of the WSPU – and wearing a new, special symbol for the ELFS/WSPU added by Pankhurst: red caps, like those worn by the revolutionary women of the French revolution.[11]

The march started at the East India Dock Gates and several brass bands played the "Internationale", "The Red Flag" and other working-class and socialist songs as the thousands marched through the East End to Victoria Park. Speaking at the rally were John Scurr (prominent East End socialist and dockers' leader), H. W. Nevinson (another well-known socialist) and Pankhurst (representing the ELFS/WSPU). The march was so successful that even the anti-feminist dockers' leader, Ben Tillett, was impressed. Though he was not known for his sympathy to the suffragettes, he was moved to say after the march that he wished that the men "had half the women's pluck".[12]

The rally was almost spoiled when some young boys attempted to heckle and to throw stones and garbage at Pankhurst. The police stood by and refused to help the demonstrators, but the women were protected by the large number of dockers who came on the demonstration.[13] At future rallies and marches, the ELFS/WSPU was able to count not only on dockers, but on gasworkers and other labourers as their allies.

This successful event marked the official founding of the ELFS/WSPU. According to Pankhurst, the ELFS/WSPU was "formally set up, to unite for greater strength the local Unions that had been formed in Bow, Bromley, Poplar, Limehouse and Hackney".[14] Unlike its parent organization, the ELFS/WSPU was democratically run, with elected officers and organizers. Pankhurst was elected honorary secretary; Norah Smythe, an independently wealthy woman who became one of Pankhurst's closest friends and comrades, was the financial secretary. Other officers were the treasurer, meetings secretaries, an advertisement manager, district secretaries and organizers and two elected representatives of the members in each district. The five or six full-time organizers were paid 30 shillings a week. Pankhurst also employed a secretary, Nellie Rathbone. The wages paid to East End women working in factories or workshops at this time were about 11–15 shillings a week.[15]

The federation was financially supported partly by dues from its members, which were 1½d. per month. The main source of revenue was contributions, especially from wealthy members or supporters. Pankhurst was aware that the ELFS/WSPU could not maintain its level of organization and activity on dues alone. "The business of our treasurers was, in short, to aid us in raising a supplementary fund, to enable us to do a larger propaganda than we could have done by the contributions of our poor membership alone, and to supervise accounts," wrote Pankhurst.[16] Norah Smythe gave most of her inherited wealth to the ELFS/WSPU.[17] In order for the ELFS/WSPU to grow and to keep its members' interest, it had to provide more than marches and demonstrations. Thus, the ELFS/WSPU trained women to become organizers and speakers for the suffrage movement. It provided services such as medical advice for women and their children and child care that enabled the women to attend meetings.

Pankhurst had an extraordinary ability to recruit to the ranks. Annie Barnes, a Stepney woman who joined the ELFS in its early years and later became a Stepney councillor, remained friends until Pankhurst left for Ethiopia in 1955. "Mind you," Barnes later said, "Sylvia was such a wonderful woman she only had to say something, and you wanted to do it."[18] Barnes's recollection of how she was recruited to militancy was not an untypical story.

At the first ELFS/WSPU meeting that Annie attended, Pankhurst gave a pep talk. "Well, you new recruits won't be any good unless you are prepared to face anything, and I mean anything. You will be sometimes in danger." Having led a somewhat quiet and sheltered life, Barnes didn't know what to make of this speech. However, at the second meeting, Pankhurst asked for a volunteer. "This box in front of you is padded," she explained. "I want someone to be put in the box and taken to the House of Commons to the tradesmen's entrance. Everything has been arranged." She then outlined the plan: "We want someone to be delivered as goods, so in the night she can get out and go up to the public gallery and hide. At ten o'clock tomorrow when the House opens you're to go to the part of the gallery immediately above Asquith's desk."

Barnes could not volunteer for that assignment, because she knew she could not risk imprisonment. She was too afraid of her parents' reaction. But another woman volunteered and threw a three pound bag of flour over Asquith's head! The next day the newspaper headlines said, "Asquith floured all over."

Barnes did volunteer for other, equally risky assignments. Her very first mission was to go with Pankhurst and others to the top of London Bridge with carrier bags full of Votes for Women leaflets to throw down at people. It was not only dangerous but exhausting, for the women had to climb up and down the narrow spiral staircases before they were caught by the police.

"Be as quick as possible," urged Pankhurst. "Throw them over and get down quickly because the police will be after you." The women were stopped by the police, but managed to feign innocence and escape. "The East End had been so quiet, and all at once it was tense with excitement. Meetings here, meetings there. It was marvellous," Barnes recollected.[19]

The women members were very busy political activists. The federation had meetings twice a week, once in the afternoon and once in the evening. This way, both housewives and working women could attend. In the spring and summer months there were fortnightly Sunday open-air demonstrations. It was always difficult to get large crowds of women to join these demonstrations because "mothers could not come out on Sundays as the children have to be looked after, and she is too tired to come out after the weary preparation of dinner".[20] The federation set up nurseries so that more mothers could participate.

Classes were set up to train women to become public speakers. A member named Rose Leo took charge of these popular and successful classes. They were held at several different locations and male speakers, often George Lansbury or John Scurr, would be invited so that the women could practise heckling and learn how to deal with hecklers.[21]

In December 1913, the ELFS/WSPU organized a week-long suffrage school. The lectures and discussions covered a wide range of social problems facing women as workers and as housewives. They included: the legal position of women, wages, housing, infant mortality, sex education, trade unionism, radical and socialist history, female psychology and the effects of hunger striking and forced feeding.[22] Lectures on such topics as sex education and female psychology were unusual at this time. They give an idea of the breadth of the ELFS/ WSPU's feminist radicalism as well as of the women's issues that concerned it. The schools and the meetings, the planning and organizing of demonstrations, marches and rallies, all trained a number of East End women who remained politically active as leaders even after the suffragette activity ended. Annie Barnes wrote, "Being in the suffragettes did a lot for me. I couldn't say 'Boo' to a goose before that. It really brought me out."[23]

Nellie Rathbone, who joined the ELFS/WSPU in 1913 (when she was 21), echoed many of Annie Barnes's comments:

> I'd never heard of anything like it – you see, coming from a Jewish family where the daughters are not thought of much. The daughters do the work. I was a bit of a rebel from early on, went to meetings on Mile End Waste with the suffragettes, and indoor meetings too.[24]

Once organized, the federation participated during the spring and summer of 1913 in massive demonstrations against new repressive legislation specifically passed to deal with the suffragettes and the problems of forced feeding. In March 1913, the home secretary, Reginald McKenna, drafted the Prisoners' (Temporary Discharge for Ill Health) Bill. Once passed by Parliament, it became known as the "Cat and Mouse Act". It provided that hunger strikers be discharged when their health deteriorated sufficiently as a result of hunger-striking and then re-arrested when their health improved. This was called being *out on licence*. The licence "expired" when the authorities decided that the suffragettes had recovered sufficiently to withstand being in prison. It meant that hunger strikers would have to serve their full term of imprisonment, with the possibility of spending years in and out of jails.

Not content with this, McKenna went further. The authorities banned suffragette meetings, arrested members of the editorial board of the *Suffragette* and finally censored the newspaper itself. George Bernard Shaw, a friend of the Pankhursts, aptly remarked: "The suffragettes have succeeded in driving the Cabinet half mad. Mr. McKenna should be examined at once by two doctors. He apparently believes himself to be the Tsar of Russia, a very common form of delusion."[25]

Government repression only made the suffragettes more determined. On 29 June, the ELFS/WSPU organized its first march from the East End to Trafalgar Square. Although several suffrage and trade union organizations were present and in her speech Pankhurst proclaimed the procession was "immense", she was nonetheless dissatisfied and urged her followers "to go and hoot the Cabinet ministers, and if they were able to do more than hoot – to imprison the Cabinet Ministers in their official residences, as they had imprisoned more than 2,000 suffragettes".[26] The demonstration ended in fierce fighting between the East End contingents and the police. Many people were arrested,despite several daring "rescue" attempts, one involving a doctor who was seized from the clutches of the police as he was being frog-marched to a waiting Black Maria.

Pankhurst's speech led the police and government to issue a warrant for her arrest. The government had recently resurrected an old statute, passed, in fact, during the reign of Edward III to deal with demobilized militiamen who refused to behave in a peaceable manner once war was over. This statute gave the government very wide powers of arrest and imprisonment when offenders were deemed to have disturbed "the peace of our Lord the King" or incited a crowd to violence, as Pankhurst's speech was construed as doing. Suffragettes indicted under this statute received harsher prison sentences than had hitherto been given. Emmeline and Sylvia Pankhurst, Annie Kenney, Mrs Cohen from Leeds, John Scurr and George Lansbury were all arrested at different times under the Edward III statute. By refusing to answer her summons, Pankhurst challenged the police to come into the East End and arrest her.

Despite determined efforts to protect her, ultimately the police succeeded in arresting her on 8 July. Sentenced to three months' imprisonment, she immediately hunger-struck and within a week was released under the Cat and Mouse Act. She went to live with Mr and Mrs Payne, who were shoemakers, at 28 Old Ford Road.[27] The small room they had prepared for her became her home for the next year. It was here that she was carefully nursed back to health after the numerous hunger strikes that were to result from implementation of the Cat and Mouse Act. It was here also that Pankhurst learned firsthand the difficulties of slum life, of decaying overcrowded houses and of fleas and rats and the hard, unremitting task of keeping these vermin at bay. From her room in the Old Ford Road she also earned a small amount of money writing articles for the press – the *Clarion,* the *Merthyr Pioneer* and the *Glasgow Forward.*

The ELFS/WSPU began to organize to defeat the Cat and Mouse Act. The idea was to render the Act unworkable by preventing the police from arresting the "mice" once their licences had expired. On 21 July, Pankhurst made the first challenge. She appeared at the Bromley Public Hall disguised with makeup, a long dark coat and a hat pulled down over her eyes. Nevertheless, police detectives grabbed her and immediately suffragette partisans began battling with them to prevent her arrest. After hiding for several hours in a deserted building, Pankhurst was finally smuggled in Willie Lansbury's wood cart to the safety of the Paynes', for the police would not pursue her inside their house.[28]

On 27 July, still out on licence, Pankhurst spoke at another Trafalgar Square rally, managing to get there undisguised. She denounced the Liberal government for doing to the suffragettes "[a] great deal more harm than I and others by the destruction of the Golden Calf, their great God Property, which was of so much more importance and value than their own veracity, honour, integrity and lives of their fellow human beings".[29] She urged the crowd to go to Downing Street, calling on the police "not to break down a working-class movement" and warned that, if people were arrested, "I shall do my best to incite the crowds to free them. I think the people of London are taking fire." Pankhurst and others were arrested. Mrs Pascoe from the East End contemptuously told the magistrate at her trial, "It is better to die in prison than to be cowards like you big pots are."[30]

After an excruciating hunger, thirst and sleep strike, Pankhurst was released, only to become involved in organizing a third Trafalgar Square rally to protest at the recent sentencing of George Lansbury under the Edward III Act. Lansbury hunger-struck and was released. His arrest and imprisonment aroused enormous anger and sympathy.

John Cruse, representing the Bow branch of the Amalgamated Toolmakers, wrote to Mrs Lansbury while her husband was hunger-striking:

> I am instructed by the Bow branch of the above organisation to express the deepest sympathy with you at the cruel and unjust sentence passed on our friend and comrade. We hope that you will be better able to stand the strain when you know at least you have friends to stand by him who gave up his liberty for the downtrodden workers.[31]

Thomas Simons Attlee, representing the Poplar Labour League, also wrote:

> That the Poplar Labour expresses its enthusiastic appreciation of Comrade Lansbury's fight for free speech and its indignation at the sentence passed on him under an obsolete and ridiculous statute![32]

The executive council of the Dockers' Union also called upon all its members to demand Lansbury's release.[33]

In the previous May, John Scurr, who had led many suffragette demonstrations, was cited under the Edward III statute and received similar support from the East End community. The London officials of the Dockers' Union passed a resolution protesting against Scurr's arrest and calling upon the Free Speech Defence Committee, an organization formed to defend the right of free speech as well as the people who had been arrested in suffragette activity, to take action. With free speech being denied by the government, the labour movement was being drawn into the suffrage struggle. The fact that two important leaders of the labour movement were indicted while working for women's suffrage prepared the ground for continued co-operation between the labour movement and the women's suffrage and feminist movement in the East End of London. Thus, the North Ward Bow branch of the Poplar Trade and Labour Representation League, the executive committee of the Printers', Warehousemen's and Cutters' Union and the Bow and Bromley Socialists (of the British Socialist Party, BSP) joined in protest against not only the jailing of Lansbury but also the treatment of all suffragette prisoners.[34]

Ben Tillett, the dockers' leader, appreciated the women's militancy even though he was hostile to the organized women's suffrage movement:

> I think the women folk are splendid. It is indeed good to know women like these live – if only for the sake of the race. I find real sympathy being diverted to the "suffragettes" and that ought to be the means of giving the "Hooligans" a real fight in the near future. I am full up with work . . . but I am going to have a hand in the "Free Speech" fight.[35]

On 10 August, the third and final Trafalgar Square demonstration was held, sponsored by the Herald League, a socialist organization affiliated to the *Daily Herald* and the Free Speech Defence Committee. Between 20,000 and 30,000 people demonstrated, protesting against the jailing of Lansbury. The speeches condemned the government and its repressive legislation and extended warm sympathy to all the suffragettes (in spite of the noticeable absence of the official WSPU from the rally).

Trade union, socialist and feminist leaders spoke – Keir Hardie, Josiah Wedgwood, Will Thorne, John Scurr, Dora Montefiore, Georgina Brakenbury, Melvina Walker, Barbara Wylie and Sylvia Pankhurst. In his speech, John Scurr carefully made the connections between the suffragette movement and the trade union movement. Both, he said, were part of the "people's fight".[36] Pankhurst, however, became frustrated by the passivity of the rally and demanded "deeds not words; it is the argument of sticks and stones from the East End women that is going to win freedom for women".[37] She went on to say:

> Though I have agreed to speak at the Free Speech demonstration, I regret very much that the resolution should not go further,

for it does not seem to me either to strike at the root of power that suppresses the right of free speech, and to strengthen and bolster up that precious right for future times, or to touch the source of present free speech trouble. . . . The only demand worth making is for absolute freedom of speech in all political questions and security from prosecution for the expression of political opinion, under any act or precedent whatever. . . . The right of free speech, free assembly, call also for the right to vote.[38]

Pankhurst urged the ELFS contingent to lead the demonstration from Trafalgar Square to 10 Downing Street. A fight with the police broke out and 18 people were arrested.

The federation believed that demonstrations and actions such as these not only helped build the organization but encouraged militancy across the country:

These demonstrations of militant popular support were a fine answer to those who were saying that public opinion was against the women in their fight for liberty. Moreover, they were doing a tremendous amount of good work all over the country, for following the cue of East London, working people from Lands End to John O'Groats were beginning, more than they had ever done before, to feel that votes for women was their question.[39]

Throughout the remainder of 1913 the tempo of militancy increased in East London and was met, naturally, with increasingly savage repression. Self-defence became imperative. However, whereas the WSPU had been relying increasingly on secrecy, intrigue and army-style discipline – or, in Christabel's case, in comfortable, self-imposed exile in Princess Polignac's palace in Paris – the ELFS/WSPU looked to its community for protection. As soon as Pankhurst went to live in Old Ford Road, detectives hoping to keep her under surveillance tried to rent rooms in the area. Despite their generous offers of money and despite the general poverty of the area, not a single person in Old Ford Road would accommodate them.[40]

Police efforts were further frustrated by the ease with which, in a close-knit community such as the East End, people could identify plainclothes policemen and throw them out of meetings. Federation members claimed that police could be detected by their smell![41] Pankhurst had one male bodyguard, "Kosher" Hunt, who had been a popular wrestler in the East End,[42] the rest of her bodyguards were all women. Since the police did not employ females as detectives, any strange male found in the vicinity of Sylvia Pankhurst was immediately suspect.[43] Police and detectives were sent in ever-increasing numbers to East London to arrest the recalcitrant "mice". For a while, complicated and ingenious disguises kept the police confused and wondering. The suffragettes often changed their clothes three or four times during a meeting.[44] Increasingly, however, Pankhurst began to feel that disguises were a cowardly way of eluding the police. They were also ineffective, for the police were beginning to recognize many of the disguised women; furthermore, a disguise was no protection against a police truncheon wielded indiscriminately in a tightly packed meeting or demonstration.

The federation proved enormously resourceful when it came to other means of defence. Firehoses were extremely effective weapons when the authorities tried to break up meetings.[45] Then there was the "Saturday Night Club," an ingenious and frightening weapon, created by an anonymous inventor. It consisted of a long piece of knotted rope dipped in tar and often weighted with lead. Saturday Night Clubs were often an effective counter to police batons.[46]

At one of her numerous trials, Zelie Emerson explained why she carried such a club:

Lawyer: Are you in the habit of carrying a knotted rope?

Emerson: Yes, since my skull was fractured I have. [In Victoria Park by a police truncheon]

Lawyer: Is this the sort of thing you carry? [produces a Saturday Night Club]

Emerson: [laughing] Yes, it is a Saturday Night. A very formidable weapon, isn't it. But it's not as formidable as a police truncheon.

Lawyer: Did you see a notice it was the duty of all friends to go armed?

Emerson: Yes, I always go to meetings armed . . . for over two years I have been closely associated with the People's Army and the WSPU in the East End. I have been called a dirty dog on hundreds of occasions.[47]

When Sylvia Pankhurst appeared at a public meeting in July in front of the East India Dock Gates, the police – seeing a hostile crowd armed with sticks and clubs – left her alone. Mary Leigh, the first

suffragette to go to prison for stone-throwing, spoke at this meeting:
Get your stones ready. Get your matches ready; get your para-
phernalia of which we are such past masters in the use and
tonight, let us light a bonfire in London which is bound to be
seen by the whole world.[48]

The audience responded with rousing cheers.

On another occasion, in response to a police attempt to break up a
federation meeting,

. . . immediately the audience rose to their feet and began to fly
through the air at the constables who flung them back into the
hall. Wooden benches were dropped from the gallery upon the
police and chairs were used to belabour them about their heads.
A table on the platform was thrown bodily by several women at
the constable.[49]

Such protection enabled Pankhurst to speak unmolested in Bow,
Bromley, Hackney, Canning Town and even the Albert Hall.

Whenever she made the mistake of going out alone, however, the
police pounced. In January 1914, the federation began to organize a
Shoreditch march. Pankhurst, the featured speaker, refused to go
accompanied by her bodyguard. "I wanted not to bring an army from
Bow but to create an army in Shoreditch."[50] But "When I said 'the
detectives are outside to take me' there were cries of 'and inside too'.
Everyone stood up and hissed and shouted and shook their fists."
However, fist shaking was not as formidable as Saturday Night Clubs
and this time the police were able to arrest her.[51] On this occasion, as
in many of her arrests, Pankhurst was handled very roughly. One
officer, Inspector Riley, grabbed her arm tightly and dragged her
across a passageway. Pankhurst resisted, yelling "Votes for women!"
A detective, also escorting her, said, "If you call out again, I'll give you
a smack across the head." "How dare you," Pankhurst replied. The
police then gagged her with a handkerchief. The detective then turned
on Pankhurst and said, "You're always talking about morals, but your
morals are down in hell. Your morals are in the depths of hell."[52]

From February 1913 until the war broke out in August 1914,
Pankhurst was arrested eight times. Each time she hunger-struck and
was released on licence for a week. When her licence expired, the
police would go into the East End and try to arrest her when she
appeared at meetings or demonstrations. Each of her captures and
arrests was marked by community fighting with the police.

It was not long, therefore, before calls for the people to defend both themselves and the suffragettes (in whatever way they could) were replaced by talk of a trained workers' army. It had not escaped the notice of the suffragettes that the Liberal government had done nothing to prosecute Edward Carson and the Ulster rebels (Irish Protestants militantly opposing Home Rule for Ireland) for actions far more treasonous than any carried out for women's suffrage. This reluctance was assumed to be due to the well-trained and disciplined army that Carson had organized to fight to the death against Home Rule. However, in this the suffragettes were wrong: the main reason for the restraint shown towards Ulster was the Liberals' desire to maintain British rule in Ireland.

Carson's tactics, though not his politics, appealed to Pankhurst, who wanted to build a citizens' or people's army which would consist of "an organisation of men and women [joining] in order to fight for freedom, and in order that they may fit themselves to cope with the brutality of Government servants".[53] The army, as its oath implied, would fight for "a vote for every woman and every man, putting women first because they are always left out altogether".[54] At a suffrage meeting in November 1913, Pankhurst explained that "there would be no fear of suffragettes going back to prison if they had an army like Sir Edward Carson's".[55]

She called upon people to start drilling. This was in fact a common practice in Edwardian Britain, advocated not only by recently formed organizations such as the Boy Scouts, but also by Robert Blatchford and the socialists around the *Clarion*. Socialist Sunday schools engaged in drill practice. The popularity of drilling had its origin in the shock and shame felt by many at the poor state of health of working-men during the Boer War of the 1890s. The idea of an "army" to carry out policies was also not unknown. In fact, Christabel Pankhurst had modelled some of her organizational ideas for the WSPU on the structure of William Booth's Salvation Army.

In that year as well, across the Irish Sea, James Connolly, the Irish socialist, labour leader and supporter of the militant suffragettes, had organized an Irish Citizen Army. He first announced the formation of a military force at a suffragette meeting in Dublin in November 1913, at the height of the great Dublin General Strike. Connolly pointed out the connections between the right of labour to organize and the right of women to vote. Women, like the labour movement, should rely not on any political party but rather on their own efforts. The Irish Citizen Army would later play a pivotal role in the 1916 Easter Uprising.[56]

This call from Sylvia Pankhurst – for an army of women and men to take to the streets in formation – should be seen in this context. Its impact, though formidable, must not be overemphasized. She did exclaim, "It is no use pretending. We have got to fight. The government is so cowardly that even the appearance of force will make it give way. Let us show we are prepared to do what is necessary."[57] However, calling her group an army was more rhetorical than realistic. At this point in her life, she considered herself a pacifist.

Pankhurst urged men to join her army:

> I hope that large numbers of men will at once respond to and form themselves into a citizens' corps for this purpose. It is but just that they should do so, for women have always been found to support men in their struggle for political and economic liberty.[58]

But Pankhurst had also always encouraged women to learn the art of self-defence. "We have not yet made ourselves a match for the police and we have got to do it. The police know ju-jitsu. I advise you to learn ju-jitsu. Women should practise it as well as men."[59] Three months later she told a Poplar audience:

> I say to you that not until there is a popular uprising will you secure for us the vote. That is necessary. There is going to be drilling in the East End. We are going to fight and we will do far more than the Ulster people. Get on with this drilling. Arm yourselves. Let us fight and we shall win.[60]

However, Pankhurst had little idea of how to train and drill an army and in one of her speeches she asked anyone who had been in the army and knew about drilling to come and help. Sir Francis Vane, an ex-captain of the British Army, responded. Vane had also been interested in the idea of a citizens' or "Labour Army". He wrote in the *Daily Herald* about the necessity of drilling and arming the working class:

> The Labour Training Corps has been instituted to provide the rank and file of the Labour Party with the means by which they can perfect themselves in that simple form of drill which will enable them . . . to protect their own comrades when unjustly attacked.

He also argued that the army would be responsible for keeping meetings orderly.[61]

Norah Smythe, who was already a leader of the ELFS/WSPU, became captain of the army, which was organizationally separate from the federation. Its inaugural meeting was held at the Bow Baths on 5 November.[62] Three hundred mounted police turned up, furious that Sylvia Pankhurst had again escaped arrest despite the expiration of her Cat and Mouse licence. She escaped this time because Daisy Lansbury dressed up as Pankhurst and was arrested instead of her. The police did not take kindly to being fooled and moved in to disperse the crowd gathering outside the Bow Baths. The newly formed army managed to unhorse some of the mounted police and drive the rest from the area. The next day the triumphant army marched through Bow.

The army drilled every Tuesday night after the Bow federation meetings and was observed and cheered on by several hundred men and women. Drilling usually consisted of 80 to 100 people marching in formation, carrying clubs. At its peak in the winter of 1914, an estimated 700 women were a part of the People's Army.[63] Sometimes the police left it alone, for, as the *Daily Herald* commented on 29 October, it had "already put the fear of God into the hearts of the special Scotland Yard variety quartered in the East End".[64]

At a November 1913 rally at the Bow Baths, Pankhurst reported on the army's growing popularity, adding that she hoped it would soon be strong enough to march on Parliament or Downing Street. At this meeting, reported the *East London News,* the crowd cheered enthusiastically, lifted her onto their shoulders and carried her home singing "The Red Flag".[65]

The People's Army came under attack, particularly by the press, which ridiculed the idea of women being in an army. Pankhurst wrote a letter defending the army, after an editorial in *The Times* strongly denounced it:

> In reply to your extraordinary editorial comments ... the People's Army is not composed of Athletic Amazons as you say but of working women and men who have been toiling all their lives for their daily bread and have hitherto found neither time, energy, nor superfluous cash to cultivate athletics ... So far as the weapons employed by our recruits have not been broomsticks but life preservers made of India rubber or rope – in some

cases weighted with lead pokers, and good stout sticks. You refer to the formation of our army as "flat-footed tomfoolery" and "the negation of everything that makes for popular advancement of advantage". You would do better to abuse the Liberal government for its refusal to grant freedom for women, its introduction of the crude and disgusting practice of forcible feeding and for its brutal treatment of the Dublin strikers.[66]

The existence of an "army" in the East End also sometimes provoked the police. On 14 February 1914, as members of the army were practising running through the streets with their arms linked, the police tried to block the road in front of them. Norah Smythe, hoping to avoid a confrontation, dismissed the army. She herself was arrested, however, for allegedly kicking a policeman.[67]

Concerned with the escalating disorder in the East End, on 6 November the Poplar Borough Council passed a resolution, forbidding any organization that sympathized with the militant suffragette movement to hold a public meeting in the Borough of Poplar. In December, the general purposes committee reiterated the council's position, which was that "Halls not be let to any person or persons unless they agree that 'militancy' shall not be in any way advocated; that no person whom the police have legal instructions to arrest shall be allowed to take part in such meetings in any way whatsoever."[68]

Whether the ELFS/WSPU meetings or the police determination to capture "mice" was the cause of the disorder was debated among people in the East End, but there was no disagreement that the police were brutal to the suffragettes. A January free speech meeting in Bow/Bromley, where Pankhurst spoke, was attacked by the police. Mrs Ivor and Mrs Forbes Roberts suffered broken arms. Mary Leigh was beaten unconscious and a detective hit Zelie Emerson with a lead-weighted club. According to Pankhurst, the detective was furious because the crowd taunted him, calling him "puss".[69]

The ELFS/WSPU showed its disapproval of the council's resolution by disrupting any public meeting held in public halls unless a suffragette speech was given. It also organized a march to the council meeting on 16 December, but it was small and unsuccessful. The unsympathetic *East End News* commented that the federation's "first attempt to serenade members of the Poplar Borough Council who decline to grant use of the public halls to the militant suffragettes ended in a most inglorious fizzle".[70] There were only about 200 people and the police were able to disperse them easily. The only casualty of this march was the beautiful gasworkers' banner, which was lost in the fracas. Several days later, the clerk of the council received letters from the Poplar Trades Council, the Poplar Labour Representation Committee, the Cubitt Town branch of the Gasworkers' Union, the Poplar Labour League and the Eastern branch of the Electrical Trades Union, "protesting against the action of the council in refusing the use of the Public Halls for suffragette meetings". The Trades Council and the Labour Representation Committee also asked that a deputation on this subject be received by the council.[71] Pankhurst wrote to the council on behalf of the ELFS. The Men's Federation for Women's Suffrage and the Rebels' Social and Political Union also requested the council to meet such a deputation.[72] The council agreed to meet members of the Herald League and the British Socialist Party and dockers' and gasworkers' representatives, as well as the federation, to discuss the situation, but at the meeting the council adamantly refused to alter its decision. (This was one of the first times that the British Socialist Party openly supported the suffragettes.)

Furious, the ELFS/WSPU decided to take matters into its own hands. It announced that the People's Army would attend the next public meeting of the council in large numbers. At this meeting, on 27 March, Lansbury tried unsuccessfully to persuade the councillors to rescind their restrictive policy. On hearing of this failed effort, the army attacked.

Crying "Shame! Shame!" the women shot off popguns and threw bags of flour, blue powder, red ochre and other substances. They rushed the councillors, overturning ink pots, ripping up agendas and other official papers and throwing chairs. Any councillor who lashed out at them was attacked with a Saturday Night Club. Three notorious anti-woman's suffrage councillors found themselves engaged in hand-to-hand combat with members of the army.

Finally, the mayor adjourned the meeting to give the councillors time to discuss the situation. Upon their return, after a brief recess, they immediately passed a resolution forbidding the public to attend all future council meetings. As this policy was announced, Lansbury, in disgust, ripped up all the papers belonging to the town clerk and the meeting ended in total confusion.[73]

At no time during these events did the police enter the council building and arrest anyone, even though the mayor had called for them.

After this success, the army marched triumphantly back through the streets of Poplar. The march ended up at Pankhurst's home, where she had been recuperating from one of her hunger and thirst strikes and some of the women told an exhausted but amused and amazed Pankhurst what they had done.[74]

Pankhurst believed that the army would be important for reasons and causes other than militant demonstrations for the vote. It had been formed partly to give women a chance to defend themselves against the police. Seen as hated outsiders in most of East London, the police enforced their rule with brutality; it seemed to the population that they were trying to conquer the area, rather than to police it. The People's Army was thus also supposed to defend free speech, to drive out police spies and to prevent wrongful arrest – particularly common in the alcoholic chaos of a Saturday night.

Even further, the federation and the People's Army had been created to involve women in other actions that would better their position in society. Therefore, in late 1913, Pankhurst announced the federation's intention of organizing a "No Vote No Rent" strike in East London, thus linking the campaign for women's suffrage to women's power as consumers:

> The working woman feels the burden of rent probably more than any other. Most of the East End tenements are rack-rented and the accommodations vile.
>
> The women now say "No Vote No Rent" and with from 3 to 4000 women refusing to pay, the landlords and their supporters will find eviction impossible. This is excellent work, and is sure to prove beneficial all round. The training in the use of a weapon which can be used at will, makes the politicians rather anxious to do as the voters request and not fool themselves as they do at present.[75]

Pankhurst knew that the strike would not be easy to organize or win, but she kept encouraging people to begin the fight:

> If working women, upheld by their husbands, who should desire to see them voters like themselves, will trust each other and stand together as sisters in proclaiming a "No Vote No Rent" strike, women will have won the vote before the year is out.
>
> The No Rent strike will need careful organisation, but it will be absolutely irresistible if women will but trust each other – and it must be clearly understood from the first that until the

strike is over no arrears of rent will be paid.[76]
The People's Army was to play a role in supporting the strike. Pankhurst outlined the plan at a rally:

> On a certain day there would be no rent paid until women get votes – (Loud cheers) – and there would be no arrears paid until the strike was over. If there was any attempt to sell the furniture of any of them the "army" would attend the sale and "rescue" the furniture. (Loud cheers).[77]

Pankhurst sought support from other feminists and suffrage organizations. Nina Boyle of the Women's Freedom League wrote to her in January 1914, agreeing to co-operate in the rent strike and asking Pankhurst to mention in her publicity that Charlotte Despard, the leader of the WFL, had initiated a rent strike six years earlier. Boyle ended her letter by explaining that such co-operation might break down the sectarianism that existed among the suffrage groups.[78]

The call for such a strike was in keeping with an already established East End tradition, in particular the rent strikes that took place during the great dock strike of 1889. The following poem had been published in the *Reynolds News* on 1 September 1889:

> Our husbands are on strike, to the wives it is not honey,
> And we all think it right, not to pay the landlords' money.
> Everyone is on strike, so landlords do not be offended,
> The rent that's due, we'll pay you, when the strike is ended.[79]

East End anarchists and socialists supported the rent strikes of the 1890s, which had perhaps been influenced by the Irish Land League's resistance in the late nineteenth century.

Tactics such as the rent strike and the People's Army show clearly that the federation was not only committed to community issues but had a real sense of East End traditions. This was, of course, because its membership, by and large, was made up of residents of the East End. Furthermore, the tradition of No Rent strikes continued through the 1930s and 1940s when anarchists and communists in Britain and elsewhere defended individuals from eviction through militant community struggles.

During November 1913 the ELFS/WSPU was involved not only in suffrage agitation but also in a trade union struggle outside England. This was based in its belief that the struggle for suffrage and the working-class struggle for trade unionism were part of the same overall struggle. The federation actively supported the men and women involved in the

Dublin lockout of 1913 in which the city's entire organized labour movement had been locked out of work by a federation of employers. In this active support, the ELFS/WSPU stood out, not just among other suffrage organizations, but among other socialist groups as well. Dora Montefiore, now working with the ELFS/WSPU, was largely responsible for organizing this support. Influenced by Margaret Sanger's example during the 1912 textile workers' strike in Lawrence, Massachussetts, she organized the evacuation of children from strike-torn Dublin to the homes of sympathetic trade unionists in England.[80]

This effort was met with considerable resistance from the Liberal government, the police and even sections of the trade union movement in England. Finally, with the help of Julia Scurr and other federation members, Dora Montefiore arranged accommodation in the East End for the young evacuees. Unfortunately, the whole idea had to be abandoned because of the intervention of the Catholic Church. Horrified that Catholic children might be harboured in Protestant homes, Irish priests and nuns went so far as to seize some of the evacuees from the boats at Dun Laoghaire before they could leave for England. The families of others were prevailed upon not to let their children go to England. The fact remains, however, that the ELFS/WSPU attempted to find homes for the strikers' children, raised money and provided supportive propaganda.[81] Few organizations of the time could match this record.

The vital necessity of supporting the Dublin strikers was also understood by the *Daily Herald*, which played a prominent part in calling for sympathetic action in England. Unfortunately, the Trades Union Congress (TUC) did little more than make dramatic gestures such as sending food ships to the starving city. A huge rally was organized on 1 November 1913 by a number of other trade union and socialist groups. Its purpose was to demand the release of Jim Larkin, one of the principal leaders of the workers in Dublin. George Lansbury asked Pankhurst to speak. She agreed:

> The Dublin lock-out was to me a poignant incident in our common struggle for a fairer, more humane society. I was glad to accept the invitation as an opportunity to show solidarity with the Dublin workers and to keep the women's side of the struggle to the front.[82]

Over 10,000 people came to Albert Hall to hear Delia Larkin, sister of the imprisoned Jim Larkin, socialist and organizer of the women's

section of the Irish Transport and General Workers' Union (ITGWU).
Charlotte Despard, George Lansbury and Frederick Pethick-Lawrence
also spoke. The crowd cheered James Connolly, an Irish socialist and
another leader of the ITGWU, who declared that he opposed the domination of nation over nation, class over class and sex over sex.[83]

The *Daily Herald* reported that Pankhurst was the best-received
speaker:

> Sylvia Pankhurst happened to have eluded the police and was on
> the platform. In response to demands from the audience, she
> rose to speak, but for some time could not be heard owing to the
> enthusiastic reception accorded to her. She said she was glad to
> speak on behalf of the Dublin strikers with her fellow hunger
> striker, James Larkin. She had to remember that Rachel Peace
> [member of the WSPU] was being forcibly fed three times a day.
> (Cries of murderers!) Revolt was imperative. Women were paid
> one penny for putting 383 dots on embroidery and could some-
> times earn 6d a day. The government is responsible and the
> working woman has got to fight. In the labour movement
> women were wanted as well as men. Women had no votes and
> could not strike. The only thing they could do was fight. (Loud
> cheers).[84]

George Lansbury editorialized: "One great result of the militant
suffrage movement has been to convince many people that the vote is
not the best way of getting what one wants . . . every day the industrial
rebels and the suffrage rebels march nearer together." Lansbury also
implied that the Herald League and the ELFS/WSPU had formed an
alliance.[85]

Pankhurst's participation in the rally, her speech and the coverage
by the *Daily Herald* were too much for the WSPU. These events pre-
cipitated the long-awaited split in the suffragette family that would
lead to the expulsion of Pankhurst and the federation from the WSPU.
Pankhurst was aware that the women at Lincoln's Inn would be outraged by the Albert Hall meeting. Mabel Tuke, an officer of the WSPU,
demanded that the ELFS leave the WSPU immediately.[86] In response,
Pankhurst wrote to the *Daily Herald* and the *Suffragette,* assuring
both that no alliance between the ELFS/WSPU and the Herald League
had been made. She further explained, in a letter to WSPU branches,
that she had attended the Albert Hall rally to show that "behind every
poor man, there stands an even poorer woman" and "to put the cause

of Votes for Women before 10,000 people" and concluded by saying that she felt it was important for the WSPU to speak to large meetings such as that one.[87]

Annie Kenney responded with another letter to the branches which argued that, although the WSPU had taken the lead in holding large meetings at Albert Hall, it was dangerous to work with the Labour Party and the ILP.[88]

Meanwhile, Christabel was furious with her sister. Having utterly rejected all co-operation with the Labour Party and trade unions by this time, she believed that now was the time for women to stand and act on their own; the labour and socialist movements would not support them.[89] No doubt her attitudes were reinforced by a letter she received from Henry Harbin, a Herald League supporter and one-time adviser to Christabel. He wrote that most of the speakers at the Albert Hall meeting were obviously giving the women lip-service and dragging them in as an afterthought. "There was no real feeling on the woman question. The ovation to Sylvia was to the rebel and not to the woman."[90]

The issue for Christabel, however, was not why Pankhurst received the ovation. Christabel basically hated the fact that Pankhurst and the East End campaign were publicly defying the WSPU policy of not working with trade union and socialist groups and not appearing on platforms with men.[91] She wrote to Pankhurst re-emphasizing, "I shall repudiate any connection between the Herald League and the WSPU in this and in every possible way make it clear that we are absolutely independent of this and all men's parties and movements." She also informed her sister that Lansbury had first asked her or Annie Kenney to speak, but they had refused. "I said no . . . which was also a refusal to have the WSPU represented on the platform. They approached you and got your consent to speak."[92]

It was becoming clear that the WSPU would split. Theodora Bonwick, a long-time member of the WSPU, wrote to Pankhurst saying she was "cut up" about the fight that was going on. "I have written a long letter to Christabel on the whole matter for I cannot bear a further division in our ranks, of what our enemies would think and what our members feel."[93] She begged Pankhurst to keep quiet about the fight until Emmeline returned from a trip she was on to America.

In December, Pankhurst was summoned to Paris. Being a "mouse" at the time, she had to travel disguised as a nurse, accompanied by

Norah Smythe. When they reached Princess Polignac's mansion, Christabel informed Pankhurst that the East London Federation had to become a separate organization, since Pankhurst and the federation operated contrary to WSPU dictates. Not only had they been represented at the Larkin meeting but, Christabel continued, "You have a democratic constitution and we don't agree with that." She went on:

> A working women's movement was of no value: working women were the weakest portion of the sex: how could it be otherwise? Their lives were too hard, their education too meagre to equip them for the contest. Surely it is a mistake to use the weakest for the struggle! We want picked women, the very strongest and the most intelligent![94]

When challenged, Christabel took back her statement that working-class women did not have a "higher fighting standard" than middle-class women. However, she told Pankhurst and Norah Smythe that, although an ELFS deputation to the Labour Party was "all right", "a deputation to the king was better for the WSPU".[95]

Christabel also complained that Pankhurst was always thinking for herself and acting on her ideas, a trait that made her incompatible with the WSPU.[96] Although Emmeline also was present in both a personal and an official capacity at this formal split of the Pankhurst women, she said little, deferring to Christabel.

Realizing that it was useless to argue, Pankhurst and Smythe remained quiet. A few days later the *Suffragette* announced that the ELFS and Pankhurst were no longer part of the WSPU, for they preferred to work separately.[97]

On 26 January 1914, at the Annual General Meeting of the WSPU, there was a discussion of the split. Pankhurst had challenged her expulsion by trying to join the Kensington branch of the WSPU while remaining a member of the ELFS. The elder Pankhursts decided at this meeting that dual membership was not allowed.[98] Pankhurst was informed of this decision by Elsa Dalglish, who had been a founding member of the ELFS/WSPU:

> I can't tell you how much I had not [sic] had to write the enclosed. It means that the difference has to be emphasised and if you had only written and resigned the whole thing could have been quietly passed over. Your resignation would not have seemed odd or weak, but only natural considering the statements that have been officially issued.[99]

But quiet resignation was not in Pankhurst's nature.

The split continued to plague the WSPU. Pankhurst infuriated her mother and sister by continuing to use the word "suffragettes" in her organization's name. On a number of occasions, Emmeline wrote to her daughter demanding that she not use the word. In one letter she said, "A little calm reflexion would have shown how misleading and ambiguous the name you have chosen is. Federation of the suffragettes means to the public that you are a department of the WSPU." She went on to attack her daughter personally:

> You are unreasonable, always have been and I fear you always will be so! Had you chosen a name we could approve, we could have done much to launch you and advertise your society's name.
>
> Now you must take your own way of doing so. I'm sorry but you make your own difficulties by an incapacity to look at situations from other people's point of view as well as your own. Perhaps in time you will learn the lesson we all have to learn.[100]

This is the last exchange between the Pankhursts on the women's suffrage movement and they had little contact with each other after this. Richard Pankhurst had often referred to his wife and daughters as the "four pillars of my house".[101] The pillars had fallen in on themselves.

The split within the WSPU and the Pankhurst family was inevitable, given both the clear political differences and the family dynamics of jealousy and dislike. The only question is why it took so long to happen. Pankhurst's reluctance to split with the WSPU arose from two sources. First, making a personal and political break with one's family or close friends and associates is always painfully difficult. Pankhurst may have needed first to organize the ELFS, which in a way had become her family by the time her mother and sister threw her out. Secondly, there were political reasons. Pankhurst was not a "quitter" or "splitter". Her political temperament was such that she preferred to stay in an organization and fight for her principles, rather than leave. She never wrote in any detail about her personal feelings regarding the divorce between herself and her mother and sister; however, she made them clear in her later writings, especially *The suffragette movement,* in which she consistently portrays Christabel in an unflattering manner. Pankhurst tended to accept unpleasant and sorrowful aspects of her life, to put them behind her quickly and resolutely and to move on.

Immediately after the split, Norah Smythe and Zelie Emerson persuaded Sylvia Pankhurst that the ELFS should start its own newspaper, a voice for women's suffrage and women's emancipation in the East End. After much deliberation over costs and printers, it was determined that this could be done. Even when the ELFS had been formally a part of the WSPU, it could not rely on funds from the national office, so its source of funding did not change after the expulsion. Norah Smythe was largely responsible for financing the newspaper with her personal income. Some debate took place over the name. Pankhurst wanted to call it the *Workers' Mate*, "mate" being a familiar term of address in East London; Emerson and Smythe preferred the *Women's Banner;* but Mary Patterson suggested *Woman's Dreadnought* and this proved acceptable to all.

The choice of name was somewhat provocative. A dreadnought was originally a fearless person, but by 1913 a dreadnought was the name for a class of battleship superior to any of its predecessors, whose main armaments were large cannons. The newspaper was originally published by the Athenaeum Press. J. Edward Francis, the publisher, wrote to Pankhurst that he would be willing to print the paper provided that, since he could be sued and arrested for libel for articles the government deemed offensive, he had certain censorship rights.[102] Pankhurst was forced to agree. Twenty thousand copies were printed each week. The newspaper cost a halfpenny and was enthusiastically sold by East End members. Annie Barnes had to risk parental wrath to get the paper out. "My father didn't know anything about this. I'm sure he wouldn't approve at all as he had a business. Mrs. Moore used to bring the newspapers to the side entrance. After the children were in bed, I used to slip out and deliver them."[103]

Other sellers complained of police harassment, the difficulty of trying to sell a paper to immigrants who didn't speak English and male hecklers who crowded around the women but did not buy a paper. These problems were countered imaginatively with late-night publicity campaigns, chalking parties – when suffragettes would write on walls and pavements telling people where they could buy the *Dreadnought* or attend the next meeting – and hiring a boat in Victoria Park from which banners and parasols unfurled, spelling out "*Dreadnought*".[104]

The *Dreadnought* was written to a considerable extent by East End women, although, as sole editor, Pankhurst made a substantial contribution to each issue. Of the other women's contributions, she said that she "took infinite pains in correcting and arranging their manuscripts, endeavouring to preserve the spirit and unsophisticated freshness of the original".[105]

Pankhurst claimed the paper's readership was about 10,000, but 8,000 appears to be more accurate.[106] Until the outbreak of war, the paper was largely London based and oriented. It dealt with East End matters: battles with borough councils, fights with the police and demonstrations. It exposed the conditions of women home workers, reported on the victims of hat-pin abortions and covered women's suffrage activities.

The ELFS was astonishingly successful during its three-year life, owing to two factors: the women Pankhurst attracted and the alliance she forged with the dockers. Pankhurst was able to gather around her a corps of working-class women who were born leaders and agitators – women such as Charlotte Drake (ex-barmaid, labourer's wife and mother of five) and Melvina Walker (a one-time lady's maid and, like many ELFS members, a docker's wife). Walker's scandalous tales of high society made her a popular speaker. Nellie Cressell, a mother of six married to a paint-factory worker, eventually became the mayor of Poplar. Other women, including Annie Barnes and Julia Scurr, later became Stepney and Poplar councillors. Some socialist women, active or once active in the ILP, SDF, Socialist League or BSP, also gathered around Pankhurst. Jennie Mackay, who had been in the SDF and was also the first woman member of the National Union of General Municipal Workers, served as a Poplar councillor from 1919 to 1945. Louise Somerville, from Islington, had been a member of William Morris's Socialist League. Amy Hicks, another old-time socialist from the SDF, began to write for the *Dreadnought*.[107]

Pankhurst's organization received support from other influential sections of the East End community, in particular the dockers. Their support often enabled the suffragettes to carry on their activities without fear of police harassment.

At first glance, an alliance of dockers and suffragettes might seem strange, if not implausible. Dockers then, as now, were not known for their feminism. But, in the pre-war East End, other considerations were involved. This connection was a matter of political conviction and of the shared experience of struggle. Many dockers were married to suffragettes. Important dockers' leaders, such as John Scurr, were women's suffrage activists. Scurr's wife, Julia, came to politics through the ELFS and was the spokeswoman for the final East End deputation to Asquith in 1914. Similar connections between suffragettes and dockers existed in Glasgow as well.

Mrs Bigwood, who had led the East End deputations to Asquith in 1912 and to Lloyd George in 1913, was an active ELFS member. Prior to her suffrage work, she had won the respect of London's dock-workers by organizing the relief fund for the families of destitute dockers during the 1912 strike.[108] In fact, many federation members had made impressive contributions to the dockers' struggles, particularly during the long strike of 1912, which ended only when the men were starved back to work. ELFS members had demonstrated on many occasions that they supported the dockers' struggles and that their fight was one and the same. In return, dockers responded. In March 1913, Zelie Emerson organized a march to Holloway to support a sister suffragette, Scott Troy, who was hunger-striking. Over 1,000 people were present, including many from the dockers' and seamen's unions, firefighters and postal workers. In recognition and in thanks for her having helped to feed thousands of dockers' children during the 1912 strike, the Dockers' Union made Scott Troy an honorary member.[109]

The ELFS *wanted* dockers to support it. Almost every day the East End suffragettes would sell the *Dreadnought* and hold meetings near the dock gates so that dockers could participate. Every Sunday in spring and summer, the ELFS staged a procession that either began or ended at the dock gates. Melvina Walker set up a branch of the federation adjacent to the East India Dock Gate. It should not be surprising, therefore, that dockers gave their support by coming to suffrage meetings and acting as stewards and bodyguards.

There were other reasons for the dockers' support of the suffragettes. Les Garner suggests that, as suffragette militancy increased in the East End, the organization of the People's Army brought dockers, other trade unionists and some socialists closer to the suffragettes.[110] Another explanation is that, although the federation stressed "Votes for Women", it also campaigned for full adult suffrage. This would make an alliance with the labour movement quite possible, especially in the East End, where so many men could not vote. Men who received poor law relief were ineligible to vote. A man had to be registered at one place for 12 months. In Poplar, where the population was

75,614, only 9,519 men were registered to vote in 1911. In Bow and Bromley in the same year, only 10,669 men out of a population of 86,994 could vote and other areas in East London showed similar voting eligibilities.[111]

At the same time, there was little if any alliance between socialist and radical organizations and the ELFS. Not until the war years, when Pankhurst built a revolutionary organization in the East End, was it possible for women to be involved in revolutionary agitation that did not deny them their right to organize as women for their own liberation.

In April 1914, shortly before Pankhurst left London to go on a speaking tour of Europe, the ELFS managed to rent 400 Old Ford Road. This building had a hall at the back capable of seating 300 people. The remaining space provided a new home for Pankhurst and Mr and Mrs Payne, as well as offices for the new headquarters of the federation. The place was fixed up by Willie Lansbury and the Rebels' Social and Political Union. Soon it housed a lending library and facilities for a choir, lectures, concerts and a "Junior Suffragettes Club".

In May 1914, the ELFS was well represented at the May Day celebrations and organized its own Women's May Day later that month. This involved a march to Victoria Park. Pankhurst led the way with 20 other women chained and padlocked to her to avoid arrest, for she was still a "mouse" with three months of her sentence for her Trafalgar Square speech still to complete. Already she had gone to jail seven times for this one offence. However, the chaining failed to deter the police, who smashed the locks and sent her back to Holloway for the eighth time. She was soon released, only to be seized once again while being carried on a stretcher to the House of Commons, to demand that Asquith meet a deputation of East End women.

By this time, Pankhurst was physically shattered by her hunger, thirst and sleep strikes. On 30 May, while out on licence, she made a dramatic announcement. She would neither eat, drink nor sleep, *in or out of prison,* until Asquith agreed to meet a deputation. Her followers were convinced that their leader was going to die.

In June, while Pankhurst was in prison for the ninth time (having once again been arrested), the East London Federation prepared itself for a massive demonstration and a deputation to Parliament. Huge meetings were held to elect representatives; constant lobbying, picketing, leafleting, chalking and marching took place. Almost unanimously the federation decided that the deputation would demand votes for all women over 21.

Because of ill health, Pankhurst was released on 18 June and driven to the House of Commons to wait outside and – if necessary – to die, right on the spot (should Asquith still refuse to meet the deputation). With a general election approaching, Asquith feared adverse publicity and finally capitulated, agreeing to receive the suffragettes. This was the first time that he had ever formally received a deputation of suffragettes, or, for that matter, non-militant constitutional suffragists.[112]

Supporters of women's suffrage had particularly high hopes at this time, because the plight of the "mice" in prison was at its most desperate. They were enduring not only forced nasal feeding but also rectal feeding and other more harrowing forms of torture. They were being drugged with bromides and hallucinogens in many of the prisons in Britain.[113]

Six women had been chosen for the deputation: Julia Scurr (by then a Poor Law Guardian in Poplar), Elsie Watkins, Mrs Parsons, Jessie Payne, Mrs Savoy and Mrs Bird. Pankhurst did not want to go. "Let these working mothers speak for themselves: It was for this I had struggled," she explained later.[114]

Predictably, neither Emmeline nor Christabel offered support for either Pankhurst or the deputation. Emmeline informed Norah Smythe while Pankhurst was in prison that she should drop the idea of a deputation. "Tell her I advise her when she comes out of prison to go home and let her friends take care of her."[115]

On 20 June, thousands of women and men marched to Parliament to await the results of the deputation. During the wait, Melvina Walker had to be restrained from making a potentially indictable speech about the "House of Humbug". She was at the time a "mouse" released from prison under licence. Her original offence had been to tell a policeman, "If there were such things as mansions in the East End, I feel we would have popped them up a long time ago, and there would not be a mansion in East London tonight." For this she was arrested, charged and imprisoned for one month under the Edward III Act.[116]

Inside 10 Downing Street, the six women were appealing to Asquith. Mrs Savoy, a brushmaker, reached down into a brown sack to show the kind of work she did. Terrified that she was reaching for a bomb, Asquith ran for the door. Chuckling, Mrs Savoy reassured him and showed him how, for a few pennies a day, she put bristles into a hairbrush.[117]

He listened to the sad, ugly facts about the poor, heard about the lives of needlewomen, cigarette packers and shoemakers, about unmarried mothers and prostitution and was impressed. "If the change has to come," he told the women, "we must face it boldly and make it thorough going and democratic." Asquith concluded by promising again to give women's suffrage "most careful and mature consideration".[118]

The women emerged convinced that Asquith had changed his mind. Adding to their optimism was the fact that, a few days earlier, Sylvia Pankhurst had met Lloyd George, who had offered to introduce a Private Member's Bill to enfranchise women in the next session of Parliament and to resign if it were not passed.[119] The East London suffragettes were elated. They believed, with good reason, that their efforts had finally paid off. Years of demonstrations, forced feeding and fighting with the police were about to be vindicated. Victory was almost in sight.

On 8 July, the federation held a victory party. The Liberal and Labour press attributed Asquith's apparent change of mind to the East End deputation. Organizations that previously had been hostile to the ELFS became friendly. The United Suffragists, an organization of militants and non-militants, led by Barbara Lytton Gould, invited the ELFS to co-sponsor a women's suffrage demonstration in Trafalgar Square.

Only the WSPU remained aloof. Though Christabel was forced to concede that Asquith appeared to have changed his mind, she warned the suffragettes that they should never trust the government:

> The government are spreading about a piece of claptrap invented for the deluding of women who want votes. It is that "there must come a negotiations stage". Not at all says the WSPU. The militant women say to the government, "When you give us the vote, we will give you peace."[120]

In fact, Christabel's uncompromising stand was short-lived. When war was declared a few weeks later, on 4 August, the elder Pankhursts suspended all suffragette activity, despite not having been granted the vote. Almost overnight the WSPU became a vociferously patriotic organization and devoted its time to agitating for industrial conscription for women and military conscription for men in order that

England, glorious England, might slaughter "the Hun".

In the end, Asquith did not draft a women's suffrage bill. The war changed the situation on the home front and delayed suffrage. Not until 1918 were all men and women over 30 (with some exceptions) granted suffrage. The "Flapper vote", that enfranchised women over 21, was not granted until 1928.

Chapter Four

❧

The Great War

When war broke out in August 1914, Sylvia Pankhurst was in Dublin compiling a firsthand report for the *Dreadnought*. British troops had fired on a crowd of innocent civilians and the incident became known as the Bachelors' Walk Massacre. Devastated by the news, Pankhurst "could not realise its full horror".[1] She had known that war was imminent; Keir Hardie had warned her, but she had been so embroiled in the struggle for the vote that thoughts about war (or, more important, about anti-war organizing) were pushed to the side. Knowing that it was coming, however, in no way softened the blow. She took the first boat back across the Irish Sea and quickly returned to Old Ford Road.

The First World War brought tremendous changes to the East London Federation of the Suffragettes and to the life of Sylvia Pankhurst. The women's suffrage movement collapsed and women who had been involved in the struggle for the vote were now equally divided amongst themselves on the issue of supporting or opposing the war.

The socialist movement, both in England and internationally, was thrown into confusion. The movement had long condemned wars as a means by which ruling classes solved their internal domestic problems at the expense of the working class. Prior to 1914, socialists, radical trade unionists and most feminists shared Pankhurst's pacifism. The Second International, an international organization of socialist parties, had resolved that, if war broke out, it was the duty of socialists not to support their government's belligerency; it called for workers of all involved countries to go out on strike against war. However, when fighting did break out, many abandoned their principles of "sisterhood" and "international working-class solidarity" to support their own national ruling class against workers and "sisters" of other nations.

In Britain, the war created a social crisis that revolutionized Pankhurst and her organization. In this period Lloyd George began to create the structure of the future British welfare state. People in Britain were uneasy about these changes, for George's policy led to benefits of social welfare but at the same time to a more coercive and repressive state apparatus.

Between 1914 and 1917, the ELFS made a shift of which Pankhurst was not fully aware. It changed from a political organization that mobilized women to fight for political demands for themselves to a feminist social welfare organization that attempted to provide the same relief that government should have provided to alleviate the misery caused by the war. In this struggle, the ELFS found itself fighting to democratize the state, as it would later struggle to find ways to democratize diplomacy as the organization's demand for suffrage changed from votes for women to universal suffrage. An indication of this change of emphasis is that, in March 1916, the ELFS was renamed the Workers' Suffrage Federation.

By the end of the war, however, Pankhurst's experiences fighting against the horrors of the war and government repression even greater than in the days of suffrage militancy had led her to a revolutionary political position. She came to realize that her organization should be trying not to provide resources for the East End but rather to fight for a socialist and feminist restructuring of society. During the war years, Pankhurst emerged as one of Britain's leading revolutionary anti-war agitators. In 1918, the organization's name and focus changed again; this time it became the Workers' Socialist Federation and was no longer an East End-based organization but a national federation with branches in England and Scotland.

Adding to Pankhurst's despair at this period was the fact that the war also further divided her from her mother and Christabel. (Adela, the youngest sister, was involved in anti-war activity in Australia.) "War was the only course for our country to take," wrote Christabel. "This was national militancy. As suffragettes we could not be pacifists at any price."[2] Emmeline and Christabel suspended suffragette activity; in return, the government unconditionally released all suffragette prisoners.

Christabel returned from Paris in September 1914 and scheduled a major appearance at the London Opera House. It was a triumphal return: her admirers placed wreaths of flowers at her feet when she appeared on the stage. She spoke not on women's suffrage but on the issues of the war. When Victor Duval of the Men's Political Union for the Enfranchisement of Women heckled with a cry of "Votes for women!" Christabel countered, "We cannot discuss that now."[3]

Pankhurst went backstage to visit her mother and sister after the meeting ended, but the reunion was cold and brief. As the Pankhursts left the Opera House, rival cheers for "Sylvia" and "Christabel" went up from various political supporters. Embarrassed at this public display of the family feud in front of the press, Pankhurst hurriedly left.[4]

Pankhurst never forgave her mother and sister for their support for the war. She believed that her mother had betrayed everything that Richard Pankhurst had stood for and wept when Emmeline wrote that she was "ashamed" to know that Sylvia and Adela opposed the war. Worse was Pankhurst's shock when she read a speech in which Emmeline said that she wished her son Harry – Pankhurst's adored brother, who had died in 1910 – had lived to march at the front.[5]

Given the widespread collapse of socialist and pacifist ideals once war had broken out, the first task facing Sylvia Pankhurst was to convince the ELFS that it must oppose the war. Upon her return from Dublin, she found that a number of the members and officers – Jessie Payne and Norah Smythe, for example – supported England's cause. Pankhurst's fierce and uncompromising opposition to the war and her determination to impose her position on the ELFS cost her dearly in terms of members. The peak of the federation membership had been reached at the height of the suffragette campaign in the East End in 1914, around the time of the formation of the People's Army and the women's deputation to Asquith. With the general overwhelming patriotism at the beginning of the war, the ELFS lost many members and supporters, both middle and working class. Elvina Haverfeld, the federation treasurer, resigned, although Norah Smythe and Jessie Payne changed their positions about the war and remained in the ELFS and Dr Barbara Tchaykovsky was so repulsed by the fanatical belligerency of Christabel and Emmeline that she left the WSPU and became a devoted worker for the federation.[6] As the East End began to feel wartime hardships, however, the original outburst of patriotism dissipated and the ELFS/WSF won new recruits. Even so, there were no more than a few hundred people actively involved in the ELFS/WSF during wartime.[7]

The problems of membership were discussed at federation meetings quite openly. East Londoners were faced with the disincentive of intolerable conditions brought on by war. For example, in October 1916 and again in September 1917, it was reported that it was difficult to get people to meetings because of the bombing of the East End. Outdoor meetings were slightly more successful, as were indoor and outdoor meetings held in provincial towns.[8]

From 1914 to 1917, all 16 of the executive committee members lived in the East End. By 1917, half had left the organization. Only four remained on the executive committee until 1920 and many of the new recruits came from outside the East End. Men were admitted as members but, unlike women, had to be nominated and seconded by the branch committee (the executive committee of a local branch) and then approved by the executive committee.[9] They also served on the executive committee after 1918, but never dominated the proceedings.[10] In 1915, the ELFS set up an associate membership category for young people aged 14–18 who wanted to join.[11]

After 1914, the ELFS expanded outside the boundaries of the East End. Before war broke out, the ELFS had branches in the North London area of Hackney. By October 1915 there was a branch in Holborn and by 1916 branches were organized in Hoxton, St Pancras, Holloway and Islington. Some of the local branches set up their own bookshops.[12] By 1917, the WSF had 30 branches in many parts of England, South Wales and Scotland. Many of the branches were in key industrial areas and by the end of the war the WSF had established links with other leading socialist and industrial militants. However, none of the branches outside London's East End had either the numbers or social influence of the original ELFS.

In the war years, the ELFS also attracted a remarkable group of women socialist organizers and agitators. Emma Boyce was a roving organizer for the ELFS/WSF. An early member of the ILP, she joined the WSF in the early years of the war. She had twelve children of whom four had survived and three of these fought in the war. She spent time organizing in Newcastle and Glasgow. Being an organizer was dangerous work. I. Renson, a colleague, described one particular incident:

When we were in Reading, me and my brother witnessed the

breaking up of a "Stop the War" meeting in the Market Place in about September 1918 by soldiers. The meeting was organised by the ILP and the chief speaker was Mrs. Boyce of Hackney. Soon after this elderly lady got on to the platform, it was pushed over and she fell off backwards, but she appeared to have been caught by her friends who were behind her.[13]

In her fifties when she worked with the WSF, Boyce was a tireless activist, speaking sometimes five times a week and travelling around the country. She was elected a Hackney Labour councillor in 1918 and after 1923 served as the governor of the London Maternity Hospital. She died in 1929.[14]

Another new member was Jessie Stephens, a Glaswegian who had been active in the ILP, the militant suffragette movement, as well as in the Socialist Sunday Schools, organizations that taught children an ethical socialism. When war broke out, she went to London, hoping to find a job and met Pankhurst, who immediately asked her to work for the ELFS. Stephens, only 20 at the time, went back to Glasgow to think about Pankhurst's offer, finally deciding to take it. The Stephens family was very poor and Jessie did not have the train fare to go back to London, but one night her mother defied her husband and secretly gave Jessie the fare.[15]

After the young woman had spent some time in London, Pankhurst sent her out to organize the provincial cities. Stephens later described her work:

There were two of us, Mrs. Boyce, a working woman who'd brought up a family of twelve kids and was going around the country, just like me. She gave me lots of hints as what to do. She says, 'always take with you a pound of candles because you'll find in some places no light, when you'll want to read in your bed and you can't . . .'

When I was working for Sylvia I got thirty bob a week and it wasn't enough sometimes to pay my digs when I was travelling through the country. But I used to go to the ILP branches as well – free lance, of course, because none of us were on salary – we had to depend on the branches to pay us what they could . . . .

You couldn't buy new clothes on that. In fact, I went to Burnley market once and bought a remnant there for 6d to make myself a blouse. My first stop on the WSF tour was Sheffield where I was lucky enough to find lodgings with Mrs.

Manion. The friendly atmosphere helped me enormously in this first provincial venture.[16]

Stephens was also successful as a fund raiser for the ELFS/WSF. She stayed on until spring 1917, when she became an ILP organizer for Bermondsey. Stephens enjoyed working with and respected Pankhurst, who she said "could charm when she liked, but at the core was inclined to be as autocratic as her mother and elder sister Christabel".[17] Like so many others, Stephens continued her political activism after she left Pankhurst's organization. She participated in the birth control movement and was the first woman president of the Bristol Trades Council. In 1975, when she was interviewed by *Spare Rib,* the English feminist magazine, Stephens was 81 and still active in the Trades Union Congress.[18]

Still another activist was Lillian Thring, a militant suffragette from London who in 1911 moved to Melbourne, Australia, where she came into contact with revolutionaries and joined the Industrial Workers of the World (IWW). She was famous for being a brilliant public speaker. Married in 1913, she lived briefly in the Sudan and then returned in 1915 to England, where she joined the ELFS/WSF. She was especially active in the "Hands off Russia" campaign and the Workers' Committee Movement. As an alumna of the WSF, Thring was active in the Communist Party, the ILP and the anti-fascist and trade union movements in the 1930s, 1940s and 1950s.[19]

Upon the outbreak of war, the ELFS had to rearrange its priorities. When its executive committee met to discuss the wartime emergency, it decided that it had three options: to continue suffragette activities as if nothing had happened; to try and alleviate suffering in the East End; and "to make capital out of the situation", meaning to exploit the issue of the war in order to gain new members.[20] Suffrage work took a backseat to defending the East End: the executive committee voted for the second choice. However, given Pankhurst's passionate pacifism, the federation did all it could to make political capital out of the wartime catastrophe. Pankhurst was aware of her political isolation; she could "not say much against the war at present as so many people have relations in it, that they will not listen yet".[21] It was not until 1915, when anti-war sentiment was developing, that the WSF took a clear anti-war position.

During the first two years of the war the ELFS/WSF was, for the most part, largely responsible for initiating what anti-war activity existed

in London. Its tactics were similar to those used during the suffrage
agitation. Meetings were usually held at the East India Dock Gates
followed by a procession to Victoria Park. Even though most of the
demonstrations were large, with numbers of soldiers and sailors participating, they were smaller than the suffragette demonstrations had
been and they were met with greater hostility than before.[22] Melvina
Walker, who lived in Poplar two doors away from the recruiting office
in East India Dock Road, wrote that Dock Road was an extremely
good spot to have chosen for that office, for it was a "parade ground
for the unemployed".[23] The dock gates, once the sacred ground of
socialist agitators, became a platform for recruiters. Pankhurst travelled to Glasgow in October 1914, thus becoming one of the first
suffragettes to speak out against the war. At a well-attended meeting
sponsored by the ILP, she said that peace must be made by the people
and not by the diplomats.[24] In December, along with 100 other
prominent English women, she signed an open Christmas letter, published in *Jus Suffragi*, an international women's suffrage publication,
from the "British Women to the Women of Germany and Austria",
that said, "We are with you in this sisterhood of sorrow."[25]

The war began with a volunteer army – in keeping with Liberal
ideas of individual freedom. But by 1915, the realities of trench war-
fare led not only to an increased need for new recruits, but also to a
need to discipline the civilian population. Early in 1915 there were
strikes of engineering workers in Glasgow and dockers in Liverpool as
workers decided they had a right to share in the increased profits that
their extra war work was creating. The government passed draconian
legislation designed to get more recruits into the armed forces and
to discipline the workers better in defence-related industries. The
Defence of the Realm Act (DORA), passed in August 1914, was continually amended. Under DORA it was illegal to spread information
"likely to cause disaffection or alarm" to anyone in the military or
among the civilian population. Suspects could be arrested without a
warrant. Power was given to search anyone's premises at any time or
place and to seize documents or anything the government deemed
suspect. Furthermore, persons arrested under DORA could be tried by
military court-martial as if the individual were a soldier on active
duty.[26] It was under this act that individual anti-war agitators such as
John Maclean of Scotland were imprisoned.

In May 1915, the government also passed the Munitions Act, which regulated the lives of all workers employed by the munitions industry. Finally, after 1915, the government began to pass a long series of acts designed to "soften up" the British public and to get it ready for "Prussian" type conscription in 1916, then full conscription in 1918. Pankhurst and a growing number of socialists campaigned against military conscription for men and industrial conscription for women; they also objected to the fact that only labouring people – workers and the military – were being conscripted, not capital, essential services and supplies.[27]

Pankhurst was particularly appalled by section 40d of the Defence of the Realm Act. This made it compulsory for women suspected of being prostitutes to be inspected for venereal diseases. It was against the law to have sexual intercourse with a member of HM Forces if one had such a disease. Pankhurst argued that this Act laid innocent women open to blackmail and false imprisonment; it punished women and led men to believe that, since they were automatically absolved from any guilt in transmitting venereal diseases, prostitution was right and necessary.[28]

The government also rushed through the National Register Act, which made it compulsory for all citizens to supply the government with detailed particulars of their lives and their trade or profession. Penalties would be imposed on anyone who did not register or falsely claimed to have registered.[29] Pankhurst, the ELFS and other trade union and radical groups opposed the act because they saw it as the first step towards conscription.

In July 1915 the ELFS announced it would march through London protesting against the Register Act and the conditions of sweated labour. Pankhurst had written Lloyd George asking him to meet this deputation, whose objective was to call attention not just to the registration of workers, but also to the high cost of food and coal and to the low level of women's wages; it would also demand equal pay for equal work. For this march Pankhurst had no support from official representatives of organized labour or from working women's groups such as the Women's Trade Union League, the Women's Cooperative Guild or the Women's Labour League. Unable to get Trafalgar Square, she settled for an indoor meeting in a small meeting room.[30]

In August 1915, the ELFS also staged a demonstration opposing registration that won support from a large number of prominent individuals and organizations such as the Suffragette Crusaders, the

United Suffragists, the Amalgamated Society of Toolmakers, Engineers and Machinists, the BSP and the National Union of Gasworkers. Speaking at the rally were Charlotte Despard; George Lansbury; Bessie Ward of the London section of the Shop Assistants' Union; Julia Scurr, Sylvia Pankhurst, Charlotte Drake and Edith Sharpe of the ELFS; W. I. Appleton of the General Federation of Trade Unions; Margaretta Hicks of the National Women's Council; and Miss L. Rothwell of the Women's Trade Union League.[31]

This demonstration was large and well received. Pankhurst, speaking for the ELFS, said that the register had been initiated "solely for the purpose of exploiting the workers and [would] be used for that object". She went on to denounce war profiteering and women's sweated labour, finally saying that she would refuse to sign the register, for she, like millions of Englishwomen, still did not have the vote.[32]

However, the demonstration had no effect on the government, which later that year passed a bill that called upon men to "attest" that they would undertake military service if and when they were called upon to do so. Known as the Derby scheme, this was the last attempt to keep recruitment on a voluntary basis. Conscription for single men was introduced in January 1916 and universal manhood conscription in May 1916.

It was at a large demonstration against conscription, in September 1915, that Pankhurst heard about the death of Keir Hardie. This was the greatest emotional devastation she had experienced since the death of her adored father. "I was not faint, but stunned and stricken. . . . [T]he world was dreary and grey, and Life was pitilessly cruel."[33] Although Hardie's death came as a shock, she had known for a long time that he was ill with pneumonia and had probably suffered a series of strokes. While in Caterham Sanitarium the previous July, Hardie had written to Pankhurst saying that he wanted to give her back her letters from her trip to America. He asked to keep a picture of her and one of her paintings and suggested that they meet one more time at his flat in Nevill's Court.[34]

Sadly, Pankhurst realized that the purpose of the meeting was that "he was announcing to me the final close of his working life, his imminent death, that he admitted no hope of recovery, expected never to return".[35] Hardie wrote her one last letter. He was clearly dying and the spelling and penmanship showed his confusion: "Dear Sylphia, In about a week I expect to be gone from here with no more mind control than when I came. Love."[36] The entire 16 October issue of the *Woman's Dreadnought* was devoted to Hardie. Pankhurst's pencilled draft of her eulogy of him says that "Keir Hardie has been the greatest human being of our time."[37]

Pankhurst never wavered in her love for and devotion to Hardie. After he died, she went out and bought a puppy (Hardie had always suggested that she have a dog) and named him Donald, after one of Hardie's favourite pit ponies. Pankhurst's friends called the dog "Jimmie", Hardie's nickname.[38]

The ELFS/WSF continued its opposition to conscription. In December 1915 the ELFS, represented by Charlotte Drake, Emma Boyce and Eugenia Bouvier, participated in a No Conscription Conference held under the auspices of the Poplar and Hackney Trade Councils.[39] This meeting led to a major No Conscription demonstration, on 9 January 1916, with 2,000 people attending. Speaking for the federation were Drake, Walker and Bouvier.[40] The rally, however, was far smaller than the earlier No Conscription demonstration. In the same month, the ELFS/WSF began to lobby Parliament in the vain hope of convincing MP's not to vote for conscription.

Because of the imminence of conscription, other radical and socialist groups began for the first time to work with the ELFS/WSF in anti-war, anti-repression activities. In February 1916, the ELFS/WSF, the ILP and the newly formed No-Conscription Fellowship (NCF) held a meeting that 500 people attended. Melvina Walker spoke for the federation and, according to the *East London Observer*,

> She dealt with the evils of conscription from the working woman's point of view and suggested that if they did not actively oppose it now it would not be very long before the women of England were conscripted and sent to make bombs by which other mothers' sons would be slaughtered.[41]

On 1 March, at another meeting sponsored jointly with the Forest Gate and District branch of the No-Conscription Fellowship, Emma Boyce spoke out for the federation against conscription. With three sons in uniform, she argued that, if military conscription was introduced, industrial conscription and the crushing of the workers would be next.[42] Also that week, Nellie Best, a woman unknown to Pankhurst, was imprisoned for violation of DORA. Hundreds of women organized by the ELFS/WSF demonstrated against her imprisonment.[43]

The newly renamed Workers' Suffrage Federation organized a demonstration in the second week of March in Trafalgar Square which demanded "human suffrage" and repeal of DORA, the Munitions Act and conscription. New provisions under DORA enabled the Army Council or the Admiralty to occupy factories that employed vital workers and to requisition and regulate their output. The Munitions Act, passed in May, was supposed to come into force in July 1915. In making provision for the settlement of labour disputes in munitions works, the Act proscribed strikes. In order to prevent wages from increasing when workers moved from plant to plant, workers were forbidden to leave their place of work. The Act also provided for limitations on profits and established Munitions Tribunals to deal with offences committed under the Act. As the government took over more and more industries and services, the scope of the Act was further extended.

The focus of the Trafalgar Square demonstration, held on 8 April 1916, was to oppose the full scope of the government's repressive legislation.[44] The WSF worked hard to build it. Norah Smythe went to the Dockers' Union for support; similarly, Mrs Walts visited the gasworkers. Miss Beamish approached the Canning Town ILP, the BSP and the Shoreditch Trade Council.[45] On 12 March, Mrs Drake and 20 other members were arrested in the Isle of Dogs area of East London for sticking publicity posters on walls. The posters said "War is Murder" and "The Soldiers in the Trenches are Longing for Peace."[46]

This demonstration, numbering 20,000, was perhaps the largest of the anti-war protests to date. The WSF led a large contingent on the familiar six-mile route from Bow to Poplar to Trafalgar Square. On the platform were leading members and supporters of the WSF: Sylvia Pankhurst, Charlotte Drake, Melvina Walker, Dr Tchaykovsky and Eva Gore-Booth. Also speaking was a Glasgow city councillor, Mr Taylor, who reported on the engineers' strike that was sweeping the Clydeside and about the situation of workers who had been arrested under DORA.[47] Despite the presence of a large number of hostile soldiers and sailors who threw red dye and physically assaulted some of the speakers, the demonstration was an indication of growing opposition to war and wartime conditions.

In May, the ELFS issued a leaflet that was distributed to women in the East End. It warned:

In a few days conscription will be the law of the land. Can the mothers realise what this means? Do they realise that henceforth every boy born of an English mother will be branded with the mark of Cain? For let nobody be deceived by this lying tale of conscription for the operation of the war. It has come to stay. Are we going to strike a blow for freedom and right. If so that blow must be struck at once. Now is the time to act. Now is the time to work. The work of the Workers' Suffrage Federation is to waken up the people to a sense of their obligation and of their rights.[48]

True to its promise, the WSF continued anti-war agitation throughout 1916. In June, it called a Women's Convention Against Conscription, where it was decided to ask Prime Minister Asquith to receive a deputation of working women – consisting of most of the women who had met him in 1914 – who would explain why they opposed conscription.[49]

This time Asquith did not agree to the demands made by the WSF. Conscription and DORA were far too important to the success of the war effort. In all probability, Asquith knew that, even though the WSF could organize demonstrations, it was not as large as in the pre-war suffragette days. Furthermore, he was aware that the East End, like the rest of the country, was divided on the issue of the war and that most working people would support the government rather than the WSF.[50]

In December, the WSF held a well-attended open-air peace rally at the East India Dock Gates that ended with several arrests. A young man named Attlee was speaking against the war when a group of angry men began asking why he was not in uniform. The men tried to throw Attlee off the stage. The police, who had done nothing to protect the speakers, ordered the meeting to end. Sylvia Pankhurst, Melvina Walker and Charlotte Drake began to speak. The police then arrested them as well as Minnie and Edgar Lansbury, the daughter-in-law and son of George Lansbury – claiming that it was for their own good. The crowds were very hostile, explained a sergeant named Loftus and they wanted to throw Pankhurst in the river.[51] The charges were later dropped.

With the inevitable passage of conscription, the WSF turned to the peace campaign, which had already been initiated by Helen Crawfurd and Agnes Dollan, ILP women in Glasgow who were involved in the

Women's Peace Crusade. They thought about bringing working women from the provinces to march upon Parliament, but it proved too expensive.[52] The organization also sent its members on a "peace canvass" in the East End, that unfortunately met with little success. The *Dreadnought* explained why the canvassers' arguments fell on hostile and bitter ears:

> It was pathetic to find poorly clad women with pinched white faces and backs bent with excessive toil, excitedly cry out, "We want peace on our own terms." It is strange that past experience has not taught them that they will be given no voice in the terms of settlement and that their interests will not even be considered. . . . [S]ome said, "we want our sons to have their revenge," and others cried, "Our sons are dead; your talk of peace can never bring them back."[53]

Nevertheless, the WSF continued its dogged anti-war agitation. It continued to hold open-air and anti-war meetings in the East End, especially by the dock gates. More and more, the WSF found itself in demonstrations with socialist organizations such as the BSP and the ILP. It picketed the 1917 Labour Party conference, where a number of delegates shouted abuse at the women.[54] The treatment the WSF members received at the hands of the Labour Party convinced Pankhurst that the party no longer represented the interests of working people, thus helping to shape her strong anti-parliamentary convictions.

Pankhurst also attended the 1918 Labour Party conference, where she moved the British Socialist Party's resolution that the Labour Party withdraw from the government because of Liberal–Tory support for the war. Again, she was rudely treated and her motion lost.[55] It was these wartime experiences with the Labour Party that convinced her of its bankruptcy and of the futility of working with it.

Pankhurst's anti-war activity was not solely confined to the East End; she also worked with women from the earlier suffrage campaign. Contrary to popular thinking – which Pankhurst herself helped create in *The home front*, a highly personal account of her experiences during the First World War – not all women in the suffrage movement supported the war. In fact, half of them opposed it and many who had been involved in the Women's Congress, an international organization of feminists, formed the British section of the Women's International League (WIL) in late April 1915.[56] Pankhurst attended a

preliminary meeting in London, was elected to the executive committee and moved that the title be changed to the Women's International
Peace League and that women who were not British citizens be
allowed to join. The resolution was defeated.[57] She was very critical of
the WIL; some of her feelings, no doubt, were due to the fact that
many of its leaders had been involved in the non-militant National
Union of Women's Suffrage Societies and Pankhurst considered them
politically timid. For its part, the WIL was cautious and did not wish to
be associated with radicals.[58]

The monthly WIL meetings lasted from 10am to 6pm and Pankhurst
would return to the East End exhausted. In October 1915, there was a
discussion as to whether the ELFS should formally affiliate with the
WIL. Despite her criticisms of it, Pankhurst argued that the League
was "the best and most ambitious interpretation of the women's
movement today", pointing out that the ELFS was "more advanced
than most of the others [women's groups] who belong to the League
and our mission is to lead them". She further suggested an East End
branch of the WIL. Charlotte Drake argued that affiliation would be
too great a drain on the federation, but Pankhurst's motion carried.[59]
The debate became moot two months later when it turned out that the
WSF had too few members; 5,000 were required for affiliation.[60]
Pankhurst resigned personally from the WIL in 1917, when it refused
to support one of its own members: Emily Hobhouse had been strip-
searched and called a traitor by the British government after travelling
to Belgium to report on the truth of British stories about German
atrocities.[61]

Pankhurst's relationship with the WIL shows that she did not want
herself or the ELFS to be "insular", as she argued at the October 1915
executive committee meeting – even if this meant working with
middle-class women and former opponents within the suffrage movement.[62] She had her differences and impatience with the WIL: for
example, it had refused to support the demonstration protesting
against Nellie Best's sentence for violating DORA (Mrs Swanwick,
WIL chair, told Pankhurst that she "didn't think the sentence was
severe. . . . [I]t might have been death)."[63] Yet Pankhurst was unchar-
acteristically charitable about its work: "It carried no fiery cross; but
tried in a quiet way, sincerely, if at times haltingly, to understand the
causes of war, and to advance the cause of peace by negotiation, and
the enfranchisement of women."[64]

During the war, Pankhurst emerged as one of the leading socialist anti-war agitators. In September 1915, she spoke at an anti-war, anti-conscription rally of 600–700 people in Bristol.[65] In July 1915, when miners in South Wales successfully struck in defiance of the Munitions Act, Pankhurst took up their cause. She spoke at meetings in South Wales and later wrote regular articles for the *Rhondda Socialist*. The ILP wanted to run Robert Smillie, the miners' leader, for Parliament in Keir Hardie's old district and the ILP asked her if she would like to campaign for him. The general membership of the WSF voted unanimously that Pankhurst should do this, for Smillie was a suffragist, supported trade union rights and opposed conscription. Another motivation for Pankhurst to campaign for the miners' leader was that her mother and older sister actively opposed Smillie because of his opposition to the war and conscription.[66] In 1915, she also took a dangerous trip to speak in Belfast, Ireland. Crossing the Irish Sea was risky during the war because German U-boats were always on patrol.[67]

In 1916, Pankhurst spoke at several meetings in Glasgow with George Lansbury and John Maclean, the pioneering Scottish Marxist and leading revolutionary on the "Red Clyde". She praised and defended women who had successfully organized a rent strike. Speaking in opposition to Emmeline and Christabel's industrial campaign, she warned shop stewards to stand firm against profiteering and conscription; they should beware, she said, of the dilution of their jobs by unskilled workers, who would be forced to do their work for a fraction of their proper wages. She also urged strike action when necessary, even though it was illegal.[68] In May 1917, encouraged by their socialist teachers, schoolchildren in Burston, Norfolk, went on strike, set up their own strike school and invited Pankhurst to come and speak.[69]

Still, none of this anti-war agitation persuaded the Labour Party, the coalition government in power, or any significant number of people in the East End either to join the ELFS/WSF or to adopt many of its anti-war positions. The ELFS/WSF was a small organization working with other small organizations and battling wartime patriotism as well as the general conservatism of the East End. Nonetheless, a small group of dedicated activists kept the issues of peace and opposition to government repression alive during this difficult political period.

During the war, Pankhurst became caught up in the contradictions of the organization she had built. Unlike other socialists who opposed the war, she had an organization that she could immediately mobilize to do consistent anti-war work – she was not an individual voice at the East End dock gates. But Pankhurst's organization had been built, for the most part, on the issue of women's suffrage (albeit in the context of other social issues) and it was embedded in one community. During the war, Pankhurst found herself creating many social welfare agencies – substituting for government agencies that did not exist – in order to serve the pressing needs of the women of the East End. She also found herself in a dilemma similar to that which faced the shop stewards' movement or the engineers during the war: do you consistently oppose the war, or do you campaign for better wages and working conditions for workers in war production? Pankhurst came to the same conclusion as the shop stewards and engineers: she fought for the rights of the community, which in her case meant advocating equal pay for equal work for women war workers.

Her concern simultaneously to continue anti-war, anti-conscription and peace agitation – as well as a limited amount of suffrage agitation – and to build social welfare agencies and to organize women workers pulled her in many different directions. In order to maintain its social work agencies, the ELFS/WSF had to appeal for money to middle-class supporters of the suffrage movement. At the same time, many members of the organization became anti-war activists and took stands opposing those of their affluent supporters. Meanwhile the ELFS/WSF was losing its exclusive East End base and gradually becoming a national organization through the *Dreadnought,* which was reaching a wider audience.

The ELFS/WSF expended a great deal of its energies in the area of public relief. It was this work that shifted the federation's focus. Although it lobbied Parliament, wrote exposés in the press and pressured individuals to do something about the conditions of women workers, the ELFS/WSF did not spend equal amounts of time and energy trying to organize these workers to change their working situation. The federation set up day-care centres and nurseries, communal restaurants, baby clinics and other types of services for the people of the East End; although all these were invaluable to those who benefited from them, they constituted a departure from the old suffragette tactic of organizing thousands of people to force the government to pass women's suffrage legislation. As the organization spent more time and energy providing community services, the ELFS/WSF lost a great deal of its earlier strength. Emma Boyce astutely commented that by 1917 the federation seemed more like "a charity organisation with suffrage tacked on".[70]

The decision to devote so much time and effort to providing services came mainly from the real needs of East End women. Melvina Walker, for example, told how Poplar women were faced with a shortage of many commodities during the war, especially sugar. Yet the dockers were unloading tons of sugar into the warehouses. Women of the ELFS/WSF went to see the president of the Board of Trade, but got nowhere. Walker also described the desperate potato shortage, which led women to get up at five in the morning and queue all day, quite often only to be turned away empty-handed. They then had to face the prospect of spending the night in "dug out" bomb shelters. Crowds of women ran past Walker's door, carrying their babies, rugs and cushions to the Blackwall Tunnel, where they stayed until daybreak. The tunnel they fled to for protection against bombs also sheltered wagonloads of munitions awaiting shipment. People were often maimed or killed when the horses went wild, frightened by the booming of the bombs.[71]

The work that was done, even though it led to greater problems, was an indication of the strong socialist and feminist convictions of the federation. Food became an increasingly important issue as the war progressed; the food queues, the profiteering and cheating by the rich, rubbed the working class's nose in the shortages. On 8 August 1914, the *Dreadnought* called for a No Rent Strike (different from the No Rent Strike called during the suffragette activity), "[u]ntil the government controls the food supply".[72] The No Rent Strike was soon dropped. Pankhurst wrote to Hannah Sheehy Skeffington, the Irish suffragette, on 24 August that "we are postponing the No Rent Strike until things get more acute as only a proportion of people are ready for it yet, but of course we still go on with our suffrage work".[73]

As soon as war was declared, the federation met and adopted a programme of nationalization of food supplies – a programme that showed its concern for working women and workers' participation in democratic decision-making regarding resources. Their programme stated:

> During the war, the food shall be controlled by the government in the interests of all the people in order that all may feed or starve together without regard to wealth or social position. To

make sure that the food supply is properly controlled, we demand that working women shall be called into consultation in fixing the prices to be charged for food and the way in which the food is to be distributed.[74]

One federation member, Mary Phillips, urged direct action. She said that the ELFS should go to the shops and buy food at the old prices, or take it forcibly if the shopowners refused to sell at low prices. Pankhurst claimed that this was already being done by women in the East End.[75]

Throughout the war, the federation campaigned alone and also with other groups for state control over food prices. In August, Pankhurst and Mrs Drake were at the Poplar Dock Gates calling for government control of food supplies with the consultation of working-class women, for equal pay for equal work and for the vote.[76] In November 1914, the National Women's Council of the British Socialist Party agreed to form a joint food supply committee with the ELFS, the Women's Industrial Council and the Rugby Housewives Committee.[77] A few months later the ELFS and the Poplar Trades and Labour Council organized a deputation to Asquith concerning food prices. The federation was represented by Julia Scurr and Walter Mackay; two Poplar councillors, J. Bands and S. March, spoke for the council. Nothing came of the deputation.[78]

In April 1915 the ELFS, along with the London Trades Council and the British Socialist Party, secured the London Opera House for a meeting to discuss food distribution.[79] Also in that month, a food deputation met with the mayor of Poplar, A. H. Warren, calling for the nationalization of food. Charlotte Drake advocated communal kitchens for factory workers and schoolchildren; Sylvia Pankhurst told the mayor that if the food supply was not nationalized there would be general unrest. The deputation ended with the presentation of a number of resolutions: an end to private trading in food; the food supply to be administered by the town or county councils; the introduction of rationing; municipal distribution of food with a ticket system for rationing; county councils to be in charge of the mills and food-preserving factories; national buying of food for the civilian population as for the military. There were other resolutions not directly concerned with food – a call for peace negotiations and a demand for votes for all.[80]

In June 1915 the ELFS further elaborated on its proposals for food distribution with another series of resolutions calling for, among other things:

An advisory committee consisting of 1/3 merchants, 1/3 representatives of organized workers in the trades concerned and 1/3 representatives of working women, housekeepers and the principal consumers of the nation, [that] shall be appointed to formulate and carry out the proposals for safeguarding the supplies and limiting the prices of food and milk. This committee shall have the power to fix both prices and profits.[81]

In spite of these numerous conferences, deputations and demonstrations, none of the plans put forward by the WSF were adopted. It was not that the population was not concerned with the food crisis. It was more that there was no working-class movement demonstrating and striking around these issues. The activities of the federation were restricted to "resolutionary" socialism or feminism because they did not have broad support to back them up. Given that the federation was committed to bettering the lives of working-class women, it is not surprising that it then itself attempted to set up the necessary social welfare services.

One of the first services set up by the federation was communal cost-price restaurants. Pankhurst thought communal restaurants were an important step towards the emancipation of women in her vision of an egalitarian society.

"Cost price restaurants!" The phrase sprang into my mind. Cost price or under cost price mattered not. The name should be a slogan against profiteering and carry no stigma of charity. ... Communal restaurants supplying first rate food at cost price were in line with our hope of emancipating the mother from the too multifarious and largely conflicting labours of the home.[82]

Two restaurants were set up. Wood from Lansbury's timber yard was made into tables by Edgar Lansbury and the Rebels' Social and Political Union.[83] Dinner (the midday meal) cost 2d. (1d. for children) and supper 1d.; they were free for those who could not afford this.[84] In one day, the cost-price restaurants served 400 people, averaging 150 people at a sitting.[85] This is a sizeable amount when one considers how small the membership of the federation was and how meagre its resources. But, popular as the restaurants were, they served only a tiny fraction of the community. Furthermore, there is no indication that the federation made recruits or won people to its activities through the restaurants. Thus, despite the federation's stress on feeding the working class communally – and that even a degree of success was admirable – it did not inspire working-class women to organize and demand that the government set up communal restaurants everywhere. The ELFS/WSF also set up a distress bureau in the Women's Hall in Bow, where members answered questions about food, rent and pensions. The idea for this came about because Pankhurst and Lansbury sat on the local committees of the National Distress Bureau. They were appalled at the complacency of the local authorities and the apathy of the councillors.[86] In the *Dreadnought* Pankhurst attacked the snooping investigators who judged whether or not women were "worthy" of allowances.[87]

The Distress Bureau fought on behalf of those people who were evicted from their homes for being unable to pay their rents. It also secured the release of several people in prison, helped others through the problems of unemployment and secured separation allowances for many wives of soldiers and sailors. The need was so great that bureaux were set up in Bromley, Canning Town and Poplar.[88]

In response to conditions resulting from the war – including the housing cutbacks, lack of separation allowances, food scarcity (combined with the inefficiency of established bodies that distributed relief) – Pankhurst in 1915 set up the League of Rights for Soldiers' and Sailors' Wives and Relatives. She approached Lansbury with the idea, hoping to involve sympathetic trade unionists and socialists, albeit in a minimal capacity; the federation would be responsible for the routine day-to-day work. In this area, it did involve women in the struggle for their rights. Many soldiers' and sailors' wives became honorary secretaries in other branches of the League of Rights. Mrs Lansbury was convinced by Pankhurst to be the honorary secretary of the league but was overwhelmed by chores and children, so she never had any time to do the work.[89] Thus, Pankhurst persuaded George Lansbury's daughter-in-law, Minnie Lansbury, to give up teaching and to replace her mother-in-law as honorary secretary. Minnie devoted all her time to the league and she and Pankhurst hoped that in time it would become a national body and take over the role of the inadequate Soldiers' and Sailors' Families Association.[90] However, this organization was not accompanied by the flashy success of the suffrage days. The meetings were attended by "quiet, earnest little women, who joined the organization with diffidence and in modest numbers. The dark streets were a growing deterrent."[91]

The League of Rights existed as an unofficial pressure group throughout the war and in the *Dreadnought* was still advertising its meetings in Walthamstow and East Ham as late as 1918 and 1919. But by this time its main functions were being handled by the other ex-servicemen's organizations.

Other community services were established by the federation, including a baby clinic and day nursery. For 3d. a day (including food), working mothers were able to leave their children in the care of the ELFS/WSF.[92] The clinic was able to hold only about 30 children, but in 1915 the ELFS took over an old pub called the Gunmaker's Arms, renamed it the "Mothers' Arms" and turned it into a day-care centre and nursery run by Montessori methods.[93]

Milk centres were also organized by the federation. The milk – or money for the milk – came from the generosity of people outside the community. At the Women's Hall in Bow, about 1,000 nursing mothers received a quart of milk and dinner every night.[94] Unfortunately, there were many problems with the milk centres. For one, many of the babies were often so ill that they were unable to digest the milk. One of the nurses was accused of buying Nestlé milk and selling it to the mothers at a profit. She was constantly arguing about the price of milk with the women who used the centre. The nurse was also suspected of stealing money and other items from the "Mothers' Arms".[95]

The ELFS/WSF was particularly concerned with child welfare, an issue with which Pankhurst would involve herself for many years. One plan urged by the federation was to send the poor children of the East End to live in the country for the duration of the war. There they would be exposed to the benefits of country life and their health would improve.[96] (This plan was adopted by the national government during the Second World War.) The federation also proposed to the Poplar Council that the council set up more maternity and infant centres. The motion was accepted.[97]

Every Christmas the ELFS/WSF organized a large party for the children of the East End, attended by 600 or so members and friends of the federation – mostly working women and children, with a "sprinkling of men".[98]

The success of the party was not completely due to the people of the East End. Maud Arncliff Sennett, a constitutional suffragist, helped arrange for gifts to be sent to the ELFS/WSF and claimed that the food and gifts had all been provided by wealthy sympathizers.[99]

Later, when political disagreements arose at a 1916 suffrage meeting, Sennett complained that Pankhurst and the East End women were not appreciative enough of their wealthy benefactresses.[100]

Here again, we see the dilemmas facing Pankhurst. She was forced to scrounge from her mother's wealthy friends for money and supplies for her projects, rather than rely on the East End community to develop programmes and services based upon their own resources. What is remarkable is that the ELFS did not change its political positions in order to appease its richer and more conservative sources.

Contradictions were also evident in its attempts to organize working women. The first initiatives taken against unemployment were straightforward but, as war increased the demand for labour, women were employed to release men for the army. The ELFS/WSF found itself both opposing the war and fighting for the working women who replaced the men who had been drafted.

One wartime institution particularly galled the ELFS/WSF: the Queen Mary's Workrooms. These had been set up in 1914 to give unemployed women useful work, although at abysmal rates of pay. Pankhurst wrote to the Queen on behalf of the ELFS, pointing out that in the workrooms bearing her name women worked long hours far into the night at abysmally low wages. She urged a minimum wage, overtime pay and extra pay for working mothers.[101]

The ELFS considered the Queen Mary's Workrooms a disgrace and called them the "Queen Mary's Sweatshops". The workrooms were disbanded in 1915 because war work had all but liquidated unemployment, so relief work had come to an end. In the meantime, the ELFS campaigned vigorously against them, but with little success or support. Pankhurst and Julia Scurr served on the Poplar Relief Committees and used that as a way to expose the conditions in the workrooms. They called upon Susan Lawrence and Mary Macarthur, two women trade union leaders who sat on government committees, to organize a strike in protest against the setting up of sweated shops.[102] Both women refused.

In an attempt to counter the sweated shops and to provide work for unemployed women, the ELFS decided to establish its own factories to serve as models. A boot-and-shoe factory, then later a toy factory, were set up in 1914. Fifty-nine people were employed at the toy factory,[103] which was run on a co-operative basis: everyone was paid 5d. an hour or 11s. a week and no one made a profit. The boot-and-shoe factory never paid for itself; it was subsidized by wealthy supporters of the ELFS. As with many of her projects, Pankhurst found herself begging for support from women she knew from her WSPU days. She even spent one miserable weekend – trying to get support from England's wealthy – at the mansion of Lady Astor, who was to become the first woman to serve as a Member of Parliament.[104] Here, again, she came up against the contradiction: without the contributions of rich outside supporters, the co-operative factories could not have continued, but Lady Astor later wrote to her that she would never have invited her to her house, or aided her toy factory, had she been aware of Pankhurst's pacifist and socialist beliefs.[105]

The toy factory prospered, although arguments arose over its method of operation. It was run by a Polish woman, Mrs Hercbergova, whose commercial expertise outweighed her socialist and feminist ideas of industrial organization. She opposed the WSF's belief that the factory should have a definite constitution and be run by a committee made up of its workers. Mrs Hercbergova wanted business management to be separate from this committee. The WSF decided that a special factory committee should be formed: outside people might be elected to it, but only those who held either socialist or co-operative viewpoints should be on it.[106]

The factories were set up to provide needed employment as well as to bring money into the East End, but they in no way helped the community's problems of unemployment and poverty. Nor, as with the cost-price restaurants, is there any indication that the people employed in the workrooms joined the federation or were involved in any kind of agitation.

After 1915, the WSF no longer had to deal with the question of massive unemployment for women because thousands were entering the workforce, which created a new set of problems. The WSF's issues became the abolition of sweating, the protection of women workers, the upgrading and training of women and the securing of equal pay. The *Dreadnought* played a major role in exposing their horrendous working conditions: in Limehouse, for example, one food factory was housed in a dank, steaming basement. Ironically, the factory made turtle soup for the royal family.[107] In this area, the federation's propaganda and agitation were better received. The Labour Party, women's

organizations, trade unions and the Liberal and Conservative government claimed that they wanted to do all they could to ensure safe,
decent working conditions for the women who were making soldiers'
uniforms or munitions. In other words, those organizations wanted to
improve the conditions of women war workers in order to win the
war. Although the efforts of the WSF brought attention to the true
position of women in industry, it was not able to bring about any real
improvements.

As soon as women's war work registration was announced, in
March 1915, Pankhurst called for a women's conference to discuss
the problems of women workers, which included the right to vote,
equal pay for work of equal value, women's representation on labour
tribunals dealing with work-related issues and safeguards relating to
hours and working conditions. [108]

A few months later, the WSF called for demonstrations protesting
against the Register Act as well as against the conditions of women
workers. The WSF wrote to Lloyd George asking him to receive a
deputation and it announced that it would lobby individual MPs.
However, the call was for the most part ignored by labour officials,
the Women's Trade Union League and the Women's Labour League
and the Lloyd George government refused to meet it. [109]

In March 1915 Pankhurst had written to Lloyd George demanding
that the government enforce equal pay legislation. Lloyd George sent
Pankhurst an ambiguous reply. Pankhurst thought she had wrung a
concession from the government. However, Lloyd George's letter
had been deliberately vague. A month later, attending a conference on
Women's Organizations and the War called by the government,
Melvina Walker and Pankhurst demanded that it live up to Lloyd
George's promise to pay women workers the same as men. Both
Lloyd George and Walter Runciman, the president of the Board of
Trade, refused to answer. Pankhurst and Walker were isolated at this
conference; most of the women present looked upon the WSF as dis-
rupters. [110]

In March 1916 Pankhurst wrote to the prime minister, asking again
that he receive a deputation from the WSF that would address him
on the question of equal pay for women workers. In her letter,
Pankhurst pointed out that neither the Home Office nor the Board of
Trade had included any mention of equal pay for women workers in its
latest report on women's war work. Also, only 4 out of 13 appointed

members of the advisory committee on this question were women; of these 4, none represented working women and one had been notorious for opposing women's suffrage.[111]

Again, the limitations of Pankhurst's work are evident. It might have been better for the WSF to concentrate on convincing women munitions workers rather than Runciman and George that they deserved equal pay. Had there been an organization of women workers calling for equal pay, backed up with strikes, rallies and demonstrations, perhaps more could have been accomplished. However, it must be repeated that on this issue Pankhurst and the WSF stood alone. Other socialist, trade union and women's organizations did little.

During the war, the ELFS/WSF remained the only organization that consistently pressured the government to grant votes to *all* women. In this area, the greatest irony is that the most vocal opponents of women's suffrage were the former suffragettes. Pankhurst remained dedicated to suffrage; whether in the food, anti-war or sweated industries deputations, the demand for votes for all women and men was always included. Pankhurst angered both suffragettes and suffragists in her determination to give all adults the vote. At a Caxton Hall suffrage meeting in 1916, she and the WSF argued for adult suffrage. The majority voted against the WSF and in response Pankhurst railed against "comfortable middle class women". Maud Arncliff Sennett complained:

> Miss Pankhurst, to my amazement and disgust, seeing the sense of the meeting was going against her, began to round on us as a lot of "comfortable middle class women". I am bound to say that her women did not applaud this charge, and I thought it a poor return to make for those kind-hearted "comfortable middle class women" whose money was going to support her organization and officers in the East End, to say nothing of those splendid gifts I have seen on her platform at the Christmas proceedings.[112]

Nevertheless, the WSF continued suffrage agitation, although with new allies. The BSP, for example, which had condemned the suffragettes during the height of militancy, praised the WSF, commented that "Sylvia comes on like one resurrected" and promised support.[113]

This new support arose because it was clear that the new Franchise Bill drawn up by the government in 1916 was intended to give the vote to women over 30 who were either householders or married to householders. This meant, in effect, votes for women who were probably more conservative than younger, propertyless women. The very fact that franchise legislation was being presented to Parliament at this time was a result of increasing public pressure for soldiers to be enfranchised. Also, the existing occupational qualifications for voting deprived many munitions workers, who moved around the country doing vital war work, of the vote. This seemed grossly unfair to many people. On top of this was the feeling that all working men had contributed equally to the war effort and that therefore the property qualification should be abolished. There was a growing demand, consequently, for votes for all men, to which was added a demand for votes for some women. To have given all women over 21 the vote would have made them a majority and this the government would not allow.

In a letter to the *Call,* Pankhurst clearly pointed out why socialists could not support the Franchise Bill:

1. A woman is not to vote until 30 years of age, though the adult age is 21.
2. A woman is on a property basis when enfranchised.
3. A woman loses both her Parliamentary and her local government vote if she or her husband accept Poor Law Relief; her husband retaining his Parliamentary and losing his local government vote if he accepts Poor Law Relief.
4. A woman loses her local government vote if she ceases to live with her husband, i.e. if he deserts her, she loses her vote, he retains his.
5. Conscientious Objectors to military service are to be disenfranchised. [114]

The BSP, sections of the Labour Party and other radical and some suffrage groups opposed this blatantly discriminatory suffrage bill and were willing to work with Pankhurst to avoid its electoral results. But only a minority of suffragists were interested in adult suffrage. At a WSF executive meeting in April 1917, Norah Smythe said that the WSF "had turned the middle-class against us by our attitude toward adult suffrage". [115]

The major reason for the change in name from East London Federation of the Suffragettes to Workers' Suffrage Federation in March 1916 was WSF opposition to the wording of the Franchise Bill. The Bill excluded men because of poverty and their political beliefs, it discriminated against working-class women and it excluded women because they happened to be young, poor, widowed or deserted. Only a law that simply gave the franchise to every person over 21 would be acceptable and therefore it was decided that the federation's name would reflect this. The federation members also hoped that the increasing sense of grievance felt by men who could not vote would prompt them to want to join an organization that fought for their rights.

The new name was also more appropriate to an organization of women and men and one that increasingly was involved in struggles other than specifically women's rights issues. As Pankhurst wrote in the *Dreadnought*, "the battle for human suffrage is part of the great struggle for upward human evolution, in the course of which dominance and compulsion, exploitation and poverty will be abolished".[116] Following a meeting called by Emmeline Pethick-Lawrence under the auspices of the Women's International League, the National Council of Adult Suffrage was formed. But although it was formally committed to adult suffrage, it was inactive and the WSF disaffiliated in November 1917.[117] With George Lansbury and other Labour leaders, the WSF then formed the Adult Suffrage Joint Committee. This consisted of four WSF members, three trade unionists and one member of the BSP.[118] Pankhurst believed that such an organization was necessary because the women's suffrage movement had disintegrated. The WSF introduced a resolution in May 1917 that shows its strong socialist feminist position on suffrage:

> We the undersigned workers, realising that if a woman can cast a shell, she can cast a vote, and that women whether in industry or as wives and mothers, have their full share of the world's work, whether or not in peace or war, call upon the government to introduce not a Registration Bill, but a Franchise Bill to give a vote to any woman and man of full age.[119]

But the days of massive frenetic suffrage agitation were over. The Franchise Bill was passed in 1918, with the approval of England's leading patriots, Emmeline and Christabel Pankhurst. Throughout the war they had argued that soldiers would have to vote – women could wait.

Pankhurst's reputation as a leading socialist anti-war agitator was further enhanced by her support of the Irish struggle. On Easter Sunday, 1916, Irish socialists and nationalists led by Padraic Pearse and Pankhurst's friend James Connolly staged an abortive rising against the British government. The WSF and the *Dreadnought* defended the rising and argued against British rule in Ireland, while the other socialist groups either denounced the rebels or were silent.[120] Pankhurst was devastated over the results of the rising and in particular the British government's execution of Connolly, as well as the silence of some of the leaders of the Labour Party. She was more aware than most socialists of the implications of Connolly's death and of the rising itself:

> To me the death of James Connolly was more grievous than any, because the rebellion struck deeper than mere nationalism. It is a truism that countries held under an alien dominance remain politically stagnant, and to a large extent are culturally repressed. Recognition of this made me a supporter of Irish nationalism. Yet after national self-government had been attained, the social problems with which we in England were wrestling would still be present in Ireland. I knew the Easter Monday rebellion was the first blow in an intensified struggle, which would end in Irish self-government, a necessary step in Irish evolution. I knew that the execution of the rebels had irrevocably ensured the ultimate success of their uprising. Yet Connolly was needed so seriously for the after building; him at least, it seemed, fate should have spared.[121]

An extraordinary member of the WSF, Patricia Lynch, pulled off a spectacular journalistic coup during the events in Ireland. Only 18, she was the first British person to go to Dublin after the rebellion. The city was closed off by the British Army, but Lynch was determined to get a firsthand account for the *Dreadnought*. On the train to Ireland, she met a sympathetic army officer who let her pose as his sister. She was thus able to evade the English authorities, who were determined to maintain a news blackout and to detain and arrest all those who were sympathetic to the Irish rebels.[122] Lynch's story, published in the *Dreadnought,* generated so much interest that the issue that carried it sold out. New copies were printed and eventually the story was reissued as a pamphlet.[123]

Pankhurst's support of and contribution to the struggle for Irish freedom was not forgotten. Fifteen years after the rising, Hannah Sheehy Skeffington, an Irish pacifist and feminist whose husband, Francis, was shot in the back by English soldiers after the rising had been suppressed, expressed her feelings about Pankhurst's work:

I know no English rebel who understands the Irish situation and the international so well. The comments and the sympathy of some English on Ireland just drive me mad at times as they show such a blind spot where we are concerned, in fact, friends are the worst! Your paper *Dreadnought* was always fine on this and other war matters.[124]

The events in Ireland contributed not only to Pankhurst's developing revolutionary ideas, but also to her political attitudes towards working with the Labour Party.

The influence of the *Dreadnought* also contributed to Pankhurst's growing reputation as an anti-war militant. The depth of its coverage made it arguably the most influential anti-war newspaper in England. In December 1914, Pankhurst was the first English socialist to reprint the analysis by German Marxist Karl Liebknecht that the First World War was caused by imperialists fighting over the world market. In 1917, the *Dreadnought* published the famous letter from the English poet Siegfried Sassoon, M. C. Third Battallion, Royal Welsh Fusiliers, to his commanding officer:

I am making this statement as an act of wilful defiance of military authority, because I believe that the war is being deliberately prolonged by those who have the power to end it.

I am a soldier, convinced that I am acting on behalf of the soldiers. I believe that this war, upon which I entered as a war of defence, has now become a war of aggression.[125]

The paper demanded nationalization of food as the only means to alleviate hunger. It consistently argued against all repressive measures taken by the government.[126] When editions of the *Dreadnought* carried articles about British atrocities in Ireland, the paper was not allowed into Ireland. Pankhurst always had difficulties raising money for the paper and more importantly, finding a printer who would risk printing possibly seditious materials.

Pankhurst and her organization might have lost many old supporters, but as the war brought changes that transformed the WSF from a socialist relief group to a revolutionary organization, the group gained new adherents. As the full horror and destructiveness of the international slaughter began to hit home, Pankhurst's anti-war propaganda began to reach more receptive ears. The Russian revolution boosted the growing militancy in Britain's factories and the WSF found itself being swept along on a swelling tide of revolutionary unrest. Indicating the changing mood, in July 1917 the *Women's Dreadnought* was renamed the *Workers' Dreadnought*. The SLP welcomed the change. Its paper, *Solidarity* wrote:

> Women and worker are on synonymous terms so there is nothing very startling about the alteration of the title of the bright little rebel paper, the *Woman's Dreadnought*. Miss Sylvia Pankhurst has succeeded in making the *W.D.* a real force in Labour politics and we wish her every success.[127]

In 1918 rumours were circulating that Pankhurst was interested in forming her own revolutionary organization, in opposition to the BSP and the ILP. In a letter to a friend she admitted the rumours were partially correct:

> I rather think Mrs Langdon Davies' news may be that our new branch wants to make our new name Workers' *Socialist* federation instead of Workers' *Suffrage* Federation. I think the branch is right, the title describes us better, but our annual conference at Whitsuntide will decide that.[128]

The war, the Easter Rising and the Russian revolution overturned Pankhurst's world; by 1918 she was no longer a socialist suffragette but a revolutionary dedicated to the struggle for socialism.

Chapter Five

ᴥᶘ

The Workers' Socialist Federation (1918–21)

Like other British revolutionaries, Sylvia Pankhurst was transformed by the Russian revolution of 1917. In the wake of the Bolshevik triumph and the British industrial agitation of 1917–19, the WSF too was transformed. These events demonstrated to Pankhurst and others that it was possible for workers to seize control of their lives. The Bolshevik revolution brought the hope that, even in the midst of war, it was possible for people to create revolution; it also showed that a workers' revolution was not just a continuation of the old ways, not a gradual transformation of government into a workers' parliament, but an entirely new form of government – soviet power.

From 1918 to 1921, the Workers' Socialist Federation was a unique revolutionary organization. It challenged the male domination of socialist politics, for even though its all-female membership changed over time to admit men, women continued to be the major leaders and activists. The WSF campaigned on a whole range of women's issues (such as women's and children's health care, schooling and domestic work) and also participated in workers' struggles in the East End, as well as in struggles nationally and internationally.

In this period of international upheaval, 1918–21, Pankhurst's ideas changed rapidly. She developed a hard anti-Labour Party, anti-electoral, anti-trade union leadership stance and discarded her former position that suffrage was the vehicle for social transformation. She also supported and built revolutionary workers' organizations, in England and around the world. Her internationalism and her role in the development of British and international communism will be discussed in the next chapter, in which I shall also examine WSF involvement in British working-class politics. During these years,

Pankhurst wrote little on her personal feelings about her work. Most of what we know of her attitudes towards the working-class movement in Britain is found in the pages of the *Dreadnought*.

The transformation of the WSF from a wartime feminist social welfare group to a revolutionary organization was reflected in the changing debates at the annual conferences. In May 1917 the resolutions adopted concerned conscription, the National Service Act, demands for municipal control of food distribution and an increase in mothers' pensions, and the WSF declared itself in favour of the "establishment of the socialist commonwealth".[1]

At the May 1918 conference, the Workers' Suffrage Federation was renamed the Workers' Socialist Federation, and its resolutions were significantly more revolutionary. The conference declared its opposition to the war and pledged itself to the abolition of armies and navies. It called upon the British government to recognize the Soviet government and upon British workers to oppose all candidates who supported the war and to elect only internationalist socialist candidates. It took a clear anti-colonialist stand (something that few other socialist organizations did), demanding self-determination for Ireland and India. Along with other socialist, feminist and pacifist organizations, the WSF protested against the increasing military activities in the schools, such as drilling and condemned the dismissals of teachers for their political or religious opposition to the war. The conference also made it clear that it had no use for the parliamentary system and advocated instead a form of local workers' control with soviets, or workers' committees, elected at local, national and international levels. Land and the means of production, distribution and exchange would be under a form of community control organized by workers in each industry. The workers' committees would render Parliament unnecessary. Finally, the conference called for the release of all conscientious objectors.[2]

By 1919, the WSF's revolutionary politics had developed even further. It had not forgotten its commitment to working women and children, calling for maternity centres to be set up along the lines of those established by the Bolshevik feminist Alexandra Kollontai, then commissar for social welfare in revolutionary Russia. The conference met shortly after the formation of the Third or Communist International (CI) and the WSF decided to affiliate immediately. Reiterating even more forcefully its opposition to working for revolutionary change through Parliament, it also came out against affiliation with the Labour Party. These were the central political positions being debated by revolutionaries in Britain at the time and the focus of the arguments around the creation of a unified communist party. At the 1919 WSF conference, the delegates decided to call themselves the Communist Party but, to avoid alienating other revolutionaries and organizations, the WSF postponed using this new name until after proposed unity negotiations with the British Socialist Party, the (SLP) Socialist Labour Party and the South Wales Socialist Society had taken place.[3]

By 1918 the WSF was fully committed to revolutionary aims, but its influence was far larger than its membership, which remained at about 300 in 1917, dropped to 150 in 1920, then rose again in 1920. The *Dreadnought* had a circulation of 10,000.[4] WSF branches were founded in many parts of England, Scotland and Wales. None of the branches outside East London, however, played as much of a political role as the original East End branches. WSF members were indefatigable. Pankhurst herself attended at least four meetings a week when she was in London, including WSF executive committee meetings, finance committee meetings and *Dreadnought* meetings. She also attended meetings of groups affiliated to or organized by the WSF, as well as local trade union, unemployed relief, rank-and-file, "Hands off Russia" and other political meetings. She was the editor of the *Dreadnought* and its major contributor. She also earned a meagre living for herself writing freelance. She was not only the honorary secretary of the WSF but also held that office for six other organizations in this period. This exhausting list of activities is even more remarkable when one considers that Pankhurst, who had never been in good health, had endured 15 arrests and 9 hunger, sleep and thirst strikes.

But she was not alone. From 1918 to 1920, the WSF held more than 800 meetings just in London. The organization had a team of regular speakers including Pankhurst, Mr Bahaduri, Olive Beamish, Minnie Birch, Eugenia Bouvier, Nellie Cressell (who later became the mayor of Poplar), Mr Hogben, Harry Pollitt, Miss Price, Miss Rickards, Melvina Walker and W. F. Watson. Other well-known radical figures spoke at WSF meetings, including the sexual radical Guy Aldred, Maud Gonne (the prominent Irish nationalist), Sam March (a well-known conscientious objector and Poplar councillor) and other important trade union, anarchist and radical spokespersons such as Tom Mann, Dave Ramsey (SLP member) and Jack Tanner.

The leftward direction of Pankhurst and the WSF was also prompted by increasing British industrial militancy. Like other individuals and organizations, the WSF was being swept along by a swelling tide of industrial and political unrest. The working people of Britain had learned a great deal from the war. The influence of the shop stewards' movement and the workers' committees was being felt throughout the country. The shop stewards' movement, which was founded in the Glasgow shipyards and spread in 1915 to munitions factories throughout Britain, consisted of shopfloor leaders elected by the workers, who were not formally a part of the trade union structure. The stewards then organized themselves into workers' committees. The movement demonstrated that the government and official trade union leaders could be defied, even in wartime and had popularized the idea of direct action. Even in London, where militancy during the war had been limited, such ideas were becoming more influential. War weariness was widespread, as was disgust with the political parties in power and their unscrupulous coalition government. The Labour Party was becoming popular and the Russian revolution stood out as a shining example of what was possible.

The beginning of 1919 witnessed an intensification of strikes and other forms of class conflict, illustrated by a general spontaneous demand for a better quality of life and for the realization of the government's promises about "homes fit for heroes" and "a world safe for democracy". Unemployment and the threat of unemployment – caused by demobilization and the slowing down of war work – hung over the industrial scene. From all over the country came the demand for shorter hours and increased wages. The trade union movement argued that only by reducing the number of hours worked could the unemployed be re-absorbed into industry. But the demand for a shorter work week was also a reaction to the excessive hours worked during the war. Socialist militants, their credibility and influence enhanced by wartime activities (particularly in the unofficial shop stewards' movement), played an important part in this agitation. Disillusionment with politicians and rank-and-file pressure for "direct action" for a political general strike pushed the trade union leadership to demand reduced work hours for bakers, cotton operatives, electrical workers, engineers, labourers, miners, railway and transport workers, shipbuilders and workers in some of the small trades.

At the close of 1918 and the beginning of 1919, union officials negotiated with shipbuilding and engineering firms for a 47 hour work week. In January there was a general strike in Belfast over the issue of a 44 hour work week. The strike committee virtually controlled the town, issuing permits for the use of gas and electricity and the distribution of food. The Clydeside engineers then demanded 40 hours. The highpoint of their campaign was the battle of George Square on "Red Friday", when a crowd was brutally beaten by the police. The strike then spread to bakers, builders, carpenters, gasworkers, joiners, miners, municipal workers, paperworkers and railway workers. Workers in Barrow-in-Furness, Edinburgh, Greenock, Leith, Perth and Rosyth joined as well. In London, shipbuilders and repairers walked out, demanding 15 shillings a day. Although these actions were taking place simultaneously, they were not co-ordinated. However, when the Electrical Trades Union (ETU) voted to come out in support of all the strikers, Britain was threatened with a complete blackout. The government responded by invoking the Defence of the Realm Act (DORA) and by declaring the electricians' strike illegal. The miners were engaged in negotiations for a charter that demanded a 30 per cent increase in wages, a six hour day, full unemployment relief, the equivalent of union wages for miners unemployed through demobilization and nationalization of the mines with joint control by the state and the mineworkers. But, in the face of disorganization and government threats, the trade union leaders retreated from the brink of a potentially revolutionary general strike. Their inability to employ bold initiatives only heightened Pankhurst's contempt for and impatience with trade union leaders. She wrote in the *Dreadnought* that "trade union officialdom is becoming a mere parasite on the workers' movement".[5]

The state was threatened from a different quarter as well. The army and navy were facing mutinous men at Calais, Dover, Folkestone, Osterly Park and Rhyl in late 1918 and early 1919. The police had gone on strike for union recognition for the first and last time in their history in 1918. Although these actions took place at the same time as the great upsurge in industrial militancy (the Glasgow strike coinciding with the Calais mutiny), this too was not by design. The armed forces and the industrial workers never joined together. If they had, the revolutionary potential of the situation would have been immense.

Having brought the country to the verge of open class war, the industrial militancy then subsided around 1919. The railway workers received an eight hour day through negotiation. The miners, granted a wage increase, consented to drop their demand for unemployment pay and in March accepted the interim Commission of Inquiry under Lord Sankey, which supported nationalization of the coal industry and reduced hours of work. The government promised to accept the findings of the Sankey Commission and the miners' anger was thus successfully cooled down.

Three months later, however, in June, the government high-handedly dismissed the findings of the Sankey Commission since it appeared to be too sympathetic to the miners' demands. A coal miners' strike loomed, which would have involved the other two members of the Triple Alliance, the railway and transport workers. Delays and retreats on the part of the Alliance leaders forced the miners to accept a compromise. A productivity deal was negotiated, under which wages were tied to output.

Workers won some other small victories. In the summer of 1919, the cotton operatives won a 48 hour work week and that September the railway workers struck – both skilled and unskilled going out in protest over a wage cut for the unskilled workers. The government, in its first attempt to smash labour after the war, was prepared to starve the workers back if necessary. However, its "divide and conquer" tactics failed. The co-operative movement (working-class organizations that provided mutual aid societies and businesses) rose magnificently to the occasion, providing the strikers with money and food; help also came from the Trades Union Congress (TUC) and the Labour Party. The compositors for the London newspapers also rallied to the cause, refusing to set or print lies about the railway workers' case. Because of support received from the locomotive workers, the railway workers won their strike and went back to work with no wage cuts and no reprisals.

During the autumn and winter of 1919–20, there were no large-scale strikes, but the municipal elections of November 1919 showed sensational Labour successes in Durham, London and South Wales. There were other indications that the working class was still combative. The dockers made good use of the Inquiry Clauses in the Industrial Courts Act, which forced the government to mediate in disputes if employers refused to arbitrate and dockers also made headway in improving conditions of unemployment. Wartime legislation decreed that dockers had to be registered to work and, ironically, this eliminated the casual labour system by drastically cutting the work force.

Meanwhile, throughout 1919 and the first half of 1920, the agitation against allied intervention in Russia was gaining ground. It culminated in the *Jolly George* incident of May 1920, when dockers prevented munitions from leaving Britain for counter-revolutionary Poland and in the establishment of the Council of Action in August to organize working-class resistance to intervention. The campaign for international working-class solidarity led to a second peak of working-class militance. By the second half of 1920 the brief economic boom brought about by the need for post-war reconstruction was over. Prices stopped rising and began falling. By the winter, severe depression set in and the government was able to force the trade union movement to retreat. One section after another of the organized working class in Britain was forced to accept reductions in wages and working conditions. The engineers capitulated after the lockout of 1921; the miners after the general strike of 1926. The brief period of revolutionary struggle was over.

These events and the response to them on the part of the TUC and Labour Party leaderships, played a major role in shaping the attitudes and policies of Sylvia Pankhurst and other revolutionaries in this period. From 1916 on, Pankhurst became more and more involved with the national working-class movement and the rank-and-file organization of workers that had grown up during the war. By 1918, she was actively involved with the London engineers' rank-and-file movement and she played a central role in persuading British workers to defend the Russian revolution. Her anti-war activities had made her a national agitator for the workers' movement; she was invited to South Wales to speak to the miners and to the Clyde, where she spoke not only to the (mainly male) shop stewards' movement, but also to the women involved in the equally explosive no-rent agitation.

Pankhurst's labours among women and around the immediate concerns facing women during the war, led to a working relationship with trade unionists (primarily men). For example, the Amalgamated Society of Engineers (ASE) vigilance committee held its meetings in Battersea Town Hall, pledging to strike for workers' control over food distribution and production. Pankhurst, who became a member of this committee, urged shop stewards to be more active in their shops and solicited support from rank-and-file engineers for the food strikers. This is another way in which her work closed the gap between traditional women's concerns – i.e. food distribution – and those of the predominantly male trade unionists – wages, unemployment and union recognition.

The WSF also developed a position with regard to the official union officers and the unofficial (shop stewards' and workers' committees) labour movement. It stood for industrial unionism; the organization of all workers in a particular industry, regardless of craft, gender, ethnicity, age or race. This stance placed the WSF squarely alongside the revolutionary wing of the British labour movement. Industrial versus craft unionism had been a longstanding debate among trade unionists and socialists and marked, for some, the dividing line between revolutionaries and reformists. The WSF argued that industrial unionism was the only way in which differences between skilled and unskilled, men and women, could be overcome.

The issue of a rank-and-file movement was of paramount concern to those revolutionary socialists who had been active in the shop stewards' movement. The minority strand of revolutionary syndicalism that had survived through the war called for resistance to the employer and the state. This struggle demanded workers' committees on a local, national and even international scale. The problem facing the small group of revolutionary socialists was how to link the rank-and-file organizations into a national organization and to remind workers of their political responsibilities to those outside paid labour – such as women, the unemployed and youth – as well as to the oppressed colonial nations fighting British imperialism.

However Pankhurst, like most other revolutionaries in Britain with the exception of the tiny Socialist Labour Party, had never worked in a factory or been active in a union. Many of the other socialist organizations did not see workplace organizing as important. Although the WSF did, its members were not in a position to begin systematic factory and trade union work, given its overwhelmingly female membership and the small industrial base of the East End. Thus, the WSF saw its role in building the rank-and-file movement as co-ordinating and directing the actions, mainly through propaganda in the *Dreadnought*. Although the WSF had few members who were active in the movement, it participated by explaining and encouraging strikes and analyzing important issues for the workers involved.

As early as 1916, Pankhurst could see the revolutionary potential of industrial unrest. In January, she wrote:

The new Trade Unionism, which is so active on the Clyde, wished to emancipate the workers from the position of incoherent dependent tools, whether of employers, Governments, or officials sprung from their own ranks. It wishes every worker in the trade to take his or her own part in moulding the policy of the union, and each trade union to take its part in making the nation a cooperative commonwealth.[6]

In February 1917, W. F. Watson (an engineer and ASE member in West London) asked Pankhurst if he could write a column in the *Dreadnought* on industrial unionism and workshop committees. He believed that industrial militants, whom Pankhurst particularly wished to involve in the WSF and in revolutionary activity, would be especially interested in this column and promised that the *Dreadnought* circulation would increase by 5,000. Pankhurst suggested that Watson be given a trial.[7] His column, "Workshop Notes", became a regular feature that, between March 1918 and March 1919, provided publicity and co-ordinated information for the shop stewards' movement. Each week, workers' committees from different parts of the country wrote in to report on their progress and activities.

Watson's political ideas coincided with Pankhurst's. He opposed the ASE establishment and was an ardent advocate of workshop committees. Like Pankhurst, he felt that craft unionism was obsolete and that the only way for trade unions to deal with the issues arising in the post-war period was through the workers' committee movement. Watson was largely responsible for the attempt to establish a London Workers' Committee (LWC) to co-ordinate all the different committees in London. At the time the West London Engineering Workers' Committee (WLEWC) was fighting hard against layoffs. The editor of their rank-and-file paper, the *West London Metalworkers' Record,* had just been fired for organizing. However, solidarity actions comparable to that which had earlier forced the Vulcan Works in Sheffield to reinstate J. T. (Jack) Murphy (a prominent SLP member and shop steward) after having fired him, did not take place and the *West London Metalworkers' Record* ceased publication. Watson pointed out that consolidated mass actions could prevent firings and prosecutions of radical newspapers. The inability of London radicals to defend their own through industrial militancy convinced him that

London lagged behind the workers' movement of the north and west.[8]

Watson's columns in the *Dreadnought* on the industrial unrest both reflected and helped to develop WSF policy and activity. His articles demonstrate that both Watson and Pankhurst understood the complicated and intricate arguments being debated by the government, the Labour Party and the TUC as well as by the unofficial bodies. The columns also reflected Pankhurst's commitment to women's equality, an issue the labour and socialist movement did not take up. Watson campaigned against the ASE policy of excluding women, arguing in two columns in July that, since women were employed in all grades of engineering jobs, they should be represented in the exclusively male Woolwich Arsenal Shop Stewards' Committee.[9]

The *Dreadnought* reported on and championed working women's struggles. In August 1918 the London Bus Girls struck for equal pay. At a private meeting at Willesden garage, the women decided to strike immediately without even waiting for sanction from the trade union officials. Willesden women were followed by Acton and Hackney women, who refused to go back to work pending negotiations, as the union leadership urged. The women's determination paid off and they won the pay increase.[10]

Later that month, the Bus Girls were followed by the Tube women, who worked in London's underground. Their case was taken up by the National Federation of Women Workers, which also accused the Minister of Munitions of discriminating against women in jobs formerly done by men.[11]

Since Pankhurst saw workers' committees as the basis for socialism in Britain, it was important to organize them in London, the capital. Although the rank-and-file workers there were not as extensively organized into committees as those in places such as Glasgow, workers' committees did exist at the DuCros factory in Acton, Davidson's in Hammersmith, Berwick's in Park Royal and Gwynnes in Chiswick. There were also committees at the Wadden National Aircraft Factory in Croydon and at other aircraft factories. Apart from the official London Aircraft Woodworkers' Council, there also existed the semi-official London District Aircraft Committee (in the process of being organized by both official trade unionists and workers' committees).

On 4 October, rank-and-file members from the Waring and Gillows airplane factory met to protest against the firing of a shop steward.

They demanded that the Airplane Workers' Strike Committee set up a co-ordinating body of shop stewards. Basil Thompson, the police informant assigned to infiltrate and report on the WSF, reported that "some extremists like Tanner, Dixie and Chapman opposed forming a London Council, as better work could be done with local organisation and decentralisation". Various other meetings were held at this time, involving metalworkers, railway workers, tram workers, Tube workers and woodworkers. At one such meeting, Watson – no doubt carried away by all these actions – declared enthusiastically (if unrealistically) that London should become the Petrograd of Britain.

The capital city was coming in for some criticism from revolutionaries in the provinces for not providing enough revolutionary leadership. However, the obstacles to setting up a London-based shop stewards' movement were becoming increasingly obvious. Watson was convinced that not enough allowance was being made for local differences and that the experience of other areas, such as the Clyde, should not be imposed upon London because of that city's peculiar industrial structure. The beginnings of an East London movement, in which Pankhurst played a significant role, largely as a revolutionary propagandist, became evident toward the end of 1918. In January 1919, an East London Committee (ELC) was formed. By now, however, the workers' movement nationally was losing both influence and members, so, although the East London movement was important, given its isolation it was unlikely to make permanent headway.[12]

The ELC, headquartered at Pankhurst's address at 400 Old Ford Road, was to all intents and purposes identical with Harry Pollitt's River Thames Shipbuilders and Ship-repairers' Committee (RTSSC). Pollitt was then the district secretary of the Boilermakers' Union and a member of the WSF. The ELC existed largely on paper until it became involved in the agitation for an increase in shipworkers' wages to 15d. a day, which coincided with the 40 hour strikes elsewhere in the country. The River Thames shop stewards called a meeting and 8,000 people filled the Poplar Hippodrome. WSF members attended and sold a considerable amount of literature.[13] Pollitt, the featured speaker, announced the appearance of a new newspaper, the *Consolidator* – the voice of the River Thames Committee. By the end of January, the RTSSC had 12,000 members and had brought the shipbuilders and ship-repairers of the Port of London out on strike.[14]

In his memoir, *Serving my time*, Pollitt describes how the strike came about. His work against intervention in Russia brought him into contact with trades other than his own in the shipyards and he began to discuss the formation of a River Thames Committee with other trade unionists. The woodworkers and electricians were eager; the boiler-makers, however, suffered from craft sectionalism – that is, they wanted only skilled workers organized into the committee. However, unity won out. Pollitt claimed that the River Committee spread from Tilbury to Chiswick and that, as the chief organizer, he "stumped every shipyard on the River".[15] Although women shipworkers came out in sympathy, strike organizers failed to convince the male dockers to join.

During the "fifteen shilling strike", *Dreadnought* speakers were called upon to speak at every meeting.[16] Great efforts were made by Pankhurst, Pollitt and other London militants to link the struggle to those on the Clydeside and in Belfast. But London was far from united in its response. The arsenal stewards were haggling over whether to ask for a 40, 44 or 47 hour week and paid no attention. An official ASE district meeting accepted a call for sympathy action, but nothing materialized.[17]

In the 15 February *Dreadnought* editorial, Pankhurst analyzed the strikes then going on in London. The electricians were out, as were the underground workers; the busmen were waiting for the miners and transport workers to join them. The ASE had dismissed the Clyde and London district committees of the union. A "no rent" strike was in progress in Woolwich; the strikers were demanding a decrease in rents from 9s. 6d. to 4s. 6d. for unrepaired homes, which they called "huts". The shipbuilders and ship-repairers were standing firm. A River Thames shop stewards' feeding committee had been set up and was being run in conjunction with the WSF from Old Ford Road. Again, the WSF's years of work among women in London's East End were bringing women's and children's issues to strikes comprised mainly of men.[18] By setting up children's food committees and by mobilizing women to aid directly in the strike actions, the WSF no doubt raised the consciousness of the male workers.

The "fifteen shilling strike" lasted five weeks but ended in defeat. The employers were able to keep the unskilled and skilled workers divided and eventually the movement collapsed. At the Hippodrome, where Pollitt had earlier received a cheering ovation from the workers' committees, he was howled off the stage as the strikers voted to return to work.[19] The defeat was a death blow to the River Thames Committee. It had tried but failed to organize a "London Workers' Council" to keep propaganda going for industrial unionism and even had its own choir and orchestra,[20] but none of its efforts bore fruit.

The fate of the East London Committee was even gloomier. Its office was raided in early 1919. Two leading members, Watson and Dave Ramsey, were arrested and imprisoned for making seditious and inflammatory speeches. Ramsey, one of London's leading shop stewards, was sentenced to five months in jail.[21] Watson was arrested in early March 1919, ostensibly for a speech he had made at a "Hands off Russia" meeting in the Albert Hall in February. According to Basil Thompson, "Among Watson's effects were found a number of notices showing his efforts to infect sailors and soldiers with seditions."[22] Watson received six months and appealed, but his appeal was dismissed in July. In the meantime, some London militants accused him of supplying information to the police. Since Watson was clearly the most vocal and visible member of the London shop stewards' movement and prominent in the WSF, it was crucial to establish his guilt or innocence. The case was far from simple.

On his release from prison, Watson admitted to accepting money from Scotland Yard. His defence was that he felt Scotland Yard might extract information from someone else on the London Workers' Committee or in the Hands off Russia movement; he thought it was better for him to provide them with useless information than for them to approach someone else. The Cabinet Reports make it clear that Watson was indeed a police informant, but not a particularly useful one, because the informant claimed he was an untrustworthy drunk.

> As an illustration of this kind of man who engineers a revolutionary strike, it may be mentioned that Watson was until recently furnishing information, for payment to the police, but was so drunken and untrustworthy that his communications were discredited.[23]

The London shop stewards were divided on the question of Watson's guilt. The majority argued that, even though he did sincerely attempt to mislead the police, he was guilty of giving information and should have informed the Workers' Committee of his decision to do so. A minority argued that he had given no real information to the police, who were simply attempting to weaken an already flagging movement.[24] Nevertheless, by introducing doubts into the movement, the

117

police succeeded in effectively undermining the committee. Watson no longer wrote for the *Dreadnought* and ceased being politically active.

In June 1919, the East London Committee tried to revitalize itself by organizing a conference but failed. Although it was well attended by representatives of the Railway Vigilance Committees, fewer than 200 delegates in all were present. The railway strike that autumn elicited little enthusiasm from London railwaymen. The failure of London's workers to act in solidarity with workers in other parts of Britain prompted J. T. Murphy, a member of the National Action Committee of the Shop Stewards' and Workers' Committee Movement (SSWCM) to suggest the formation of another central body for London consisting of delegates from local committees; he also suggested that a conference of such delegates take place. It was held on 22 September 1919, but very few attended. As a result of it, however, *Solidarity* replaced the *Dreadnought* (or, more accurately, Watson's column) as the official newspaper of the London movement.[25]

A genuine mass-based shop stewards' movement never developed in London, so the WSF was unable to involve itself in such a movement, although its leading members were well aware of the need for these committees. Through the columns of the *Dreadnought*, the WSF reported on the shop stewards' movement nationally and contributed significantly to the movement's theoretical development. It provided the shop stewards with publicity, encouragement and a degree of co-ordination.

In March 1918, Sylvia Pankhurst organized the People's Russian Information Bureau (PRIB). Its formation was first discussed at a WSF committee meeting after Edward Soermus, the famed Russian violinist, begged Pankhurst to convene a conference and found an organization to disseminate the truth about the Russian revolution.[26] On 24 July, the conference on Russia was held at Chandos Hall. A committee to run the PRIB was elected, with Pankhurst representing the WSF. Other representatives came from the SLP, the BSP, the National Union of Railwaymen (NUR), the Labour Representation Committee (LRC) and the ILP. The hard work of running the bureau offices, which were located in Fleet Street above the *Dreadnought* offices, fell to May O'Callaghan, the subeditor of the *Dreadnought* and Nellie Rathbone, Pankhurst's secretary.[27]

According to Home Office intelligence records, the bureau "issued leaflets containing letters alleged to have been received from Russia without passing through censorship".[28] Detectives searched the premises of the PRIB's treasurer, T. C. Hollowell, in October. Among the letters seized was one from Captain Sadoul of the French military mission in Moscow. This letter and other documents, the Home Office alleged, were proof that the main objective of the PRIB was "to work up an agitation against the Allied intervention in Russia".[29] Pankhurst received and sent communications from and to Russia via the shipping lines. She was the first to translate into English and publish the constitution of the Soviet Republic, brought to her by a ship's physician on the Cunard line.

By February 1919, 100 societies and trade union branches had affiliated with the PRIB; by July this number had increased to 347. Affiliates included the local Labour Party and Labour Trades Councils, the ILP, BSP, SLP, Herald League, NUR, ASE and ETU, plus Co-op Guilds, the Communist League and one branch of the Catholic Crusade.[30]

The Information Bureau produced a great number of pamphlets and leaflets. It translated the writings of communists abroad and circulated them to affiliated groups. Funds were received from Russia to facilitate the work: Basil Thompson of the Home Office estimated that the PRIB received £300 in October 1919 and £300 in October 1920.[31] The bureau provided publicity and information for the growing movement against Allied intervention in Russia. In early 1919, the British had sent troops to Archangel to help the White Armies. News of increasing help for the counter-revolutionary generals Denikin and Wrangel caused great disquiet among organized labour. The Labour Party conference in June voted by a substantial majority to demand an immediate end to intervention and to initiate a general strike, if necessary, to enforce its demand. The TUC parliamentary committee, however, refused to sanction such a strike. In January, the WSF, BSP, SLP, IWW and ELC circulated a leaflet signed by Sylvia Pankhurst, Arthur MacManus (a prominent SLP member), Watson and Ramsay calling for workers to fight against Allied intervention. That same month these organizations held a Hands off Russia conference, which set up a steering committee of 15 (including Sylvia Pankhurst) to oversee the anti-intervention activity.[32]

Despite great efforts by these individuals, the movement was slow in getting off the ground. A large number of resolutions condemning intervention were passed at union and Labour Party meetings up and down the country. However, they were not backed up by any kind of action. In June, the Labour Party issued a joint appeal with the BSP, the South Wales Socialist Society (SWSS) and the WSF for a 24 hour strike in support of Russia and Hungary. In the same month, a meeting was held in Old Ford Road to raise £200 for agitation in London's dockyards. Tom Mann, a prominent socialist labour leader since the 1890s, was asked to work among the dockers to persuade them not to load munitions bound for the enemies of Russia. The WSF campaigned in many different parts of London in a "great push against intervention". Open-air meetings were held regularly and successfully.[33]

On 20 and 21 July 1919, an international "ultra-left" conference (comprised of those revolutionaries who opposed parliamentary or electoral activity) met in Amsterdam and called for a 24 hour international strike against intervention in Russia. Pankhurst, one of the conference organizers, was very hopeful about the outcome of the resolution, as were many others. But the international strike turned out to be a fiasco. The French General Confederation of Labourers (CGT) and the Italian unions backed out at the eleventh hour and thus the strikes on the Continent were only partial. In Britain, the only strikes of significance were those of the London dockers, the Norwich boot-and-shoe operatives and the Merthyr miners. Demonstrations were held in Trafalgar Square, Victoria Park and Bethnal Green, where Sylvia Pankhurst and George Lansbury spoke, but they were small, numbering only in the hundreds.[34]

As part of the campaign to oppose intervention – as well as the effort to publicize events in the Soviet Union – Pankhurst printed Lenin's "Appeal to the Toiling Masses" in the *Dreadnought* in May 1920. She did so at great personal risk since the tract was blacklisted by the Home Office.[35] Nonetheless, this appeal for international working-class solidarity – to save the new soviet state from defeat by the forces of reaction – was circulated extensively in the docks. Pollitt says he stored copies of it in his mattress and worked with WSF members distributing leaflets:

> Many of the comrades could be seen outside the London Docks and shipyards selling "Hands Off Russia" literature and our members were also selling inside. Day after day we posted up placards, sticky backs and posters on dockside, in ships and lavatories.

Walker was unbelievable – she was always talking to groups of women shopping in Chrisp Street . . . telling them about Russia, asking them to tell their husbands to keep their eyes skinned for munitions.[36]

In February 1920, the WSF called meetings in Trafalgar Square and in Poplar Town Hall. Some of the speakers, according to the Home Office records, made use of a report originally published in the *Rote Fahne* (the newspaper founded by Rosa Luxemburg) which had been reprinted in the *Dreadnought*. The gist of the article was that the defeat of the counter-revolutionary Russian general Yudenich was partly due to the fact that British workmen had removed essential parts of guns being shipped to the White Armies.[37]

In March and April, the WSF and dockers in London learned that barges in that city and in Belgian ports were being loaded with munitions. They made tremendous efforts to persuade the men working on the barges to refuse to load them. Pollitt remembered how saddened he was when the dockers ignored his pleas. Then an old docker approached him, telling him not to worry. As the cargo was being loaded onto the ships, the tow ropes snapped and the cargo was lost in the North Sea.[38] On 10 May, a ship named the *Jolly George* was being loaded at the East India Dock with cargo labelled "OHMS Munitions for Poland". It took the dockers a good 20 minutes before they fully realized that they had been loading counter-revolutionary cargo. By then a considerable number of guns had been loaded. The coal heavers refused to fuel the ship until the munitions were unloaded. A deputation of dockers went to see Fred Thompson and Ernest Bevin, the general secretaries of the dockers' union. They received assurance that the union would back a strike if the munitions weren't taken off the ship. On 11 May, the export branch of the Dock, Wharf and Riverside General Workers' Union passed a resolution calling on the Transport Workers' Federation and the Parliamentary Labour Party to take such action as might be necessary to prevent the *Jolly George* from being loaded in any British port with munitions for Poland. On 15 May the munitions were unloaded back onto the quayside.[39]

"The strike on the 'Jolly George' was the result of two years unremitting work on the part of a devoted band of comrades in the East End," wrote Pollitt.[40] Pankhurst agreed. In an article in the *Dreadnought,* she wrote that Melvina Walker, Harry Pollitt and others had "kept the communist flag flying at the East India Dock Gates week in and week out all through the Russian war".[41] Pollitt, who later served as a leader of the British Communist Party (an organization that came to deny Pankhurst's contributions to the working class and to the communist movement), had only kind words about Pankhurst:

> Sylvia Pankhurst was, of course, the leading spirit of the federation and she had a remarkable gift of extracting the last ounce of energy, as well as the last penny from everyone with whom she came in contact to help with the work and activities she directed from Old Ford Road. She was loved in Poplar and though I have often heard that she was very difficult to get on with, I never found it so . . .[42]

The example set by the London dockers led by the end of May to a refusal by the dockers' and railway unions nationally to load munitions. In 1919, the British government faced its greatest crisis since the time of the Chartist movement.[43] Not only was the labour movement at its revolutionary and militant peak, but unrest among elements of the military led revolutionaries such as Pankhurst (not to mention government officials) to believe that they were justified in preparing for revolution. Demobilization of the armed forces brought about new problems. On the one hand, the army and navy hoped demobilization would rid them of some of their more disgruntled conscripts. On the other, demobilization meant that the armed forces' resources were stretched even thinner since imperial commitments had increased because of continuing civil strife in Ireland, counter-revolutionary intervention in Russia and occupation of the Rhineland, as well as other parts of the Empire. The loyalty of young working-class soldiers was also in doubt, especially as far as domestic unrest was concerned. In addition, British politicians and officers were alarmed by revolutionary discontent among European soldiers and sailors, which served as an example for British soldiers. German workers and soldiers, for example, were in a state of open rebellion. The sailors of Kiel, Cuxhaven and Bremen refused to take orders and the German fleet was in the hands of a workers', soldiers' and sailors' council. Pankhurst too was acutely aware of the significance of these developments and hailed them as the beginning of the German revolution. Pankhurst exulted in the *Dreadnought*, "It is the beginning of the Revolution. As it was in Russia, so it is in Germany!"[44] In November, a republic was proclaimed in Germany and in January the unsuccessful Spartacist Rising took place in Berlin. Bavaria declared itself a soviet republic in April 1919, with Munich as its capital, only to be suppressed a month later.

As soon as the Armistice was signed in 1918, British soldiers had clamoured to return home. The War Office's mobilization scheme of last in first out, fuelled discontent. Although Winston Churchill stepped in with a more rapid, fairer plan, it did not prevent unrest among the battle-weary, disillusioned troops. Militant demonstrations at Le Havre at the end of 1918 were mistakenly dismissed by the Home Office as being a "drunken spree", not political. In January 1919, 10,000 men mutinied in Folkestone and refused to return to France, 4,000 demonstrated in solidarity in Dover, as did others across the Channel. In the same week, 1,500 Royal Air Corps men from Osterly Park seized trucks, drove to London and demonstrated at Whitehall. Demonstrations became widespread; 20,000 soldiers refused duty in Calais. In March 1919, 5 men were killed and 2 officers and 21 soldiers injured in rioting at Rhyl. There were reports of soldiers' councils organized in Egypt.[45]

While these military disturbances were raging, sailors hauled the Red Flag up the mast of HMS *Kilbride* at Milford Haven, in protest against the lowness of their wages and intervention in Russia. The WSF circulated a leaflet entitled "To British Sailors", appealing to them not to sail to Russia. In his history entitled *Mutiny*, Tom Wintringham tells of refusals to sail to Russia and of ships being sent home.[46]

The WSF's anti-intervention work prompted harassment from the police. Dave Ramsey was jailed for five months for inciting disaffection among soldiers and civilians in May 1920. As noted, W. F. Watson, who had organized a Soldiers', Sailors' and Airmen's Union (SSAU), had received a similar sentence for an inflammatory speech at a Hands off Russia meeting. The police claimed to have found leaflets on his person proving that he was sowing disaffection among His Majesty's Forces.[47]

On 14 May 1920, the *Dreadnought*'s offices were raided and Harold Burgess, its business manager, was arrested and sentenced to six months for subverting the Irish Guards. The offices were raided another six times in the eight days following his arrest. At a 2,000 strong demonstration outside the Polish Embassy protesting against intervention in Russia, Lillian Thring and Bertram Colonna, both WSF members, were arrested at the end of May.[48]

The timing of the raids and arrests was suspicious. According to intelligence reports, the leaflets Burgess was accused of distributing – announcements calling for "Soviets for the British" – had been circulating both before and after his arrest. Hence, the arrest was a setup. It turned out that Burgess had met two Irish Guardsmen in a pub who told him, probably rather drunkenly, of their opposition to British policy in Ireland. Burgess invited the two men back to his place and gave them the pamphlets, which told how to form soviets. He also gave them some money to help spread propaganda in Ireland. The soldiers told their officers about the incident and, under orders from them, trapped Burgess into writing incriminating letters about getting machine guns to Ireland. During Burgess's trial, the guardsmen testified that they had attended a meeting in the *Dreadnought* offices with Pankhurst, where again they were promised that guns would be smuggled into Ireland. Under oath, however, they conceded that Pankhurst was not pleased by any mention of guns.[49]

Despite such harassment, anti-intervention agitation was taking hold of the labour movement all over the country. Even the Home Office reluctantly admitted that "there were remarkable demonstrations against the war [of intervention in Russia] in practically every part of the country in spite of the holiday season".[50] Even in August, the peak of the summer vacation period, meetings attracted audiences of 1,000 or more, culminating in the formation on 9 August of a Council of Action by the TUC and the Labour Party. The council was set up to mobilize the industrial power of organized workers to defeat any war between the Allied powers and Soviet Russia.

A political general strike to force the government to alter its foreign policy was on the cards. This was "direct action" at potentially its most militant and political. The Council of Action called a peace demonstration in Trafalgar Square in late October and 15,000 people attended. However, with the conclusion of peace, the council disappeared. In the rebellious years following the First World War, militancy spread far beyond the industrial centres of Britain. Quite threatening was the foment that arose among the domestic security forces. Almost incredibly, it reached the police force. The Metropolitan Police struck in August 1918, demanding recognition of their union (the National Union of Police and Prison Officers), an increase in wages and the reinstatement of their fired union organizer, ex-police constable Tommy Their.[51]

The next strike occurred in May 1919 and, though it failed, it resulted in stoppages in Liverpool, London and other cities. All the strikers were fired and union members, once identified, were immediately dismissed. Estimates in *Solidarity* show that the police union was 50,000–55,000 strong, with members throughout the provinces as well as in London.[52] During these months, when industrial unrest was blazing in nearly every important industrial centre in Britain, the government could at no time rely on the complete loyalty of the police.

Along with the defence of the Russian Revolution and the creation of a rank-and-file workers' movement, the issue of unemployment became an explosive one in post-war Britain. Nationally, the unemployed figures showed a sharp increase after the end of the war, reaching a peak of 1,828,223 in 1922. In London, unemployment more than doubled between 1 September and 1 November 1920.[53] Pankhurst and the WSF were involved in the unemployment agitation, especially in London and, through the *Dreadnought*, in the national campaigns. In particular, the WSF agitated among workers discharged from the Woolwich Arsenal, a large employer for the East End. By the beginning of 1920, Woolwich's ex-servicemen and discharged munitions workers were seething with discontent.

In October 1920, activists from the Hands off Russia Committee and unemployed servicemen's organizations met at Bookbinders' Hall in Clerkenwell. Delegates from 12 London organizations of the unemployed were present and decided to form the London District Council of the Unemployed. Wal Hannington became the London organizer, Percy Hayne the secretary and Jack Holt the chairman.[54] The formation of the council marked the beginning of more radical and militant activity by the unemployed. Soon they were occupying buildings all over London and raiding factories to prevent employers from cutting wages and making workers work overtime.[55]

During these turbulent months, a policy advocated by George Lansbury – "go to the Guardians" – was becoming popular. All over Britain, the Guardians (elected local officials in charge of administering relief under the archaic Poor Law) were harassed and sometimes terrorized by a ragged army of unemployed men and women. Families not covered or insufficiently covered by employment benefits or stranded during the gaps between periods of unemployment benefits (which often lasted a month) were forced to resort to the Guardians. Many Guardians sent men to the workhouses, often separating them from their families; others doled out miserly relief rates – well below the Ministry of Health's minimum scale.[56]

The London District Council adopted Lansbury's policy and as a result the Bermondsey, Bethnal Green, Camberwell, Clerkenwell, Finsbury, Holborn and Islington Guardians were forced to accede to the demands of the unemployed and to increase relief. A trend-setting generosity was shown by the Poplar Guardians and "Poplarism" subsequently came to haunt those for whom parting with money presented grave moral difficulties. Brentford, Deptford, Hackney, Hammersmith, Hendon, Islington, Lambeth, St Pancras, Shepherd's Bush, Shoreditch and Woolwich Guardians all received visits from the organized unemployed workers of East London.

The famous battle between the Poplar Borough Council and the London County Council took place in the summer of 1921. The Poplar Council protested against the unfair burden placed on industrial and working-class boroughs, which had to pay a greater portion for relief because of the greater number of unemployed and relatively low rates (local taxes paid for social services) in the borough. On these grounds, Poplar flatly refused to hand over the proportion of its local rates due to the London County Council (LCC) annually.[57] Instead, it demanded that London rates be pooled and distributed equally so that London as a whole – including the wealthy Royal Boroughs of Kensington and Chelsea – shared the burden of unemployment. Poplar councillors continued to pay their "generous" unemployment benefits. They stuck to their principles and refused to let the unemployed suffer because of the relative poverty of the borough.

In July, the councillors were summoned to the High Court and Lansbury and 29 others went to prison on 1 September 1921. Of the 29, 7 were or had been active members or very close supporters of the ELFS/WSF: Nellie Cressell, Edgar Lansbury, George Lansbury, Minnie Lansbury, Jennie Mackay, John Scurr and Julia Scurr. The councillors remained in jail until 12 October despite the enormous embarrassment this caused the government. Demonstrations of sympathy and support took place, with marches from the East End to Holloway and Brixton. Parliament subsequently passed a bill spreading the cost of relief over London as a whole.[58]

The December issue of *Out of Work*, the newspaper of the unemployment movement, carried an article entitled "To the Coppers", appealing to the police not to attack forcibly the unemployed marchers. The paper's editor, Lillian Thring (no longer a member of the WSF), was charged with "inciting disaffection amongst the metropolitan police". Appearing in Bow Street Court, she was fined £10 but, on refusing to pay, was sent to prison for three weeks. The action against her was seen by the unemployed movement as a deliberate attempt to thwart the publication of the increasingly popular *Out of Work*.[59]

As a result, in August 1922 30 unemployed workers marched all the way from Birmingham to the Ministry of Labour in London. They were put up by the councillors of Poplar and the mayor, Charlie Sumner, welcomed them, saying he hoped that more unemployed marches would come to London.[60] And come they did. The first Hunger March on London, including contingents that had marched from as far away as Glasgow, arrived in November. This was the beginning of the movement that led to the famous Jarrow Crusades of the unemployed in the early 1930s.

Sylvia Pankhurst and the WSF were in the vortex of all this agitation. But she paid the price for her revolutionary ardour and commitment. Police and government informants spied on her and other members of the WSF during Britain's post-First World War "Red Scare". At the end of October 1920, shortly after her return from a trip to Russia, Pankhurst was arrested under regulation 42 of DORA for:

> An Act calculated and likely to cause sedition amongst HM Forces, in the Navy and amongst the Civilian Population by publishing and causing and procuring to be published in the city of London, a newspaper called the *Workers' Dreadnought*, organ of the Communist Party, dated 16th October, containing articles called "Discontent in the Lower Deck", "How to Get a Labour Government", "The Datum Line", "The Yellow Peril and the Dockers".[61]

The first article had been written by an unnamed sailor from HMS *Hunter*, the second by a man named Rubinstein (alias Veltheim alias Anderson) later arrested as a Russian spy. "The Datum Line" referred to an agreement between the government and coal miners regarding wages and working conditions; written by Sylvia Pankhurst, it reiterated her belief that Parliament was "part of the oppressive machinery of the bourgeois state". She further argued that it was the duty of revolutionaries to destroy Parliament and, as William Morris had suggested in *News from Nowhere*, to turn the buildings into storehouses for manure.[62]

"The Yellow Peril" was written by Claude McKay, under the pseudo-nym *Leon Lopez*. He was a Jamaican revolutionary poet who became acquainted with Pankhurst after trying to get a number of his articles published in socialist journals such as the *Daily Herald*. When he came to London, McKay was horrified by the racism in the *Herald*. "The headlines were harrowing," he recalled: "Black Scourge in Europe", "Black Peril on the Rhine", "Brutes in French Uniform", "Black Menace of 40,000 Troops", "Appeal to the Women of Europe".[63]

> I wrote a letter to George Lansbury, the editor of the *Daily Herald*, and pointed out that his "black scourge" articles would be effective in stirring up more prejudices against Negroes. I thought it was the duty of his paper as a radical organ to enlighten its readers about the real reasons why the English considered coloured troops undesirable in Europe instead of appealing indirectly to illogical emotional prejudices. Lansbury did not print my letter, but sent me a private note saying that he was not personally prejudiced against Negroes.[64]

McKay was then introduced to Pankhurst, who liked his style of writing. She wanted him to write articles about life in the London docks, from an anti-racist perspective and about the experiences of black and white sailors. He was also assigned to read articles in the American, Australian and Indian press and to comment on those that might interest *Dreadnought* readers. Pankhurst's hiring of McKay is another example of her unique position among socialists on the subject of race. Like socialists in the United States, the overwhelming majority of white British socialists were not sympathetic or sensitive to the issues of race and racism. Some, like Hyndman, were out-and-out racists; others, like Hardie, believed that race relations would automatically be solved once there was a socialist revolution. But Pankhurst was aware of racism and supported the activities of people of colour in their struggle against racism and colonialism.

The *Dreadnought* was the only British socialist newspaper that had black correspondents. McKay was not the only one; Reuben Samuels, a black sailor, was also a frequent correspondent.[65] McKay wrote on a whole range of issues, including the Garvey movement and Black Nationalism in the United States, the revolutionary coal miners in the Rhondda Valley and the conferences of the Trades Union Congress.

In early 1920, he met a young English sailor named Springhall, a devoted reader of the *Dreadnought* who told McKay that the sailors on his ship were eager for more revolutionary literature. Springhall visited the *Dreadnought* offices and McKay gave him many copies of the paper. Springhall later wrote him a letter containing some crucial information about the level of discontent among sailors in the navy and he shared the letter with Pankhurst, who also saw its importance.[66] McKay and Pankhurst edited the letter and published it as "Discontent on the Lower Deck", using the pseudonym "S.000 (Gunner)". The article discussed the growing unrest on the unnamed battleship, listed the pay grievances of the men and noted that free railway passes and marriage allowances for men under 25 had been abolished. Furthermore, the article urged:

> Men of the Lower Deck: Are you going to see your class go under in the fight with the capitalist brutes who make millions out of our sacrifices during the war? Comrades, here is fertile ground for propaganda to win the Army and Navy to the cause of the workers . . . . You are the sons of the Working Class, therefore it is your duty to stand by that class and not the class of the Government which is responsible for the starving of your ex-service brothers. Hail the formation of the Red Navy, which protects the interests of the working class, and repudiate the dirty financial interests which you are protecting now![67]

A few days later, the *Dreadnought* offices were raided by the police. McKay escaped by pretending he had nothing to do with the *Dreadnought*. But Pankhurst could not get away with that and was arrested. Refusing to name her sources or to reveal the names of the people who wrote the offending articles, she was sentenced to six months in jail. She was released on £2,000 bail. At her appeal, Pankhurst defended the sailor's article and also "The Yellow Peril":

> This article is a plea that the workers should not turn around and assail their coloured brethren. . . . I was returning home one evening down the West India Dock Road and I found the place thronged. I asked, "What is the matter?" And I was told "They are stabbing coloured men." Some were killed that night and for three nights that went on in Poplar. Out of work soldiers and other unemployed were stabbing the coloured men. This is some time ago now, though it was since the war; we have had it in other towns and docks as well as East London. The fact was that the trade union was objecting to the employment of these coloured men. They were left here in this country, and the men

out of work, seeing, they thought, they were going to get their jobs, took to stabbing them. . . . Leon Lopez, being himself a coloured man – who is not a British subject perhaps – felt this keenly, and he put his letter in this paper; and I, as editor, felt he had a right to put it there and point out to the workers that unemployment is caused by deeper things than this.[68]

Pankhurst understood how racism was used to foster further divisions among working people. McKay never forgot Pankhurst's loyalty to him, nor her commitment to anti-racism. In his autobiography, *A long way from home*, he wrote:

Pankhurst herself had a personality as picturesque and passionate as any radical in London . . . . And in the labour movement she was always jabbing her hat pin into the hides of the smug and slack labour leaders. Her weekly might have been called the Dread Wasp. And wherever imperialism got drunk and went wild among the native peoples, the Pankhurst people would be on the job.[69]

Springhall did not forget Pankhurst's bravery either and tried to visit her but was told by McKay that, since she was enjoined from political activity and was under extensive surveillance, he should not go to the *Dreadnought* offices. The sailor stayed active in revolutionary politics and for that was eventually court-martialled. He travelled to Russia and became active in the British Communist Youth Movement.[70]

Rubinstein, the author of another offending article (under the pen name of "Veltheim"), was detained after Pankhurst's arrest, while trying to leave London. On his person was found a letter, allegedly from Pankhurst, showing that she and Veltheim were involved in what Pankhurst later described as "fantastic and absurd adventures".[71] These allegedly included gun running, currency smuggling and inciting violence among the unemployed in the East End. The incident was damaging to Pankhurst's reputation, even though most people believed it was a police provocation. John Maclean (Scottish Marxist, member of the BSP and friend and admirer) wrote in his newspaper, the *Vanguard*:

The report of the trial of a Finn who is alleged to be a courier between Lenin and revolutionaries in this country has brought to light a letter supposed to be written by Sylvia Pankhurst. She is supposed to tell Lenin that she got lads to create disturbances amongst the unemployed whilst Lansbury and the other London mayors were discussing matters at 10 Downing Street.

If she wrote it, then Sylvia acted as a police provocateur, consciously or unconsciously. At any rate whether guilty or not, the work was that of the police to head back the dangerous outburst when unemployment grows worse as the year proceeds.[72]

Pankhurst did at this time receive a tremendous compliment from Lenin, a man she admired enormously while differing with him politically. Lenin's article in the 17 June 1920 issue of *Pravda* no doubt enhanced her revolutionary reputation:

Sylvia Pankhurst has been arrested in England. This is the best possible answer the British government could give to this question which the non-communist British Labour "leaders" who are captives to bourgeois prejudices, are even afraid to put, namely against which class is the terror directed – against the oppressed and exploited or against the exploiters and oppressors? When they speak of "freedom" do they speak of freedom for the capitalists to rob, to deceive, to befool the toilers from the yoke of the capitalists, the speculators and the property owners? Comrade Sylvia Pankhurst represents the interests of hundreds upon millions of people who are oppressed by the British and other capitalists. That is why she is subject to White terror, deprived of liberty etc.[73]

Not surprisingly, Pankhurst felt bitter about her arrest and imprisonment, especially since – due to a police plant – she had been suspected of acting as a police agent. Furthermore, this time she had been terrified of going to jail. It would not be the same experience as during the heady days of suffragette militancy, when there were other sisters in struggle in the prison with whom she could secretly share conversations. Besides, her health was precarious. She suffered from endometriosis and serious digestive disorders brought about by her nine hunger and thirst strikes during the decade of suffrage agitation.

In her appeal, she argued that she should not go to jail because of the serious state of her health and also because the articles in the *Dreadnought* were misconstrued. Pankhurst defended herself, using her trial as a platform for her ideals and reviving the old Pankhurst fireworks. She pointed out that she was being tried for publishing articles which contained ideas found in the writings of Karl Marx and William Morris. All her ideas, like those of Morris and Marx, were available in bookshops and libraries. She explained that she had been brought up by a socialist father and had been a socialist all her life. Her struggles among working women in the East End had led her to realize the futility of working within the system. She concluded, "You cannot frighten me with any sentence you may impose. . . . You will not stop this agitation. The words that are written in my paper will be as common as daily bread."[74]

Her appeal was dismissed and she spent all but one week of her five-month sentence in an infirmary cell of Holloway prison. At first she thought about hunger striking, but after the British government allowed the Irish Lord Mayor of Cork, Terence MacSwiney, to die from a hunger strike, she decided against it.[75] She was subjected to searches for writing materials every two weeks and was not allowed to write or to receive outside literature. She continued to protest against prison treatment, in particular the abuse of pregnant and nursing women, the ugly clothes prisoners were forced to wear and the indigestible and unhealthy diet.

Despite the searches, she managed to write an anthology of poems based upon her observations, called *Writ on a cold slate*. They reflect the cold desperation and depression that she was experiencing at the time. The poems also express her understanding and respect for the other women prisoners. The anthology was named after its most evocative poem:

> While many a poet to his love hath writ,
> boasting that thus he gave his immortal life,
> My faithful lines upon inconsistent slate,
> destined to swift extinction reach not thee.
> In other ages dungeons might be strange,
> with ancient mouldiness their airs infect,
> but kindly warders would the tablets bring,
> so captives might their precious thoughts inscribing,
> the treasures of the fruitful mind preserve,
> and cutting this its flowers, postpone delay.
> Only this age that loudly boasts Reform,
> had set its seal of vengeance gainst the mind,
> decreeing naught in prison shall be writ,
> save on a cold slate, and swiftly washed away.[76]

At 8am on 30 May 1921, the doors of the prison opened. A small crowd gathered, waving red flags and singing revolutionary songs.

Pankhurst, pale and wan, emerged unsteadily. She was in tears and could barely walk. Jessie Payne and Norah Smythe rushed up to greet her, to kiss her and to help her walk to a car. A welcome-back breakfast was held at Eustace Miles's restaurant, an old suffragette haunt. On the wall was a large banner stating, "Six Months for Telling the Truth". She had spent most of her five-month sentence in the prison hospital, fed a diet of eggs, milk and bread, Pankhurst said, adding that the suffragettes had been given better treatment than this. "I've been to Russia and prisoners are better off there than here."[77]

Chapter Six

ᴥ

International communism

In the period 1917–24, revolutionaries throughout the world were attempting to organize communist parties in their own countries as well as strengthening and building the Third or Communist International (CI) based in Moscow. Sylvia Pankhurst was at the centre of this revolutionary activity as her politics continued their leftward transformation into what Lenin labelled in 1920 as "ultra-left". Ironically, Pankhurst had come such a long way since her work for women's suffrage that she now believed in abstentionism – that *on principle* revolutionaries should never participate in bourgeois parliamentary activities such as voting or running for Parliament. She also argued that revolutionaries should not affiliate with reformist organizations such as the British Labour Party or the official trade union organizations. Initially, she attempted to argue these positions as a left-wing opposition within the Communist International.

However, although Pankhurst was in the centre of activities surrounding the formation of the British Communist Party, she was not able to influence or to lead it and she was expelled in 1921. This meant she was not only politically separated from the British Communist Party and the Communist International but also viewed by communists as a political pariah. Although she could now argue her positions more "freely", she recognized the difficulties of operating as an unaffiliated left-wing individual oppositionist in a hostile socialist milieu and amid a declining working-class movement.

Between 1918 and 1921, the *Dreadnought's* wide coverage of international events set it apart from other newspapers. In July 1917, when the paper's name was changed to the *Workers' Dreadnought*, the subtitle became "Socialism, Internationalism and Votes for All".[1]

No less impressive were Pankhurst's own widespread international contacts. She was in close touch with leading revolutionaries in Russia (Alexandra Kollontai), Germany (Clara Zetkin), Holland (Herman Gorter, Anton Pannekoek, Henrietta Roland Holst), Italy (Antonio Gramsci and Amadeo Bordiga) and even Hungary (Bela Kun). When Maxim Litvinov and Theodore Rothstein (representatives of the Third International) came to Britain, they sought her out as an important and influential revolutionary.

Also indicative of Pankhurst's importance was the extent to which her articles appeared in leading foreign socialist journals. In early 1918, she was slipping material past the censor to *Avanti*, the journal of the Italian Socialist Party. These articles concerned the secret wartime treaties between czarist Russia and the other Allies, outlining the proposed carve-up of Europe and the Middle East following the successful conclusion of the war. Throughout 1919, Pankhurst was the British correspondent for the *Communist International*, the official journal of the Comintern executive. Four articles of hers appeared between June and September, although the last one – her celebrated letter to Lenin on the question of participation in parliamentary elections – was printed anonymously. The first article was about the war of intervention. She appealed to British workers and soldiers to oppose intervention and to abandon any illusions that Labour MPs would take a strong anti-intervention stance. For in Parliament, she wrote, "courage seems to evaporate like a child's soap bubble".[2] The article accused all nations involved in the war of imperialist designs and called on the working classes of all countries to wage an international civil war against capital. Her other two articles were "The Workers and the League of Nations" and "The Workers and the Social Traitors in England". In the latter, she discussed nationalization and the betrayal of the miners and railwaymen.[3]

Pankhurst was also the only regular foreign correspondent to Antonio Gramsci's *L'Ordine Nuovo*, for which she wrote at least eight articles between August 1919 and July 1920.[4] She may have written more, for other articles from London do appear in the paper but they are anonymous. She and the WSF were reported on and supported by Amadeo Bordiga's *Il Soviet* and she wrote an account of the Bologna conference of the Italian Socialist Party for the theoretical journal *Communismo*, which appeared in December 1919. Not only did Pankhurst write for foreign journals; she also published articles by foreign communists in the *Dreadnought*. These included pieces by Gorter, Zetkin, Kollontai, Luxemburg and Liebknecht.

One of the first socialists to welcome the Russian revolution enthusiastically, she had studied and commented on it from the outset. The WSF was the first socialist group to establish links with Moscow. "Working in the East End of London to alleviate the hardship of the poorest people, [I viewed] the Russian upheaval . . . [as] the first ray of dawn, after a long and painful night."[5] She described how, as the earliest news appeared she rushed through the piles of revolutionary newspapers: searching every line of them for news of the revolution – "the Social Revolution as I at once recognised it and affirmed it to be – seeing in it, but the starting point of the World War I revolution, the rising of the masses against war which would usher in the Socialist order of universal fraternity – that bright hope of the multitude which from childhood I had shared."[6]

On 19 March 1917, the WSF held a meeting that passed resolutions on the events in Russia. A message sent to Kerensky and Tchiedze, two leaders of the February revolution, congratulated the Duma for overthrowing the "autocratic domination of the Tsar" and looked forward to an early election of a constituent assembly by secret ballot and adult suffrage. At this point, adult suffrage was still a central WSF concern.[7]

A second message was addressed to socialists, the press and Russians living in Britain and France. It congratulated the Russian workers on "the partial measure of success which has already rewarded their efforts", rejoiced in the announcement of the Constituent Assembly and hoped that the election would "result in the return of an overwhelming majority of class conscious representatives of the workers who, whilst establishing a genuine democracy will be used to bring about a speedy end to the war".[8]

Pankhurst's initial hope was that the Russian revolution would open up prospects not only of peace but also of universal suffrage, in Russia and in Britain. At the same WSF meeting, a third resolution was passed, intended to embarrass the British government. In the light of Russian intentions with respect to the Constituent Assembly and the German Chancellor's recent announcement that Germany was initiating adult suffrage, it called upon the government to introduce a new measure that would provide for adult suffrage.[9] Two weeks later, the *Dreadnought* advertised a mass meeting to be held at the Albert Hall. The headlines announced: "Russia Free! A Great Mass Meeting to

Congratulate the Russian People on their Charter of Freedom which includes ADULT SUFFRAGE."[10]

Pankhurst anticipated the overthrow of Kerensky and the rise of the Bolsheviks, which, considering the general ignorance of Russian affairs, showed her ability to catch on quickly to the changing situation. Before 1917, the *Dreadnought* had mentioned the labour or socialist movements in Russia only three times. The first reference appeared on 26 December 1914, in a report on anti-war protests in Germany and Russia, which mentioned Lenin's now well-known article "The war and social democracy" as simply "the manifesto of the Russian Socialist Party".[11]

The next article on Russian socialism appeared in April 1915 in the form of a long review by Pankhurst of the autobiography of Marie Sukloff, whose death sentence for the assassination of General Kvostoff had been commuted to life imprisonment. It traced her progress from the Jewish Bund to the Social Democratic Party and then to "the new party" she had joined apparently because of her commitment to the peasants' cause. The new party was the "Social Revolutionist Party". The article did not mention the Bolsheviks.[12]

More information appeared in another long article summarizing and reviewing the study *The socialists and the war* by the American socialist William English Walling. This article noted that the Russian socialists and the Peasant Party, or Labour Group, had received 10 million votes in 1907, when the last election with a semi-democratic franchise took place. The article reported that 14 socialist members of the Duma had abstained on the war credits vote in August 1914. It mentioned political disagreements and called the Russian Social Democratic Party the "largest Socialist Party in Russia". But it did not mention either the Bolsheviks or the Mensheviks.[13] Until 1917, the only information about the Russian socialists provided by the *Dreadnought* was in these two reviews and from reading the articles one has the impression that the *Dreadnought* was as uninformed about Russia as its readers.

The first reference to Lenin and the Bolsheviks appeared in the *Woman's Dreadnought* on 30 June 1917, when Pankhurst stated that "we deeply sympathise with" the view held by the "Maximalists and Leninists" who wanted to "cut adrift from the capitalist parties altogether, and to establish a Socialist system of organisation and industry in Russia before Russian capitalism, which is as yet in its infancy, becomes more difficult to overthrow".[14]

As early as March, Pankhurst had diagnosed the situation of "dual power" in Russia, understanding immediately that the soviets might become the next government of Russia. She argued that revolutionaries should support this soviet form of government. In an article written just weeks after the overthrow of the czar, she said that "there are virtually two Governments in Russia, the Provisional government appointed by the Duma and the Council of Labour Deputies which is responsible to the elected representatives of the workers and soldiers".[15]

By the beginning of June, she was predicting the overthrow of Kerensky, who had "failed to realize the greatness of the movement he would lead".[16] At the end of the month, she identified herself with the Bolsheviks. Her comments were prophetic. Could a socialist republic "be established and maintained in the midst of a capitalist Europe with a great war raging?" The main problem, as Pankhurst saw it, was that moderate socialists wanted to wait until there was a socialist Europe, rather than struggling for a Russian socialist government. The moderates argued for building a strong socialist bloc in the Parliament to force the Liberals to adopt many of their programmes. The Bolsheviks, Pankhurst reported approvingly, rejected that approach.[17]

In August, Pankhurst wrote that the Petrograd soviet or "workers' council" was coming around to "the position of Lenin (a position we ourselves have advocated from the first), namely that Free Russia must refuse to continue fighting in a capitalist war".[18] When the Bolsheviks came to power in October–November 1917, Pankhurst welcomed the socialist revolution and defended the Bolshevik dissolution of the Constituent Assembly,[19] a turning point in the Russian revolution, acknowledged as such by its supporters internationally. It divided moderates from revolutionaries, social democrats from communists, because it marked a clear rejection of any form of parliamentary democracy. Thus, Pankhurst's defence of the Bolsheviks moved her even further leftward.

This position did not, however, represent that much of an abrupt change in her politics, for it was consistent with her belief in *soviets* or *workers' councils* as the new form of revolutionary government. Pankhurst quoted from the Bolshevik decree, which stated that "the old bourgeois parliamentarianism has seen its day" (since it was unable to cope with the tasks of socialist reconstruction) and that soviets were the only organizations of the "exploited working classes" and were in a "position to direct the struggle of these classes for their complete political and economic emancipation".[20]

Given this unequivocal support for the Bolsheviks, Pankhurst had to counter objections from both the capitalist and the social democratic press. The *Dreadnought* carried articles of explanation by Bolsheviks and their sympathizers, including Louise Bryant, the American supporter of the Bolsheviks, Kamenev, Litvinov and Lenin – people whose views would be respected and believed. After a year of exhausting activities in support of the Russian revolution, Pankhurst embarked in 1919 on an equally exhausting and far more dangerous six-month tour of revolutionary Europe. Even though she was in the thick of revolutionary activity in London, she knew that she had to be involved in some of the international debates about building a revolutionary organization. Her trip to the Continent was facilitated by a new development in Pankhurst's life – her relationship with Silvio Corio.

A left-wing anarchist who had been forced into exile some 20 years earlier,[21] Corio was born in October 1875, in Saluzzo, near Turin and he was known to the police for his anarchist views by the time he was 20. Drafted into the armed services, he engaged in political activities and fled to France after Italian police tried to get him to inform on other socialists and anarchists. He was expelled from France after being sentenced to two months in jail for his political activities.

Before becoming involved with Pankhurst, Corio had a tumultuous relationship with an Italian socialist, Clelia Alignani. In 1902, she gave birth to a son, who died shortly thereafter. Corio and Alignani separated and reconciled periodically. He fathered another son and a daughter, Beatrice Roxanne; the mother(s) of these children is/are unknown.[22]

From France, Corio went to London, where he became active in a West End anarchist group consisting largely of Italian and Jewish comrades who met regularly in Soho. In 1902, he began publishing the biweekly *Socialist Revolution*. In 1907, at an international anarchist convention in Amsterdam, he met the anarchist and sexual radical Guy Aldred, who got him a job as a typographer for the *Voice of Labour*. In 1911, Corio and Aldred published the pamphlet *Herald of revolt*, which argued against the pro-war nationalism of H. R. Hyndman, the leader of the Social Democratic Federation. At this time, Corio was signing his articles "Crastinus". He was also a correspondent for *Avanti*, the Italian socialist newspaper, writing against Italian militarism and colonialism and he wrote as well for the *Star, Justice* and the *Daily Herald*.[23]

Pankhurst met Corio in 1917 when he was working on the anarchist monthly *Freedom*. He had become friendly with L. A. Motler, a printer who also wrote for the *Dreadnought*. It was probably through Motler that they met. Corio began to write articles for the *Dreadnought* in late 1917, signing them "S" or "S. C.". He was a skilled typographer and printer, an expert researcher and writer and he had a deep understanding of anarchism. When Italian revolutionaries came to London, they sought him out for help. Much to the chagrin of Pankhurst's close friends, especially Norah Smythe (who resented his intrusion into the tight-knit group of women), he took over management of the *Dreadnought* offices.[24] Not much is known about the personal side of Pankhurst and Corio's relationship. He was stateless and his name did not appear in radical journals; he appears to have been very careful not to give interviews or to be quoted in the press. There is little information about him in the Pankhurst papers. Perhaps one or both of them, or their son Richard, destroyed or withheld information about Corio for their own protection or that of the family.

The evidence about Corio's personality is contradictory. May O'Callaghan (one of Sylvia's secretaries) and Nellie Cressell (a WSF member) thought him repulsive.[25] Others in the WSF or at Agenda Press, the company that published the *Dreadnought* (e.g. Edgar Whitehead), claimed that he mismanaged the books and caused political trouble. He was ill for a good part of his life and this no doubt added to Pankhurst's responsibilities. On the other hand, David Mitchell, a biographer of the Pankhursts, believes that Corio and Pankhurst had a warm and comradely relationship.[26] Whatever the truth is, they remained together until his death in 1954.[27]

It was through Corio's political connections with European revolutionaries that Pankhurst was able to make her clandestine trip, which was dangerous because socialists were being pursued by authorities and meetings had to be held secretly. In the summer of 1919, she attended the conference of the Italian Socialist Party (PSI) in Bologna. The PSI at this time contained within its ranks a broad spectrum of left-wing opinion: the reformist or parliamentary socialists led by Filippo Turati and Lodovico d'Aragona; the "maximalists" or "electionist maximalists", as they called themselves, led by G. M. Serrati; the revolutionary left-wing socialists led by Amadeo Bordiga; and other revolutionaries such as Gramsci, Angelo Tasca and Palmiro Togliofli.[28] At this conference the PSI declared its allegiance to the Communist International.

An ultra-left, abstentionist, anti-parliamentary faction led by Amadeo Bordiga was formed at this conference. Bordiga wanted to make the PSI truly worthy of membership in the CI, which meant defeating the reformists and getting the conference to take a clear anti-parliamentary stand. However, his group was routed by 3,300 votes to 6,500.[29] Despite this defeat, the Bordighists continued their organized opposition and Pankhurst supported them.

This conference shows how Pankhurst fits into the context of international socialism in this period. Far from being a lone crackpot, as some of her detractors claim, she shared identifiable political positions with many in the movement. At the conference, she made a brief speech, bringing greetings from British workers and welcoming the revolutionary upsurge in Italy expected in the following spring. She also said:

> All the more reason, therefore to recognise that the attitude of the abstentionist faction is most logical. It is difficult for me to understand how you can possibly make propaganda to win seats in parliament – a body which you mean to abolish in a few months – when you ought to be absorbed in the work of revolutionary preparation and when the most urgent need is to convince workers that the time for Parliament has passed.[30]

Pankhurst later wrote that diverse tendencies were making themselves felt in the party. In the centre was Serrati and on the left there were two rival factions. One led by Gramsci was editing *L'Ordine Nuovo* and pinning his faith on workshop committees and a workers' militia, looking for inspiration to Soviet Russia. The leader still further left was Bordiga, a young lawyer from Naples who was more incisive and extreme in thought than the other; he too was thinking of the Russian example but was independent and unwilling to accept dictation from Moscow.[31]

Pankhurst clearly identified with Bordiga on the question of abstention from parliament and admired his independence from Moscow. However, at this period, her abstentionism was a response to the circumstances of that moment; that is, that the situation was so revolutionary that elections were unnecessary. It would soon harden into a political principle. She admired the factory council movement of Gramsci and the Turin metalworkers and also saw the Italian cooperative movement as a positive socialist example. It is difficult to assess the relative impact of Bordiga and Gramsci on Pankhurst's political development. Aspects of both appealed to her and, in the light of their respective contributions to the communist movement in Italy, this is not surprising.[32] Rather than seeing Gramsci and Bordiga as being locked in sectarian conflict, Gwyn Williams, a leading Gramsci scholar, argues that they were "twin, if tautly dialectical polarities of Marxist-Leninism".[33] That is, while Bordiga failed to recognize the potential of factory councils, Gramsci was slow to realize the necessity of a revolutionary party.

Pankhurst may or may not have conceptualized the interrelationship between Gramsci and Bordiga in such a way, but it is interesting to examine the similarities between her thinking and theirs. At the time of the Bologna conference and the April 1920 factory uprisings in Turin, she was writing for Gramsci's paper, *L'Ordine Nuovo*. She saw the factory council movement as a far more developed expression of the workers' committee movement in Britain and therefore judged it to be revolutionary, considering the councils to be the forerunners of the soviets and an integral part of the revolutionary movement. Bordiga, however, dismissed the workers' council movement as a "reformist modification of trade union structure – a deviation from the job of creating a homogeneous party".[34] On the other hand, Bordiga's concept of a rigid, proletarian, uncompromising communist party may have influenced Pankhurst – at least temporarily. The similarity between his writings in *Il Soviet* and Pankhurst's in the *Dreadnought* are sometimes startling and may not be entirely coincidental.

Gwyn Williams, who wrote on Gramsci's communism, argues that Bordiga believed the Communist Party should be free from all bourgeois contamination, all reformism and any alliances and blocs with social democrats; it was to be committed to revolution and to the dictatorship of the proletariat. The proletariat was so strictly defined as to exclude even trade unionists who were artisans. Furthermore, argues Williams, Bordiga's party would marshall against bourgeois society all the hosts of the "disinherited seizing on grievance and rebellion and mobilising them in a perhaps simplified, schematic and dogmatic form of communism".[35]

Bordiga stressed *individual* commitment to the party, stating that people should not join as components of a professional category, a factory or a local group. A powerful sense of conversion, of total rupture with the bourgeois world, permeates Bordiga's writings. He did not care if the party consisted of only an "audacious minority".[36]

Pankhurst's political beliefs contain similar feelings of individual commitment to politics, an almost religious dedication to what she believed to be right. She made all her major decisions alone. "I never consulted anyone" is a recurrent theme in her writings about her life. When she abandoned a potentially successful artistic career, she did so totally and without hesitation. Living in the East End, she totally rejected bourgeois trappings, even to the point of wearing only clothes that women there gave her. In February 1920, she wrote about the necessity for revolutionary purity:

> The Communist Party must keep its doctrine pure, and its independence from reformism inviolate; its mission is to lead the way without stopping or turning by the direct road to Communist Revolution. Do not worry about a big Communist Party yet; it is better to build a sound one. Never let us hesitate, lest we should make it too extreme.[37]

Preparing to build social soviets in East London, she stressed the "quality not quantity" of the membership. Perhaps the similarities between Bordiga and Pankhurst can to some extent be explained by the social situations in which they worked: both worked with non-industrialized and non-unionized workers. However, there was a gulf between them as well. Pankhurst worked mainly with women, Bordiga mainly with men. But Pankhurst also worked with dockers and engineers and understood the importance of industrial organization as well. Although she fervently and theoretically believed in activity by workers and opposed "leaders", she was, after all, in temperament a Pankhurst and accustomed to leading a group of devoted followers.

While in Italy Pankhurst attended another "secret conference" in Imola but wrote nothing about it in detail. She also spent time in Bologna observing "municipal socialism" visiting gardens, schools, rest homes in the mountains, communal restaurants and land reclamation projects and enjoyed "a brief interlude" reading the poetry of Dante.[38]

At the Bologna conference, Pankhurst got an early glimpse of fascism when the delegates, on entering a Town Hall reception at the mayor's invitation, were attacked by the Arditi, a group of thugs, the fore-runners of the Blackshirts. The Arditi were inspired by Mussolini (who at the time was rumoured to be in hiding in Bologna).[39]

Pankhurst then crossed the Alps *on foot* (aided by a woodsman) and arrived finally in Zurich. In her manuscript "In the red twilight", she wrote that when she arrived in the city at night she could not find a place to stay. Finally, a schoolteacher gave her a bed and then she met an editor of a socialist paper who gave her lodgings.[40] From Switzerland she made her way into Germany, this time with the help of a young Swiss man. Again, the journey was perilous and her writing about it has a cloak-and-dagger aspect, no doubt owing to Pankhurst's love of the dramatic. She was forced to travel at night over fields and constantly fell into ditches.[41] Germany was even more dangerous; most of the socialists were in hiding because the authorities were raiding people's homes. She stayed with Clara Zetkin, whom she described as "a remarkable woman". She was impressed by "[h]er enormous power despite her chronic illness", also "[h]er devotion to the cause".[42] Zetkin dictated to her "The life and times of Rosa Luxemburg," which was reprinted in English in the *Dreadnought*. Pankhurst also met Paul Levi Bronsky and other refugees who were in hiding after the fall of the Munich soviets.

Pankhurst then travelled with Zetkin to Frankfurt for a secret con-ference organized by the western bureau of the Third International. She was not impressed by the "idle comrades of Germany" or by their talk of revolution. Zetkin shared this reaction, pointing out that, dur-ing the meeting, "[w]aiters come in and out with beef and beer whilst comrades talk revolution".[43] In Frankfurt, the Russian representative from the CI gave her encouragement as well as money for her work and travels. On the basis of her discussions with the Germans, Pankhurst concluded that the Russians had been "grossly misin-formed of the strength of the movement in these countries", which was much weaker than they believed.[44]

From Frankfurt she travelled to Amsterdam to attend what subse-quently has been called the "ultra-left" conference, because of the uncompromising nature of the resolutions passed there. The British delegates were J. T. Murphy (SLP), Sylvia Pankhurst (WSF), a man named Hodgson (BSP) and another man named Willis (BSP).[45] At this conference, Pankhurst proposed that preparations be made for an international general strike in defence of Soviet Russia. Herman

Gorter, from the Dutch CF, seconded the motion, adding that the German revolution must be defended. Both were accepted. The last stop on Pankhurst's trip was Berlin, where she met members of the Spartacist group.[46]

Upon her return, Pankhurst plunged into a whirlwind of revolutionary activity. Her experiences in the revolutionary centres of Europe and her participation in the debate over soviets in Italy helped her to clarify her political position on soviets and to integrate her feminism with her communism. This integration can be seen in her proposals for social soviets, which were a practical and direct way to make feminism central to working-class life.

The arguments for social soviets outlined by Pankhurst represent an important aspect of socialist theory that has been neglected by both feminist and Marxist historians.[47] Pankhurst's social soviets represented a way to involve the *entire* working class – in particular women who were not involved in paid employment outside the home as well as unemployed men, children and the elderly – in the creation of a revolutionary organization. Her advocacy of social soviets shows not only her continuing commitment to women's liberation but also a rather advanced understanding of the relationship between oppression and exploitation. She was attempting to integrate the politics of feminism and those of working-class revolution.

Pankhurst first raised the idea of social soviets in the wake of the Russian revolution. In June 1917, the British Socialist Party (BSP), the Labour Party (through the *Daily Herald*) and other left-wing labour groups and leaders organized a conference in Leeds to discuss the revolution's ramifications.[48] The meeting coincided with massive mutinies in the French army. The May strikes of the engineers, involving 200,000 people, had barely subsided. From the tone of the conference, it seemed that even orthodox Labour leaders such as Ramsay MacDonald and Philip Snowden were preparing to play a role in the formation of an alternative revolutionary organization in Britain. One proposal involved setting up local "Councils of Workmen's and Soldiers' Delegates" on the Russian model, but it turned out to be largely hot air.[49]

Pankhurst was an active participant in the conference and she tried unsuccessfully to amend the phrase "Councils of Workmen's and Soldiers' Delegates" to refer to non-gender-specific *workers*, claiming that the offending word was in any case a mistranslation of the

Russian original.[50] The WSF further insisted that these organizations be called the Workers', Soldiers' and *Housewives'* Councils.[51] Like today's feminists, WSF members knew that words and titles in the male generic that claimed to be inclusive of women as well as men were in fact *exclusionary*. Furthermore, Pankhurst argued that unemployed women and housewives were also members of the working class and therefore must be included in any and all organizations that claimed to be socialist. Although she did not specifically use the term *social soviet*, the germ of that idea is present in this proposal.

Nominated to serve on the executive committee of the Workmen's and Soldiers' Councils, Pankhurst at first declined the position because she did not believe that those who advocated the organization were serious. She was also contemptuous of the tokenism involved in her nomination. In an observation that sounds all too familiar to women today, she acidly pointed out that "they cast their eyes round for a woman. One woman was enough to put on a committee these days, but one woman they must have to placate the suffragists."[52] Despite her refusal, she was elected by a large majority as the sole representative for London and the southern counties.[53]

When Ramsay MacDonald complained that there was little working-class support for the conference and that only one sailor had been elected to the executive committee (owing in part to the high cost of the conference and railway fares), Pankhurst replied that she was sorry that her being there had "robbed them of a soldier or trade unionist", but she had been elected against her will. "The twelve other district representatives would have doubtless said the same thing had they been present."[54]

The councils were instructed to carry out a great number of tasks, including defending civil liberties, safeguarding trade union rights, controlling profiteering and helping to employ and to maintain discharged and demobilized soldiers. Born in a flush of revolutionary enthusiasm and high hopes, the conference ended up accomplishing nothing. Pankhurst arrived 20 minutes late for the fourth meeting of the council to find it had disbanded.

In January 1920, the National Administrative Council (NAC) of the shop stewards' movement, a national co-ordinating committee, decided to call a rank-and-file convention to be held in London. All the shop stewards' and workers' committees in the country were invited. The conference was to run concurrently with the TUC conference scheduled for March. Pankhurst, a central figure in the working-class movement by this time, was delegated to draw up the agenda for the conference, which was to discuss theories of soviet power. This convention was important because it devoted most of its time to this discussion, particularly to the idea of *social* soviets or *social* committees. It was here that Pankhurst first used the term *social soviet*.

Pankhurst's belief in soviet power was a result of her long-held faith in both workers' control and a localized or decentralized form of socialism. As mentioned earlier, she had become disillusioned as well as impatient with parliamentary government, believing that it could not solve the problems of war, poverty or women's oppression. Her commitment to soviets was strengthened by the revolutionary upsurge that took place not only in Russia but throughout Europe. Soviets were formed on the Continent and Pankhurst believed that they were the basis for both a future socialist organization and a democratic socialist society. Pankhurst was quite explicit about why soviets were superior to other forms of government:

> As a representative body, an organisation such as the All-Russian Workers', Soldiers', Sailors' and Peasants' Council is more closely in touch with and more directly represents its constituents than the Constituent Assembly or any existing Parliament. The delegates ... are constantly reporting back and getting instructions from their constituents; whilst Members of Parliament are elected for a term of years and only receive anything approaching instructions at election times. Even then it is the candidate who, in the main, sets forth the programme, the electors merely assenting to or dissenting from the programme as a whole.[55]

The soviets, Pankhurst believed, had an advantage over other forms of democracy in that they were elected along occupational lines and so they would reflect the organization of the working class itself. She explained, in an article in the *Dreadnought*, that the soviet was, in fact, the only organization that truly represented the working class. This was precisely what the Bolsheviks wanted – and something that all socialists should support, since under socialism "everyone will be a worker and there will be no class save the working class to consider or represent".[56]

After 1918, soviets were central to Pankhurst's politics. They were, she said, "the most democratic form of government yet established".[57]

Accounts of soviets and how they worked, or were supposed to work, appeared frequently in the pages of the *Dreadnought*.

The appearance of soviets, or workers' councils, in Fife, Glasgow and Methel in Scotland, in Cork in Ireland and in Bologna in Italy and in Bulgaria and parts of Germany, as well as in Russia, posed new challenges for revolutionaries. Marx and Engels had not specified in their writings the particular forms of working-class organization that would be necessary for a working-class revolution. The Paris Commune of 1871, which gave socialists throughout the world a glimpse of what the form and content of a socialist society would be, was not based upon soviets. It was during the 1905 Russian revolution that the first soviets sprang up, when factory workers organized themselves into councils. Soviets became the backbone of the revolutionary movement in Russia then and in 1917. They were democratically controlled, with elected and recallable leadership. However, although they existed separate and apart from any one political party, members of the differing parties – Bolsheviks, Mensheviks and Social Revolutionaries, for example – worked within them, trying to win a majority of delegates to their particular programmes. This form of working-class organization was far more democratic, revolutionaries argued, because it was based upon the Marxist concept that real social and political power resided at the point of production, in contrast with the bourgeois and social democratic conception that political power rested in the electorate. In Russia in 1917, soviets posed a threat to the government because the allegiance of the working class had shifted to the soviets and away from the government.

Pankhurst's socialism and feminism always contained a strong belief in local, or community, control. This was reflected in her war work in the East End, where the ELFS/WSF advocated and fought for local control of the distribution of food, welfare and relief agencies and of children's centres. She had also always been interested in how socialists would run a city, a nation and the world. That was why, during her 1911 trip to the United States, she made a special visit to Milwaukee, with its socialist mayor. Pankhurst wanted to see if and how municipal socialism worked. She was critical of many of the elitist aspects of municipal socialism, aware that the people who ran Milwaukee and made the decisions were largely middle-class professors and businessmen; she commented that ordinary working women and men played little role in the day-to-day workings of the city. During her 1919 tour of revolutionary Europe, she was far more enthusiastic about the revolutionary soviet she visited in Bologna than she had been about the social democratic vision of Milwaukee.

Sylvia Pankhurst was one of many British revolutionaries who intently studied and argued the nature of the organization they should build. The debate heated up as more information from revolutionary Russia became available and defence of the Revolution intensified. Above all, every British revolutionary wanted to know how to apply the principles of the Bolshevik revolution to British conditions. The difference between the reformists, who still believed in gradually changing society though parliamentary democracy and the revolutionaries, who believed in abolishing parliamentary democracy for the real democracy of the soviets, became clearer.

There was another pressing reason for the rank-and-file conference's discussion of social soviets. By this time, the power base of the shop stewards had been whittled away because many of the workers had been laid off and their movement was in retreat, searching for an identity and seeking support outside the immediate confines of the engineering and munitions factories. Revolutionaries were looking for a way to save and revitalize what remained of the movement. Organizations called *social soviets* or *social committees*, based on organizing workers where they lived rather than where they worked, provided a possible answer. Unemployed engineers could be brought back into the mainstream of the movement since belonging to a social committee or soviet would not depend on being employed in a particular workshop.[58]

The idea of soviets had been discussed even before the setbacks of 1919. Pankhurst had written about the Russian and Italian soviets in the *Dreadnought*. In early 1919, the Socialist Labour Party published its "Plea for the reconsideration of socialist tactics and organisation" in the *Socialist*. This article pointed the way to a new society based on soviets, as did *Direct action*, a pamphlet by William Gallacher, a prominent member of the BSP and chair of the Clyde Workers' Committee. J. T. Murphy's pamphlet *The Workers' Committee: an outline of the principle and structure* also provided a far-sighted account and assessment of workers' committees. However, none of these writings discussed the role of working women or housewives.

The *Socialist* article was adopted as the basis for a new party structure in January 1919, in an attempt to adapt the traditional ideas of industrial unionism to the SLP's experiences in the workshops and the developing revolutionary situation.[59] The concept of soviets or some equivalent came naturally to the British rank-and-file movements and was given a boost by the Russian revolution. However, the relationship of soviets to the revolutionary party was not as clear to Pankhurst, Gallacher, Murphy and other revolutionaries as it was to Lenin in Russia. Most British revolutionaries, including Pankhurst, believed that soviets were simply workers' committees that were synonymous with local branches of a revolutionary party. The British radicals did not comprehend that the soviets in Russia – because they were in a position to contend for state power – were independent of a revolutionary party and took up broader political issues than did the workers' committees on the Clyde.

The rank-and-file convention appointed a small group of 14 people to set up committees for propaganda purposes throughout Britain and called them *district soviets*. The committees were also supposed to compile lists of food supplies and machinery in order to prepare for the revolution believed to be near.[60] However, these committees were not directly engaged in any truly revolutionary actions. James Hinton, a historian of the shop stewards' movement, argues that the formation of social soviets was merely a form of revolutionary social work.[61]

Following the convention, Pankhurst and the WSF embarked on an intensive campaign to found social soviets.[62] Joe Thurgood, a WSF member from Ashford, Kent, was a bootmaker and keen supporter of the Bolsheviks and had considerable influence among postal and railway workers. He became the WSF organizer of the workers' committees, which were to look after the men in the workshops, while Pankhurst was to organize revolutionaries socially – where they lived. These soviets were to be transformed into branches of the Communist Party as it formed. Pankhurst believed that soviets already existed in Scotland in the form of social committees and the WSF urged that the Scottish example be followed throughout the country. In London, Pankhurst hoped to organize a group of sympathetic comrades to canvass local trade union and socialist organizations on the issue.[63]

Pankhurst attempted to connect Lenin's and Trotsky's analysis of soviets with her vision of feminism:

> These are the workshop committees of the mothers for the streets and the houses they live and work in are *their* workshops.

The women must organise themselves and their families and to help in the general struggle of the working class to conquer the power of government.[64]

In March 1920, Pankhurst spoke on soviets at the Bow Baths, to a meeting reported in the outraged *East London Advertiser*. The hall was decorated with WSF banners proclaiming "Welcome to the soviets". Pankhurst praised the German and Italian soviets, claiming that they were gaining ground. She argued that the continuous rise in food prices was bound to make people rebel. "We have got to have soviets in our streets, in our workshops, and in our factories." At the same meeting Harry Pollitt urged the women of East London to raid the docks as one sure way of bringing down prices. Melvina Walker, who chaired the meeting, called upon everyone to follow the example set by Russia. "[T]he WSF wanted the young men and women to push the Labour leaders along and out of the way."[65]

Towards the end of March, the *Dreadnought* published Sylvia Pankhurst's "Constitution for British soviets". As evidence that forming such soviets was a real possibility, she cited the East End women's ability to organize children's parties that celebrated peace. These parties were very elaborate involving concerts and pageants. All the women in the East End streets co-operated to make them a success. Street organization was the key to both the success of these parties and the organization of women into soviets, "so as to bring together a convenient number of women, not too many, so all women know each other, to direct things and elect and instruct their representatives".[66]

Pankhurst argued that women had to organize to protect themselves and their families against rising prices and rents. The Food Controller and the Ministry of Food were useless. The Labour Party, through the local councils, had failed to keep down food prices. The only remedy was to place the land, industry, food supplies, milk, trams, buses and houses in the hands of workers' committees or soviets. As always Pankhurst's appeal was made in terms of problems of direct interest to women. Her whole argument and frame of reference centred on involving women in the revolution and her "constitution" emphasized "household" soviets:

The population of Poplar at the 1911 census was 162,449 and there were 35,179 families or separate occupiers. Each of these would mean a member of the Household Soviet. Fifty members of the Household Soviet would make 701 Soviet areas. The Poplar District Household Soviet would therefore subsist of 701 members. As the number is rather large, Subdistrict Household Soviets could be formed in Bow, Bromley and Poplar.[67]

This would become the basis for town soviets, regional household soviets, household soviets in rural areas, county rural household soviets and industrial, public health, educational, army and agricultural soviets.

Pankhurst's vision of the soviets was a product of her long-held belief in local organization of a socialist society, her practical experience in working with the women of the East End and her understanding of soviets in Russia and Italy. Her vision was important, although unrealistic. She herself was acutely aware of women's lack of industrial power and hence of their relative lack of social power.

Pankhurst's concept of social soviets is problematic in other areas as well. She had not in any way intellectually grappled with the concept of the sexual division of labour or the question of the exploitation of and the production of surplus value by women working in the home. Or she may have approached women's activity from an assumption of difference. The basis for her formulation of the social soviet was that women's work was located in the home and the community. She acknowledged that, although provision had to be made for individual men who did not have housekeepers, the household soviet was for women. Men worked in factories and therefore would be represented in the industrial soviets. She also believed that women who worked outside the home for pay would be adequately represented by the workshop or industrial soviet. But she never took on the issue of women's double role at home and in the workplace.

Pankhurst certainly was aware of and did write and agitate around, the issues of women's housework. She was dedicated to revolutionizing the home, community and work situations of women in the East End. She was particularly concerned with the health and welfare of mothers and children. Especially from 1918 to 1924, the *Dreadnought* carried many articles about women and socialism, asserting the need for communal laundries, restaurants and clothes mending shops staffed by professional houseworkers (again, the implication being that the majority of these would be female) and for the children to be cared for by the state.[68] But these ideas reflected Pankhurst's acceptance – perhaps tacit, perhaps grudging – that there was men's work (the factory) and women's work (the home and family). She never acknowledged the possibility that women and men might share housework and child rearing.[69] There had been some interest in this issue by some ILP women but it was viewed as a personal question having to do with a sense of socialist decency. Although Pankhurst did not write as much on the issue of the gender division of labour as did Hannah Mitchell, for example, it must be pointed out that it was not the central focus of socialists and feminists at the time.

In spite of Pankhurst's determination to build soviets, neither she nor the WSF was able to do so, either in the East End or in other areas where the WSF had chapters. Pankhurst seems not to have realized the impact of the difference between the situation in Britain – where the working class was in retreat – and that in Germany, Italy and Russia – where soviets developed out of a period of revolutionary working-class upheaval. Revolutionaries cannot create soviets either by calling for them or by wishing for their existence. Even Pankhurst's inexhaustible will could not create soviets amid the British working class in this period. Nevertheless, Pankhurst's concept of social soviets shows how, in this period, she tried to reconcile her desire to organize working-class power with her knowledge – born of experience – that those members of the working class who were not skilled white male factory workers must also be represented and active participants in their own revolution. What is more, Pankhurst focused on a problem that other socialists ignored or omitted: the participation of women. In this respect, she can be considered an intellectual foremother of today's socialist feminists.

At the same time that Sylvia Pankhurst was developing her theory of the social soviets, she was making preparations for another trip – the most dangerous but perhaps most important and exciting of her political career. During July and August 1920, she travelled to Moscow as a delegate from the WSF to the Second Congress of the Third International. The official British delegation included William Gallacher, J. T. Murphy, Dave Ramsey, Jack Tanner, William MacLaine and Tom Quelch, the last two from the BSP.

Pankhurst had exchanged letters and received a radio message from Lenin on the question of participation in Parliament and affiliation to the Labour Party. In his message Lenin condemned her action of unilaterally and prematurely forming a communist party in June 1920, based upon non-affiliation and non-participation in elections.

Pankhurst's somewhat sarcastic reply came in the *Dreadnought*:

> My reply to you is that I would like to defend my tactics in the Moscow Congress, but I have been refused visas by two intervening countries. If you, through your influence in the Labour Party and your parliamentary friends can obtain for me a passport, I shall gladly meet you in debate.[70]

Unable to get a visa, Pankhurst made preparations to go illegally. With the help of a comrade, Dick Beech, she stowed away on a Norwegian ship, writing later that the "engineers treated me like a queen". The crossing to Murmansk was dangerous, especially between Norway and Soviet Russia. At one point a group of fishermen warned her not to travel on one of the small boats. She disregarded their advice but found out after arriving back in London that three French delegates and some of the same fishermen had drowned in one of these boats on their return voyage.[71] Pankhurst arrived in Moscow to find that the British delegation had already arrived and the meeting was underway. Nonetheless, she was welcomed as an important participant and immediately whisked off to the Russian Communist Party headquarters, where she received her credentials.

It was clear right away that her opposition to parliamentary activities was going to be a minority position. The German KAPD (Communist Workers' Party of Germany) had already walked out because they disagreed with the majority resolutions passed at the conference. Nonetheless, the tone of Pankhurst's pamphlet, *Soviet Russia as I saw it*, gives the impression that she thoroughly enjoyed her trip and participation at the conference.

And why not? She was working and discussing politics with hundreds of revolutionaries from a variety of nations. The delegates were warmly welcomed by the Russians, who plied them with gifts (mainly cigarettes, cigars and food). Pankhurst commented that the foreign representatives also wore Russian peasant blouses although, she wrote, they didn't look as good in them as the Russians did. She also commented that the English delegation was unaccustomed to Russian food: "caviare to them was not a luxury, but merely distasteful".[72] She arrived to find a meeting going on at the Kremlin. Lenin made a positive impression upon Pankhurst: "Lenin, with smiling face came quickly forward from a group of men waiting to get a word with him." He seemed to her "more vividly vital and energetic, more wholly alive than other people".[73]

She was ushered into the czar's former bedroom, where she sat at a round table. Lenin was on her right and Wynkoop from Holland sat on her left and translated. Pankhurst especially admired Bukharin, the editor of *Pravda*, and John Reed, the US journalist and revolutionary. Radek and Zinoviev were also there. Pankhurst did not particularly like Zinoviev: "He was a little impatient with the opposition and criticised with a tinge of contempt. . . . One of the American delegates said of Zinoviev that he always talks to one as though he was taking a bath."[74] At this first meeting, Lenin appeared to be almost bantering with the British delegates about the issue of parliamentary action. However, for Pankhurst and the other British delegates, the matter was serious; and in reality Lenin did not take any kind of political difference lightly.

The debate centred on whether or not the soon-to-be-formed Communist Party of Great Britain (CPGB) should affiliate with the British Labour Party and engage in parliamentary action. Gallacher and Pankhurst were the two abstentionists in the British delegation and both had a significant political base back home in Britain. Lenin's concern was that British revolutionaries had to differentiate themselves from the reformists and convince the working class of the futility of reformism and parliamentarism. However, he was convinced that, in order to do this, the CPGB had to engage in a political discussion with the working class, which required affiliation. He explained at the congress, "Millions of backward members are enrolled in the Labour Party, therefore Communists should be present to do propaganda amongst them provided Communist freedom of action and propaganda is not thereby limited."[75]

In this respect, as Raymond Challinor, a British historian, has argued, Lenin's "theoretical position seems acceptable; where it fell down was in practical tactical application".[76] Challinor goes on to explain that Lenin incorrectly believed that the British Labour Party was a mass party, with millions of activists who were trade unionists and other members of the working class. He also believed that the Labour Party would allow free full political discussion. Lenin wrote:

> Comrades Gallacher and Sylvia Pankhurst cannot deny that. They cannot deny that while remaining in the ranks of the Labour Party, the British Socialist Party enjoys sufficient liberty to write that such and such leaders of the Labour Party are traitors, champions of the interests of the bourgeoisie and their

agents in the Labour movement; this is absolutely true. When Communists enjoy such liberty, then taking into account the experience in all countries, and not only in Russia (for we are not a Russian, but an international congress), it is their duty to affiliate with the Labour Party.[77]

Lenin further asserted that, in order to expose the futility of reformism and the bankruptcy of Labour officials, the Labour Party must have a trial run in office. Therefore, British communists should affiliate with the Labour Party, give it critical support and demand the formation of a joint parliament and mutual sharing out of constituencies. In this way revolutionary workers would see that the reformists could not and would not grant their demands and would then look to the communists. Pankhurst disagreed:

We assert that the Labour Party will in any case come to power, that the British Socialist Party cannot disassociate itself too clearly from the Labour Party's reformist policy, and must by no means enter into alliances or arrangements with it. We believe that Communists can best wean the masses from faith in bourgeois Parliamentarianism by refusing to participate in it.[78]

Elsewhere she elaborated on her position:

When the workers have passed through trade unionism and Labour Parliamentarianism, through industrial unionism and developed a Marxian appreciation of the class war, and are striving to build up amongst the workers within their own industries, the organisation and consciousness from which the soviets will spring, they are unlikely to turn their attention back to Parliamentarianism in any form.[79]

At subsequent meetings, the British delegation debated the issue. Lenin and William MacLaine of the BSP debated against Pankhurst and Gallacher. They were originally given five minutes, but Pankhurst persuaded the Congress to give her half an hour. "Of course we were badly beaten," she wrote to an anarchist comrade in 1921.[80] Alfred Rosmer, the French revolutionary, wrote later that Pankhurst's speech was "suitable for a public meeting rather than a Congress; it was an agitator's speech. She spoke fierily, throwing herself about dangerously on the rostrum. But she wasn't a good advocate of our viewpoint."[81]

Her arguments were lost in the flood of her rhetoric and Lenin's thesis won the day, as did his arguments against Jack Tanner, who

suggested that a revolutionary party was unnecessary and that workers' committees were the only organizations needed by revolutionary
workers. Lenin later bolstered his arguments with the publication in
1920 of his now-famous pamphlet *Left wing communism: an infantile disorder.* The title alone was enough to defeat the Pankhurst–
Gallacher position.[82] There is no indication that the proceedings were
unfair or undemocratic. Lenin's resolutions passed unanimously and
at the end of the conference Pankhurst claimed that she was in full
agreement with the bulk of the accepted resolutions.[83] However, it is
clear from her activities once she returned that she was not.

At the conference, the executive committee of the Communist
International ordered the formation of a united party within four
months of the delegates' return to England. This they pledged to do.
Pankhurst hoped that the anti-parliamentarian delegates still might
"bring the Third International round to a better understanding of
what was necessary for our revolutionary struggle in this country".
In terms reminiscent of her reluctance to break with her mother and
sister, she wrote:

> Moreover, I was loathe to break with those who had placed the
> Soviets in power without great consideration. I felt they had
> been through the fire of battle, they had the courage to rise and
> had at least achieved something, whereas we were only talking
> still.[84]

After the Congress ended, Pankhurst travelled with John Reed
through parts of Russia, where she studied the social aspects of the
revolution: local soviets, workers' self-management, schools and hos-
pitals. She paid special concern to the issues of maternal and infant
care and commented on the role of women in social, economic and
political life. *Soviet Russia as I saw it* does not compare at all with
John Reed's *Ten days that shook the world,* the classic journalistic
account of the day-to-day events leading to the Bolshevik victory.
Pankhurst's account is a rather starry-eyed pamphlet. However, it
gives a great deal of essential information about conditions in Russia
as well as insightful glimpses of the revolutionary personalities.
Pankhurst could not refrain from criticizing her British comrades,
who she claimed were constantly acting as if they were tourists,
complaining about their food and lodgings. She even accused them of
eating her food when she was ill.

The trip home, during which Pankhurst was sometimes alone and sometimes with other British delegates, was even more dangerous and agonizing than the trip to Russia. The British government had asked the Norwegian authorities to detain Pankhurst upon her arrival in Norway and, in order to elude them, she was smuggled into a tiny fishing boat and was drenched during the entire voyage. With the Norwegian police after her, she was smuggled by Danish comrades onto another ship bound for Christiana in Denmark. She was then put on a third ship and told to say she was a stewardess who had deserted her ship. The sailors on this ship were neither comrades nor sympathetic and probably tried to rape her. After a physical struggle with them, she left the ship for another. This final boat ride was equally harrowing. At last she returned to London, evading the police who were searching for her.[85]

On this return voyage, as during their travels in Russia, Pankhurst found herself at odds with the rest of the British delegation, for she was the only woman delegate. Nellie Rathbone thought Pankhurst's conflict with her male comrades stemmed from her concern for privacy. Rathbone also thought that the male delegates felt that because Pankhurst was a "suffragette she should put up with everything they did".[86] But she was a woman in fragile health, travelling primarily with men in a country that had few hygienic facilities. For Pankhurst, who had been used to the companionship and camaraderie of women in the East End, this experience must have been a considerable jolt.

Was Pankhurst the "infantile" ultra-leftist described by Lenin? She had not always opposed participation in electoral politics. Her political shift came about as a result of her experiences fighting for women's suffrage and supporting the Labour Party as the political vehicle by which working women would gain some political and social power. She distrusted the Labour Party, not only because of its lack of commitment to women's suffrage but because of its support for the war and its refusal to help James Connolly and the other martyrs of the 1916 Easter Rising. Pankhurst was not alone in her distrust of Labour. Other left socialists and feminists, such as Alice Wheeldon, became disillusioned with the Labour Party before the First World War. Nonetheless, Pankhurst had urged people to vote Labour in the 1918 election and even praised the SLP for using the elections as an effective means of disseminating socialist propaganda. She had even considered running for Parliament.[87]

Her change in attitude came about as a result of the day-to-day difficulties of working with the Labour Party in the East End. From Pankhurst's point of view, it was the reformists in the Labour Party who refused to work with revolutionaries. In spite of their political differences, the WSF tried to co-operate with the Labour Party and the trades councils. In April 1918, Pankhurst reported to a general meeting of the WSF that its representatives had been elected to the Poplar Trades Council and the local Labour Party. The delegates included herself, Miss Lagsding, Mrs Pascoe, Norah Smythe and Miss Watts. Pankhurst "thought it was well for the WSF to be on the local Labour Party to start with, though a time might come when they could not continue in the party".[88]

In October 1918, the WSF board elected Sylvia Pankhurst and Melvina Walker as delegates to the Labour Party women's conference. In May 1919, Miss Lagsding wrote to the executive of the WSF about affiliation of her branch with the Poplar Labour Party. Pankhurst replied that "branches had free autonomy to affiliate to local Labour parties – it was one way of doing propaganda among trade unionists which we otherwise would not do".[89]

However, WSF work within the Labour Party did not continue for long. Its experience belied Lenin's belief that it would be possible to work as revolutionaries in the Labour Party. On 20 July 1919, the Labour Party held a rally in Victoria Park. The WSF decided to have a platform there and they hired a flatbed truck that they decorated with a "Welcome to the soviets" banner. They used the truck as a soapbox. Shortly afterwards, Norah Smythe received a letter from the assistant secretary of the Poplar Trades Council informing her that, because of this action, she was expelled from the Poplar Trades Council. Melvina Walker received a letter informing her that she too was expelled from the executive of the Poplar Trades Council, withdrawn as a delegate to the London Trades Council and no longer allowed to attend Central Labour Party meetings in the capacity of a delegate. Both Walker and Smythe protested against their expulsions but to no avail. Miss Lagsding said that the Poplar Labour Party objected to the soviet banner.[90]

There were other reasons for Pankhurst's developing abstentionist politics. She saw even at this early stage that electoral politics put socialist principles under tremendous pressures. The status quo set the agenda and led to an opportunistic tendency to play according to the rules. In a September 1919 letter to Lenin published in the

Communist International, she wrote:

> The Labour movement in England is being ruined under my eyes by parliamentary and municipal politics. Both leaders and masses are only waiting for elections, and, while preparing for the election campaign, quite forgetting the socialist work. Nay, they totally suppress all socialist propaganda in order not to frighten the electors. The BSP takes pride in the election of members to the Municipal Councils; but their election is not a signal for revolutionary agitation therein. They accepted the departmental office and became part of the machinery of capitalism.[91]

Indeed, Pankhurst was outraged by the behaviour of communists and socialists after they were elected to public office. Here, too, her disagreement with Lenin is reasonable. She had an understanding of British politics that Lenin didn't have. She knew firsthand the corrupting influence of Parliament. After all, she lived in a country with one of the oldest traditions of parliamentary government. Lenin, on the other hand, came from a country with no tradition of bourgeois government. Lenin argued that after the working class seized power they would face even greater temptation to weaken their principles. Thus, they needed to be tested before the revolution or else they would not meet the test after it occurred.[92]

Although Pankhurst's suspicion of the dangers of electoral politics was well founded, as Lenin noted, she was unnecessarily rigid in her resolute opposition to participation in elections. Her position led her into the trap of asserting pure principles from the sidelines. However, whether or not Lenin was right and the abstentionists wrong about joining the Labour Party became a moot question within a very short time. In 1921, the Communist Party made a formal application for membership into the Labour Party and was overwhelmingly rejected, with the Labour Party leaders arguing that the communists could not abide by the party's constitution.

The debate over parliamentary participation made the road towards building a united Communist Party long and tortuous. It involved bringing together a number of socialist organizations – the BSP, SLP, SWSS and WSF – along with a large number of unaffiliated socialists. Each of these organizations had its own politics and traditions as well as its own leaders, with their individual egos, suspicions and hostilities towards each other and other groups. The result was not the kind of Communist Party Pankhurst had in mind. Furthermore, the WSF had neither the numbers nor the stature to affect the course of events that led to the formation of the Communist Party.

Negotiations for a united Communist Party began when the British Socialist Party suggested, in May 1918, that the *Call* and the *Workers' Dreadnought* be amalgamated.[93] However, Pankhurst later took the credit for initiating the move, writing that "members of the WSF, hearing that almost the entire executive of the BSP was affected by the raising of the conscription age, approached the BSP with a tentative offer of fusion and were very cordially received".[94] The WSF withdrew its offer when it discovered that E. C. Fairchild of the BSP – who would have been joint editor of the combined paper – would not commit himself to soviets and to the dictatorship of the proletariat. Nevertheless, relations between the two groups remained amicable. Pankhurst was a member of the BSP delegation to the 1920 Labour Party conference and spoke on behalf of the BSP in the debate on whether or not members of the Labour Party should withdraw from the coalition government.[95]

In February–March 1919, the Communist International was founded in Moscow and at their Easter conferences both the BSP and the SLP passed resolutions in favour of a united Communist Party. The BSP leadership remained divided, however, in its commitment to the Soviet revolution and ordered a ballot on affiliation to the Third International. The rank-and-file voted overwhelmingly in favour.[96]

For its part, the WSF declared itself a communist organization and voted allegiance to the Communist International at a WSF meeting in June 1919 but "decided in view of these negotiations not to make use of the name 'C. P.' for the present in order that the new organisation might not feel that in taking the name 'C. P.' it was becoming absorbed into an already existing organisation".[97]

With a great deal of prodding from the Russian representatives of the Third International, Theodore Rothstein and Maxim Litvinov, two meetings were held in June 1919 with the four parties interested in unity. There was little serious disagreement on issues of principle – commitment to soviets, dictatorship of the proletariat and affiliation to the Third International – but the issues of Labour Party affiliation and parliamentary participation rapidly took up more and more of the debating time and proved to be real stumbling blocks. The WSF delegates had been instructed to stand firm on these issues, particularly on the question of non-affiliation to the Labour Party. The BSP favoured affiliation but stood alone and in the minority. It was decided to allow the membership of the new party to vote on affiliation by secret ballot three months after its formation.

Before unity negotiations reopened, internal fighting broke out. The SLP was in favour of unity, but some would not accept the proposed ballot. Since this was one of the necessary preconditions for the BSP to remain at the negotiating table, a deadlock ensued. When the BSP called a conference for January 1920, only three members of the SLP attended: Thomas Bell, Arthur MacManus and J. T. Murphy, who constituted themselves as a breakaway group of the SLP. The SWSS and WSF refused to go ahead without the SLP and it was agreed to adjourn, "pending an important event".[98]

The "event" was the long-awaited publication of Lenin's reply to Pankhurst's letter of September 1919, in which she had criticized the tactics of the BSP, ILP and SLP. Lenin replied, "I am personally convinced that refusal to participate in parliamentary elections is a mistake on the part of the English revolutionary workers, but it is better to accept this mistake than postpone the formation of a strong Communist Party."[99]

The WSF yielded to some extent, agreeing that participation in Parliament would be left to the future party to decide upon as the situation arose. However, the WSF remained adamant about non-affiliation with the Labour Party and announced further that, should unity negotiations fall through again, it would immediately get together with the SWSS, the Communist League and other groups willing to form a left-wing Communist Party.

At this time Pankhurst was in Amsterdam at the "ultra-left" conference, which decided that no communist party would be recognized if it affiliated with the Labour Party. This resolution added fuel to the WSF's fire. Pankhurst wrote a piece in the *Dreadnought* saying that, of course, work in the Labour Party and trade unions should be done but that affiliation was not necessarily a revolutionary responsibility. She further argued that the experience of the Clyde and Italian soviets demonstrated that industrial power lay in the workshops: "The working class must be reached by direct appeal to the workshops. Until we have done the propaganda amongst the rank-and-file workers we shall neither influence the Labour Party nor expel officials from its head."[100]

Although Pankhurst and the WSF were continually accused of being anti-trade union, she was not at this time opposed to working within unions for greater democracy, although she emphasized that this would be a hard, bitter struggle, especially within trade (as opposed to industrial) unions. It was important, however, to realize that no trade union could be revolutionary. Rather, she said, revolutionary organization took the form of soviets. Insisting that power in Russia lay in the All-Russia Congress of Soviets, she asserted that democracy within the unions could be achieved by creating workers' committees – which were the forerunners of soviets. For Pankhurst, soviet democracy was central to a socialist government.[101] When, later, she decided that power no longer resided in the Russian soviets, she ceased supporting union work.

On 24 April, a unity conference, which included the BSP, SWSS, WSF and the SLP unity group (the faction of the SLP that accepted the ballot proposal), voted for non-affiliation and no parliamentary action, but the BSP refused to accept the first decision and demanded a national convention of the membership of the groups.[102] Having the largest membership, the BSP would have an advantage in such a vote.[103]

Before this took place, yet another meeting was convened and the Labour decision was reversed. The SWSS had not had time to mandate its delegates and was therefore not represented. It was decided that the decisions made at this meeting should be binding on the national convention. Delegates would have to agree to them in advance. The WSF withdrew in disgust but continued to urge people to attend the convention.[104]

It was obvious now to the WSF that the united Communist Party would be dominated by the BSP and would therefore be essentially right wing. In an unpublished letter, Pankhurst accused Rothstein of manipulating the change in the vote on affiliation by promising the delegates money from the International if they agreed with Lenin's positions.[105]

Having withdrawn from the unity negotiations, the WSF immediately called a conference of its own for June 1920, which was also attended by seven other small left-wing groups and some individuals. The groups were the Aberdeen, Croydon and Holt Communist groups, the Stepney Communist League, Gorton Socialist Society, the Labour Abstentionist party (led by Edgar Whitehead) and the Manchester Soviet. D. A. Davis was in the chair. The meeting – held in the apartment shared by Nellie Rathbone, May O'Callaghan and Daisy Lansbury – constituted itself as the Communist Party (British section of the Third International), CP (BSTI), with 25 people on its provisional council and an initial membership of 150, which grew to 430 in three months.[106] Edgar Whitehead became secretary and Robert Stott treasurer and the *Workers' Dreadnought* became the official newspaper.

The first letter of the CP(BSTI), circulated to all its branches, urged them to organize propaganda, industrial literature and information subcommittees, with the emphasis on the industrial subcommittee. The goal was to organize the branch in building up workers' committees and in pushing rank-and-file movements and unofficial reform movements within the unions (so as to weaken the power of the permanent union officials) and to alter the structure of the unions (so as to allow the rank-and-file to have complete control and to spread the doctrine of the revolutionary general strike).[107] Quite an ambitious, unrealistic programme for a subcommittee in an organization with a membership of 150.

A month earlier Sylvia Pankhurst had attempted to launch a communist youth movement around a journal called the *Red Flag*. The editor was Nathan Whycer, it was printed by the Agenda Press and the secretary's address was the same as the *Dreadnought*'s.[108] The project was very short-lived; only one issue appeared, which consisted of a combination of socialist stories and information about the Young Socialist and Communist Internationals. It claimed branches in Bethnal Green, Bow, Croydon, Hackney, Hoxton, Islington, Poplar and Stepney.[109]

One can only speculate as to the reasons for this venture. Perhaps Pankhurst was trying to build up her alliances to attain better political leverage at forthcoming unity negotiations. Or perhaps she saw the handwriting on the wall – either the futility of a united Communist Party or, more likely, a united but right-wing Communist Party, with herself outside it. She began publishing material in the *Dreadnought* from the German Communist Worker's Party (KAPD), which had never affiliated with the Third International.

Much to the relief of the BSP, Lenin's radio message condemning Sylvia Pankhurst for unilaterally setting up the CP(BSTI) came in autumn, leaving the way clear for the BSP's own conference, which was finally held in November 1920. The timing of the August 1920

London unity conference was peculiar, for it met while the Second Congress of the CI was in session and a strong British contingent – including William Gallacher, Sylvia Pankhurst, Tom Quelch, Dave Ramsey and Jack Tanner – was in Moscow. Also absent from this convention was John Maclean, the Scottish Marxist and left-wing member of the BSP, arguably the most respected revolutionary in Britain at the time. He claimed that the BSP had prevented him from attending.[110] The barring of Maclean – not to mention the absence of some of Britain's leading revolutionaries – did not bode well for a "unity" conference.

The WSF was present at the unity conference via the *Dreadnought*, which circulated an open letter urging communist unity, containing a brief account of the aims of the left-wing Communist Party and urging delegates to attend a CP(BSTI) inaugural conference in Manchester in September. At this point the CP(BSTI) did not envision merging its identity into a united Communist Party, which it rightly expected would be dominated by the right-wing members of the BSP. Instead, the CP(BSTI) saw itself forming a left-wing bloc or faction that would enter the Communist Party (CP) and attempt to change it. Pankhurst thought it "might be best to join it to consolidate the Left Wing, and then if there were no prospect of changing the policy to come out of the party".[111]

At a further informal meeting, the CP(BSTI), the South Wales Communist Party and the Communist Labour Party of Scotland heard Gallacher and Ramsey urge them to join the CP. They were promised that they would be fully allowed to raise their criticisms and ideas.[112] At this time, Pankhurst was serving her six-month prison sentence for sedition. Gallacher, who was a leading figure in the unity negotiations, wrote her a long letter pleading with her to join and promising that "[t]here can be no question at all about the right of discussion within the organisation . . . . We certainly would be free to advocate our own peculiar views on a public platform." He urged her to continue her fight against parliamentarianism from within, as he promised to do himself. "Surely your members in such serious times as these would not allow a matter of so little importance to stand between them and the great world movement?" Begging her to take part in shaping the movement, he signed himself, "your sincere comrade".[113] This sincerity did not last long: within months, he was leading the slander campaign against Pankhurst.

Believing strongly in the validity of her political perspectives, Pankhurst urged her members to agree to join the united CP. However, an additional complication arose because the united Communist Party was to be based upon the Twenty-One Theses of the Communist International which had in the meantime been adopted by the Moscow Congress (whose delegates had, however, not been allowed to see them). CP(BSTI) branch members were told they had to accept them on faith. The majority agreed to go along with this test of loyalty and voted to join, but four CP(BSTI) branches refused to accept such terms and resigned from the organization.[114]

Two more meetings were held in December between the CPGB, the Communist Labour Party, the CP(BSTI) and what remained of the shop stewards' movement to work out organizational details. Sufficient progress was made and common ground found to call a unity convention in Leeds on 29 and 30 January 1921. As well as she could, Pankhurst had followed these events from prison. She "saw in advance that there would be no strong fight put up for the Left Wing. I realised that the Left Wing would collapse, for the time being."[115] In fact, during her imprisonment, she was all but deserted by the CP(BSTI). By January 1921, the left-wing bloc that she had envisaged within the CP, with its own paper, the *Dreadnought*, had little support – so little, in fact, that when she was expelled later that year, very few people rallied to her defence.

How could Pankhurst – with an organization that she had built herself and with the editorship of the *Dreadnought*, one of the most influential socialist newspapers – be deserted by her own members? Part of the reason was personal, most of it political.

Much of it involved a severe clash between members of the CP(BSTI) and Corio. As in so many conflicts arising within political organizations, it involved temperaments as well as ideals. The dispute was over the running of the Agenda Press and the management of the *Dreadnought*. Corio ran the press and edited the *Dreadnought* even though he was not a member of the CP(BSTI). Worse, he was an anarchist. May O'Callaghan claimed it was Corio's behaviour that led to Pankhurst's political isolation:

> He was working the Agenda Press with a couple of other people and they couldn't stand him. He used to get drunk. . . .Once they got mad and pretended to hang him. . . . I know she used to go to the Press and find life very difficult.[116]

The Agenda Press had been subsidized with money from the CI. It was under the trusteeship of Norah Smythe, Pankhurst and Corio, who was paid £5 a week to manage it. Joe Thurgood accused Corio of mismanaging the paper, politically and financially, charging that he mismanaged funds, refused CP orders even though the *Dreadnought* was a CP paper, underestimated and overcharged work done for the movement and acted as editor of the paper even though he was not a member of the CP.[117]

There is no evidence either way to determine the validity of Thurgood's allegations. His political charges are probably true. Corio was an anarchist; philosophically he did not agree with the formation of communist parties and probably tried to convince the Agenda Press printers of his point of view. This made Corio's position at the press somewhat untenable and Pankhurst politically vulnerable.

Matters came to a head at an executive meeting of the CP(BSTI). A repudiation and boycott of both the *Workers' Dreadnought* and the Agenda Press was again considered and by a unanimous vote it was decided to repudiate the *Workers' Dreadnought* as the official organ of the CP(BSTI) and also to institute a boycott of the WD and the Agenda Press. Edgar Whitehead, the National Secretary of the CP(BSTI), wrote to Pankhurst:

> I would therefore ask you to remove from the *Dreadnought* . . .
> the intimation that the *Dreadnought* is the official organ of the
> Party.[118]

In fact, at the Manchester conference of the CP(BSTI), Pankhurst had said that she was prepared to submit herself to the wishes of the party and to give up editorship of the paper. No one came forward to assume her responsibilities and she was re-elected editor.

What eventually brought about her expulsion from the CP was the contents of the *Workers' Dreadnought* and its relationship to the party. By January 1921, the *Dreadnought* was heavily in debt. Norah Smythe, who did most of the editing while Pankhurst was in prison, went to Moscow in June 1921 as a Communist Party representative to the Women's Communist International Congress. While there, she met Kollontai, who promised to send money for Pankhurst's publications.[119] In fact, the *Dreadnought* owed its existence largely to outside funding and Pankhurst was very dependent on money from revolutionaries outside Britain.

The paper's content was also changing noticeably. It was becoming increasingly theoretical and published fewer and fewer articles about domestic struggles and actual events in the trade union movement. Literary criticism and poetry were replacing stories of strikes and mutinies. Although this change was in part a tacit recognition of the decline in the class struggle, it was clear that the contributors were no longer a part of or even in touch with workers' struggles as they had been a few years before.

The *Dreadnought* did remain alive to international issues. Pankhurst published Alexandra Kollontai's articles on women, prostitution and the development of the Workers' Opposition, a left-wing, semi-syndicalist faction that wanted to operate within the Russian Communist Party. Pankhurst's political position was close to Kollontai's and it is likely that she agreed with Kollontai's political assessment of the events in Russia. Pankhurst emphatically agreed with the right of a left faction to exist within the Communist Party. The *Dreadnought* also printed articles by the KAPD, including the entire text of Herman Gorter's "Open letter to Comrade Lenin", which was a reply to *Left wing communism*. The views expressed in articles such as these were becoming intolerable to the CP, which was evolving rapidly into an organization that would accept only one point of view. In this case, the point of view came more from the CI than from the British CP members. This orientation contradicted everything Pankhurst had ever believed.

At its January conference, the CPGB had discussed the fate of the various socialist papers and determined that the *Worker* and *Solidarity* were suitable for CPGB members and could continue but that the *Spur*, an anarchist paper and the *Socialist* were barred as being unorthodox and not to be read by loyal comrades. The matter of the *Dreadnought* was left in abeyance until Pankhurst got out of prison. Many branches of the CP took this to mean that it should not be circulated.[120]

The CPGB was afraid not only of ideas but of other socialists who were not ready or willing to join. Gallacher, now a leading CP functionary, embarked upon a campaign to wreck the left-wing SLP. He and some political allies gatecrashed an SLP meeting in Glasgow organized by John Maclean on Christmas Day, 1920. They repeatedly heckled the speakers and it seemed the meeting would end in a fight. Violence was avoided, but the Gallacher group continued heckling.[121]

Upon her release, Pankhurst met right away with a subcommittee of the Communist Party Executive:

The sub-committee put it to me that "as a disciplined member of the party" I should hand the *Workers' Dreadnought* over to the Executive, to stop it or continue it, and should I continue the paper, to put it to any use or policy it chose, and to place it under the editorship of any person whom it might select; I was not to be consulted, or even informed, till the decision should be made.[122]

These were the brutal terms that Pankhurst had to face. She replied that she would not accept such a proposition right away but would give it thoughtful consideration, arguing that, having just been released from prison, she needed time to look around and hear other points of view. She also asked if she could meet the full executive committee. This request was ignored and she was issued a directive to cease publication within two weeks.

Pankhurst was not about to accept the dictates of such an executive. Comrades brought messages warning of her pending expulsion. "I waited patiently for the event, not troubling to sign a membership card."[123] On 10 September she was finally summoned before the Executive and staunchly argued her case for a left-wing faction within the CPGB. Appealing to international events – such as the formation of the Workers' Opposition in Russia and the KAPD in Germany – to bolster her case, she pleaded with it not to stifle left-wing ideas. The executive replied that it could not tolerate any communist newspaper independent of itself. "'We are not here to consider what good the *Dreadnought* might do, but the harm it might do', said Comrade MacManus – his red silk handkerchief showing so smartly from his pocket."[124]

Discipline, party discipline and more party discipline were the watchwords of the meeting and on this issue the expulsion rested. Pankhurst assessed the situation thus: "The Communist Party of Great Britain is at present passing through a sort of political measles called discipline which makes it fear the free expression and circulation of opinions within the Party."[125]

A resolution was moved to expel Pankhurst. Before it was voted on, she informed the executive committee that the *Dreadnought* was about to fold anyway, owing to financial pressures. One member of the committee suggested that, in light of this disclosure, they might simply drop the case. But this was ruled out of order. When Pankhurst insisted that it was financial pressure and not obedience to Communist Party discipline that was persuading her to stop publication, she was expelled.[126]

Pankhurst wrote about this action:

> I do not regret my expulsion; that it has occurred shows the feeble and unsatisfactory condition of the Party; its placing of small things before great . . . . I desire freedom to work for Communism with the best that is in me. The Party could not chain me. I, who have been amongst the first, as the record of the papers published, both in this country and abroad, will prove, to support the present Communist revolution and to work for the Third International, shall continue my efforts as before.[127]

As it turned out, the *Dreadnought* did not fold. Even more determined now to keep it going, Pankhurst went to her former suffragette friends, the Pethick-Lawrences, who gave her the needed funds. The loyal Norah Smythe and a few others resigned from the CPGB in protest. William Gallacher bitterly accused her of getting herself deliberately expelled in order to get money from opposition groups abroad to finance the *Dreadnought*.

Chapter Seven

The red twilight

In September 1921, Sylvia Pankhurst wrote a lengthy article in the *Workers' Dreadnought* explaining her differences with the Communist Party. It ended "And so I leave the Party but not the movement. I am tired, comrades. I have had a long and hard struggle."[1] Her struggles in the communist movement were not over, however. From 1921 until 1924, she continued her efforts to build a left-wing communist organization, to keep the *Dreadnought* alive and to organize the unemployed in the East End. But her expulsion from the Communist Party, combined with her sectarianism toward the developing Labour Party, only contributed to her growing isolation from the labour movement and the East End community. By 1924, Pankhurst was financially, politically and emotionally exhausted.

Even though she had told the CP Executive Committee that the *Dreadnought* was about to fold because of financial difficulties, she was able to keep it going. The ever-faithful Norah Smythe dipped into her savings and Pankhurst begged from old friends such as the Pethick-Lawrences. She also received an initial £50 from Herman Gorter, the left-wing German communist.[2]

Pankhurst believed that it was important to keep the *Dreadnought* alive as an "independent communist voice":

> An independent organ is a guard against the corruptions, opportunisms and tyrannies which are apt to attend on parties and especially parties formed as the Communist Party of Great Britain has been from groups of conflicting tendencies, brought together by outside pressures and largely comprised of persons as yet untried in the political struggle.[3]

Shortly after her expulsion from the party, Pankhurst received the manifesto of a newly formed Fourth International.[4] This umbrella of left-wing communist organizations, which had been founded by Herman Gorter of the German Communist Workers' Party (KAPD), included Belgian, Bulgarian, Czech and Dutch left-wing communists. It condemned the development of a bureaucracy in Russia, the lack of democracy there and the attempts by the leadership of the Third International to impose the Russian experience upon the communist parties of other countries. The manifesto argued that revolution in the advanced capitalist West, with its traditions of parliamentary democracy, legal trade unions and (in some countries) legal social democratic parties, could not follow the same course as revolution in semi-feudal Russia.

Pankhurst declared her agreement with this manifesto, for although she considered herself a revolutionary socialist, she was becoming more and more critical of developments in the Soviet Union and, in October 1921 the *Dreadnought* called on communists to leave the Third International and join the Fourth, known as the International of Opposition Parties. Pankhurst was initially somewhat hopeful about its success. "I think and hope, it is still in a fluid state, ready to grow and develop. I hope it is still moving leftward." She went on to explain her position about the right of criticism within a communist party as well as her ideas about "party loyalty":

I shall never adopt the motto "The Party Right or Wrong" – I shall always go for what I believe to be best. I think that is the only way to avoid becoming a hindrance to progress. A Communist Party, a Party of Revolution, must, I think be very stern, very unyielding, very exclusive towards the Right elements, but ever tolerant toward the Left elements".[5]

Because of her international reputation and the contacts she had made in the previous ten years, Pankhurst remained well informed about events in Russia:

I was getting news from Russia that showed me reaction was developing steadily there. Workers' control of industry was less and less of a reality there. House rent, rates, charges for fuel and light were being reestablished, concessions to the principle of private capitalism were being made every day. A "Workers' Opposition" of some of the best revolutionary fighters had been formed within the Russian Communist Party.[6]

Not surprisingly, Pankhurst took up the cause of the Russian

Workers' Opposition, a left-wing faction organized by Alexandra Kollontai and others that called for political power to be vested in the organizations of workers – soviets, trade unions, workers' committees – and not in the Communist Party machine. In June 1922 the Russian Workers' Opposition affiliated with the Fourth International and the *Dreadnought* printed its entire manifesto for the first time in English.[7]

The *Dreadnought* was one of the few revolutionary newspapers that could provide information about left-wing, syndicalist and anarchist criticisms of the new Soviet Union; in addition, it continued its extensive coverage of events in Russia, of paramount concern to socialists everywhere. Pankhurst also used the *Dreadnought* to explain and justify her political positions. She analyzed what she considered to be the reintroduction of capitalism into Russia. Very critical of Lenin's New Economic Policy, she accused the Communist Party of a number of capitalist compromises, such as the trade agreements with capitalist countries, concessions to foreign capitalists operating in Russia and the definite shift of the Soviet government towards state capitalism in the enterprises under its control. She asserted that the abolition of free food, housing, light, fuel and clothes (which made workers entirely dependent on their earnings) increased wage differentials and quickly eroded socialism.[8]

These decisions had been guided by the overwhelming pressures of circumstances: the near destruction of Russian industry as a result of the First World War and the civil war, a series of catastrophic famines and the Allied blockade. Although realizing this was the case, Pankhurst nevertheless argued that Lenin and the communists did not thereby achieve any substantial famine relief. "For my part, I would have risked a collapse rather than make concessions."[9] She further did not believe that the Bolsheviks were reluctantly imposing such measures as a last-ditch effort to prevent the overthrow of the communist government and a more violent capitalist restoration. "It is difficult and it seems very churlish to criticize those who have made a big fight and recorded many achievements," she admitted.

> But is it not very sad to find the soviet government proceeding on the assumption more can be done by people who are working for their own private gain and employing wage slaves than by free workers cooperating on equal terms to supply common needs?[10]

Pankhurst continued publishing articles concerning the development of state capitalism in Russia, the decline of workers' control and attacks on Lenin and the Communist Party, as well as reports on political persecutions from anarchists, syndicalists and other left-wing critics and opponents of the new soviet state. One of Pankhurst's last comments on the Russian communists was that "they pose now as prophets of efficiency, trustification, state control and discipline of the proletariat, in the interests of increased production".[11]

In 1921, Pankhurst formed her own group, which she called the Communist Workers' Party (CWP). A few loyal friends, including Melvina Walker and Norah Smythe, joined. The CWP tried to hold regular meetings at the old WSF haunts in the East End – the East India Dock Gates, Grundy Street and Poplar – but the group never really amounted to anything in the East End and Pankhurst immediately began trying to find other prospective CWP members in the London area. She also came in contact with an ex-Communist Party member named Braddock who had just formed a Revolutionary Industrial Union Propaganda League, which joined the CWP.[12] By early March, Communist Workers' Party groups had been formed in Portsmouth and Sheffield as well as London and Dick Beech, another ex-Communist Party member, was trying to build a CWP branch in Hull. In April, there were the beginnings of a branch in Glasgow.[13]

The Communist Workers' Party was not a political party in any sense of the word. It was rather a tiny propaganda sect, trying against all odds to stay alive as a revolutionary organization while maintaining its distance and differences from the Communist Party of Great Britain. Based on the principle of opposition to parliamentary or local government action, the CWP advocated revolution through the creation of soviets. It called not for higher wages for workers but for the abolition of the wage system. It opposed trade unions' negotiating with employers and demanded an end to the entire employee/employer system. There could be no compromises or alliances with the Labour Party. Finally, the CWP maintained that a single revolutionary industrial union should embrace all workers, with working women and men organized on industrial lines rather than on a craft basis. The locals should resemble the shop stewards' organizations.[14]

Although these principles were consistent with those of a "purer" communist party, they were totally unrealistic for the period and they demonstrate that Pankhurst was seriously out of touch with political reality. In July 1922, Pankhurst received a letter from a left-wing Russian communist, telling her of a proposed conference of the Fourth International that would take place in Berlin in August. Another urgent invitation came from Gorter, who told her that, if the British government did not issue her a passport, she should get a visa in Holland and meet him there, where "everything would be arranged" for the conference.[15]

Pankhurst tried to get in touch with Gorter, but her messages were intercepted by the authorities. Unable to attend the conference, she wrote to the organizers: "As far as the Communist Workers' Party is concerned, we have three good groups actively at work. One is in Willesden in London, one in Sheffield and one in Portsmouth with scattered comrades."[16] She added that the South African section of the Fourth International was using the *Workers' Dreadnought* as its newspaper, since it was the only surviving journal that stood for industrial unionism (*Solidarity* had ceased publication in May 1921).[17]

Pankhurst also kept in touch with revolutionaries in Ireland. She was very critical of the Communist Party of Ireland because it had called first for a national revolution – throwing the British out – and only then for a socialist revolution. Instead Pankhurst advocated an Irish Socialist Republic: "Irish workers against Irish landlords and the Irish bourgeoisie" as well as the British Empire.[18] A member from the economic section, a faction within the Irish Industrial Workers of the World, wrote to Pankhurst that he hoped his group would be backed by the Fourth International because "our fight is your fight and this country is the key to the world".[19]

Pankhurst was active in the CWP, but the task of trying to build such a group, to keep it together and to keep the *Dreadnought* afloat was superhuman, even for the iron-willed, indefatigable Sylvia Pankhurst. She was always scrounging for money and bills for the *Dreadnought* and office rent often went unpaid, so that she frequently wondered if each month would be the last. In a letter to a Dutch comrade written in July 1922, she said that the *Dreadnought* had just won a slight reprieve since the print shop had received a large work order. "Otherwise, there was no prospect of paying the balance of the rent within a reasonable time, to say nothing of the other liabilities. It was really looking like the end – but now we have another lease on life."[20] A year later, she wrote a letter to John Maclean, promising she would keep a speaking engagement in Glasgow, but begging for some help in paying her travel costs since her financial problems were desperate. She ended the letter, "I often wonder whether I'll be able to keep on."[21]

Pankhurst pointed out in the *Dreadnought* that, because of the economic depression and the defeat of the working-class movement, revolutionary activity was becoming more or less impossible. Yet, instead of searching for actions that would be possible within these circumstances, she resorted to a half-hearted and vain appeal for people to join the Communist Workers' Party.[22] However, the CWP, like other tiny revolutionary organizations, simply did not have a chance to grow in this period. Not only did external forces militate against recruitment, but so did the presence of the Communist Party. It had the official seal of approval from the Comintern and, even if it did poorly in Britain, Moscow would do all it could to shore it up. Indeed financial support from the Comintern was essential for the CPGB's survival. J. T. Murphy, who was a CP functionary in the 1920s, admitted that, had the Communist Party not received big financial shots in the arm, it would have been reduced and probably gone out of existence within a year or so of formation, just as Sylvia Pankhurst's organization and its paper died when they got no money from external sources.[23]

In 1923, Pankhurst became involved in one last burst of political activity, with the unemployed in the East End. The Labour Party still controlled the Poplar Borough Council and the agitation over rents and relief for the poor and unemployed continued. In participating in the unemployed movement, Pankhurst came up against the Communist Party and the organizations it controlled. Many of the former stalwarts of the WSF, such as Harry Pollitt, Minnie Birch, Lillian Thring and Sidney Hansen, were now active members of the Communist Party, but Pankhurst continued in her fiercely independent direction even when it led her to oppose them.

Since 1921, Pankhurst had been particularly critical of the Poplar borough councillors, demanding that they lead the fight against unemployment, because she thought such a struggle might lead to the creation of soviets.[24] In response, the Bow branch of the Communist Party censured her for her continuous criticisms of the councillors.[25]

The major organization of the unemployed, the National Unemployed Workers' Committee Movement (NUWCM), decided at its third national conference in April 1923 to organize rent strikes and mass marches to factories and to call for a general strike to enforce its demands. The NUWCM also voted to affiliate to the Red International of Labour Unions (RILU), which was itself affiliated to the Third International. The Communist Party was an important political force in the NUWCM but did not completely dominate it, for the same conference voted down (by 55 to 52) a resolution calling for a united front – a political term referring to co-operative work among organizations – with the Communist Party. In the East London branches of the NUWCM, political opposition to the Communist Party was significant.[26]

In March 1923, a rival organization to the NUWCM had been formed – the Unemployed Workers' Organisation (UWO), led by G. A. Soderberg, an ex-member of the Communist Party. Neither the *Workers' Dreadnought* nor the Communist Workers' Party was instrumental in forming the UWO, although they agreed with most of its programme. According to the *Dreadnought,* UWO members asked for space in the newspaper to publish their manifesto. "Having read their manifesto," Pankhurst wrote, "we saw that their programme was similar to our views and we allowed them space."[27]

The UWO manifesto attacked the NUWCM for limiting itself to improving conditions for the unemployed and accused it of being dominated by professional politicians. Instead of the NUWCM's slogan "work or maintenance at trade union rates", the UWO offered the more revolutionary "abolition of the wage system". The UWO stood for direct action, opposed what it labelled the "counter-revolutionary" Labour Party and the "reformist" Communist Party and opposed affiliation either with the Trades Union Congress (TUC) or the Communist International-dominated RILU. The Communist Party, declared the UWO, was "dominated by middle class politicians". The UWO proposed to build a "genuine working class revolutionary movement".[28]

In an editorial in the *Dreadnought,* Pankhurst cautioned about "one phrase that has crept into the UWO constitution – support for the dictatorship of the proletariat", pointing out that, "when Marx originated the term, he meant the suppression of the bourgeoisie after a socialist revolution. Today, in Russia the 'bureaucrats' use it to justify the dictatorship of a party clique over party members as well as the masses."[29] This comment indicates that, although she supported the UWO, it was clearly not under her political control.

In the late summer of 1923 the Bow, Bromley, Millwall and Poplar branches of the NUWCM joined the UWO. There was also discontent in the Edmonton branch, 600 of whose members joined the UWO and defections from Lambeth and Camberwell.[30] The *Dreadnought* reported a number of large, open-air meetings in Bow and Millwall and in one week in August 50 new members joined in Poplar and Bow, increasing the membership to 80.[31] By September, the UWO membership had passed the 500 mark.

Wal Hannington, a member of the Communist Party and chairman of the NUWCM, understandably grew upset at these losses when he returned from Moscow in the late summer of 1923, since these East London branches were the "largest and strongest movements in the country".[32] Speaking at a UWO meeting in September, he called for unity and solidarity. A debate was organized between Hannington and Soderberg, the UWO leader. Not surprisingly, the biased *Dreadnought* claimed that Soderberg, having proved that the NUWCM was indeed controlled by the Communist Party, won the debate.[33]

The UWO was involved in one major activity in Poplar, which brought it into direct conflict with both the Communist Party and the Labour Party. On 26 September 1923, the UWO sent a deputation to meet the Poplar councillors to ask for a restoration of the coal allowance and an increase in relief for single men and women. Previously Poplar had been renowned for its generosity in this respect. But this time the councillors refused the request.[34] Immediately, the unemployed locked the main doors and organized a "sit-in". There were about 200 unemployed in the building as a whole, 20 of whom occupied the room where the councillors met.[35]

The police were called to remove them and upwards of 40 people were hurt in the riot that ensued. Unarmed women and men were brutally batoned by the police, some of whom were reported to have been drunk. About 100 others were slightly injured. The councillors looked on, ignoring pleas such as "George [Lansbury], can't you stop it?" even though the beatings were vicious and indiscriminate.[36] It was never known exactly who called the police, but noted East End left-wingers (most of whom were former members of the ELFS or the WSF) were probably involved: Julia Scurr and her husband John, a member of the ILP and mayor of Poplar; A. A. Watts, an ex-BSP and present CP member; Edgar Lansbury of the Communist Party and his father George, a member of the Labour Party. On 3 November John

Scurr went to a meeting at the Poplar Town Hall of unemployed ex-servicemen and other unemployed, called by the UWO, which demanded that Scurr defend the position taken by the councillors. He argued that refusing to increase relief was the only way to keep rates down and asserted further that the police had simply come in; he did not know who called them.[37] During the question-and-answer period, A. A. Watts and Julia Scurr were pointed out as the culprits. To Pankhurst, the councillors' action was only proof of the correctness of her anti-parliamentary position. Editorializing in the *Dreadnought* on 6 October 1923, she wrote:

The result of working-class representatives taking part in the administration of capitalist machinery is that working-class representatives become responsible for enforcing the regulations of the capitalist system itself.[38]

A week later in the *Dreadnought*, another UWO activist agreed: "The policy of the UWO is definitely anti-parliamentary and we can claim victory for our defeat by being able to prove the fallacy and futility of local governing bodies in their endeavour to abolish poverty and distress."[39] Communists, members of the Labour Party and other socialists were not supposed to call the armed forces of the state against members of the working class and the Communist Party attempted to downplay the event. However, in many parts of Britain the workers were not so forgiving. When Wal Hannington, substituting for Lansbury at a meeting organized by the Trades Council in the Glasgow Town Hall, attacked the UWO for going to the councillors, he was angrily howled down and the meeting broke up.

John Maclean, equally disgusted by the sectarianism and use of violence by the communists and Poplar councillors, organized a meeting with the Scottish Republican Workers' Party as well as unemployed workers and invited Pankhurst to come up and present the UWO's point of view. Maclean described the meeting: "Sylvia came in on Friday, and after tea at Ca'Dora she arrived at City Hall all right, but naturally tired. The City Hall was filled and if it had been free for the unemployed we could have filled it three times over."[40]

Pankhurst's accusations regarding the effect of the councillors' accepting positions in government may have been strictly accurate; when socialists assume responsibilities in a capitalist government – whether local or national – they usually wind up, willingly or otherwise, maintaining aspects of capitalist law and order. However, observers in defence of the councillors, such as Noreen Branson, make a different point:

> This assertion, valid in some areas, hardly fitted the facts of Poplar where the Guardians [councillors] still had the threat of surcharge and possible prison hanging over them because of their refusal to operate the regulations and, moreover, were soon to be taken to court for their defiance of the law over the dock strike.[41]

In retrospect, the UWO was wrong in its assessment of the Poplar councillors. Although there obviously was a better way to deal with the UWO demonstrators than calling in the police – who had a well-established reputation for being brutal with East End protestors – the Poplar councillors of this period were and are known and respected for their determination to equalize the disparity between rich and poor in terms of rates and relief in London.

The life of the UWO was very short. By January 1924, it claimed 3,000 members but even if that figure is accurate, its membership was slowly either rejoining the rival NUWCM or dropping out. The NUWCM was steadily applying pressure upon UWO members in the East End, downplaying its association with the Communist Party and emphasizing the importance of belonging to a national organization. In early 1924, the NUWCM had successfully proposed joint work with the TUC. The UWO could raise no opposition and soon it folded.[42]

Pankhurst's efforts with the UWO were her last flurry of activity in the East End – at least for a decade. There is no question that by 1924 she was politically disoriented by events. Although she correctly analyzed and predicted the consequences of the destruction of the international revolutionary movements, the collapse of the Russian revolution and the retreat of the British working class, she was not able to readjust tactically. Thus, in this period of working-class retreat, she called for immediate revolutionary demands such as the creation of soviets. As her group of political supporters and allies dwindled, she became more sectarian, refusing to work with former friends and comrades, now members of the Labour or Communist parties and she became isolated from the working class she so desperately wanted to liberate.

The *Dreadnought* reflected Pankhurst's political dilemma. By 1921, it contained scant coverage of industrial news and the stories it did cover no longer had the flavour of the workers involved. After the

Labour victory of 1923, Pankhurst argued that this would only prove the sham of parliamentary politics. She saw the election of eight women to Parliament as no advance for women:

Women can no more put virtue into the decaying Parliamentary institution than can men: it is past reform and must disappear. The woman professional politician is neither more or less desirable than the man professional politician: the less the world has of either, the better it is of it.[43]

This comment measures the tremendous political change Pankhurst had undergone. Neither did she now advocate special activities and organizations for women. Frank O'Connor, writing in the *Dreadnought,* summed up Pankhurst's political philosophy: "Even as far as work for women is concerned everything is to be accomplished by concentrating on the proletarian movement."[44]

In spite of Pankhurst's political isolation and sectarianism, the *Dreadnought* continued to be exemplary in its international coverage. It championed the causes of Irish and Indian independence. Every issue carried news about the Irish struggle, the Black and Tan war and British atrocities against the Irish. The *Dreadnought* opposed the partition of Ireland and in March 1923 carried a front-page interview with Constance Markievicz, the Anglo-Irish woman who became the first female to be elected to the British Parliament and a leading participant in the 1916 Easter Rising.

Pankhurst continued to cover the German and Russian revolutions, publishing Luxemburg's *History of the Russian revolution,* her letters from prison and Karl Liebknecht's letters from prison.[45] She continued publishing and defending the rights of left-wing Russian dissidents. In 1924, she appeared at a political rally for the Russian anarchist Nestor Machno.[46] She also spoke at concerts with two well-known exiled Russian left-wing musicians, Edward Soermus and Bohumir Ulman.

As Pankhurst became distanced from the day-to-day struggles of the working class, her paper took on a more literary flavour. Beginning in 1921 it carried regular articles about learning an international language – Esperanto. She serialized Emile Zola's *Germinal* and published Ezra Pound's poetry.

Pankhurst's writings about communism looked more to the past than to the future. She wrote long historical articles about the Chartists, Ernest Jones, William Morris and Edward Carpenter.

She reprinted tracts on anarcho-communism from Prince Peter Kropotkin. She gave evening classes about William Morris's *News from nowhere* and the French revolution of 1789.

She also published her own poetry, which, like so much else in the *Dreadnought*, was out of sync with the political and literary times:

I sing of revolt,
I sing of the burning sun,
I sing of thee and thy heat waves,
Thy heat waves that stir men's hearts to revolt,
Arousing a storm of passion, barriers overthrowing.

Burst ye the bonds of wagedom,
Burst ye the bonds, O people,
Stirred by the sun that burns,
O life giving sun that burneth.

Why will ye chaffer by the market barrows,
Or show your wares behind glass when the sun
Is raging,
Faded and spoilt are the paltry wares ye are selling.
Abandon this tedious barter in which ye waste your lives![47]

Pankhurst also tried to publish a revolutionary socialist journal named *Germinal*, after Zola's novel, as an attempt to create a literary voice for the people of the East End. The first issue carried a short story by Maxim Gorky and a story and poems by Pankhurst, neither very good. The publication was a failure; only two editions were published.

By 1924 the *Dreadnought*'s masthead reflected Pankhurst's political confusion. It no longer proclaimed "International Socialism" but the meaningless phrase "Going to the Root". In one area, however, Pankhurst did display a clear understanding of important events. She began writing systematically about Italian politics in 1921 and the 19 August 1922 issue of the *Dreadnought* first warned about the fascists: "Now Mussolini dominates the situation with his fascisti . . . . [T]hey have broken the back of the working class movement."[48] These articles show that Pankhurst was one of the first to comprehend the danger of fascism. She had, after all, seen Mussolini firsthand in Bologna in 1919.

Pankhurst described how fascism in Italy thrived on the chaos that followed the abortive revolutionary year of 1919 and faced little resistance from the defeated soviets and the disunited revolutionary organizations. The frightened middle classes looked to Mussolini because he promised stability, order, Italian unity and strength. In her articles Pankhurst correctly assessed the use of violence in the fascist movement and analyzed why women joined it and what their position in it was.[49] She also railed against the Labour Party for not understanding the fascist menace and on 25 March 1923 spoke at an anti-fascist rally.[50] Had she not been so isolated politically, had the Communist Party been less sectarian, perhaps there might have been greater appreciation of these warnings.

As Pankhurst looked around her, she saw little hope for continuing the kind of socialist propaganda and agitational work she had been doing. The Communist Workers' Party had collapsed and many of her friends were in the Communist Party. Some, like Jessie Payne, had died. Norah Smythe, her devoted, loyal friend and comrade, wrote Pankhurst a long letter begging her to rethink her priorities.[51] The WSF office, once a hub of revolutionary and feminist activity, was desolate. No longer was Pankhurst the suffragette "mouse" evading the police and confronting Asquith, or the heroic figure of the war years who battled bureaucracies to ameliorate suffering, or the brave and lonely defender of Bolshevism, struggling to save Russia from Allied intervention.

In July 1924, after a decade of revolutionary activity in the East End, Pankhurst stopped publication of the *Dreadnought*. She and Norah Smythe had found a four-room cottage in Woodford Wells, outside London, where they could live with Corio. They renamed it "Red Cottage", for their intention was to serve tea and offer revolutionary discussion there. Pankhurst's departure from the East End coincided with the election of the first Labour government; this event, which she had once dreamed of, she now denounced as a fraud. The move also came at the same time as the defeats of the Russian and German revolutions, the ebbing of working-class struggle in Britain and internationally and the rise of fascism.

Pankhurst's health continued to plague her and she was desperately poor. She needed some time to think, to recover from the collapse of her revolutionary dreams, to earn some money and to recoup her health. She wrote:

> I toiled till I saw that the voiceless women about me, the poorest and the most oppressed had roused themselves from a hopeless, helpless misery and subjection, had grown to speak and think

for themselves. From the mean streets of the East End, the women were coming forth for elections as councillors and Guardians. They were Parliamentary voters and a Parliamentary seat for the poorest was not beyond their hope.

I opened my eyes and saw that my youth had fled. Then I said that I should have a child of my own in whom I should live again.[52]

Chapter Eight

ᴥ

Conclusion

When Sylvia Pankhurst, along with Norah Smythe and Sylvio Corio, moved to the suburban rusticity of Woodford Green in 1924, her politics and her commitments were in flux; her life as an activist was far from over.[1] Besides serving tea to lorry drivers to earn some money, she also began to write extensively. In 1926, she published *India and the earthly paradise,* a meticulously researched 600-page book that discussed Indian nationalism. In it, her communism leaned toward Indian communalism, advocating Gandhi's emphasis on preserving the rural co-operative village life as the key component of Indian nationalism.

In 1927, she published *Delphos, or the future of the international language:* again, searching for a way to encourage international co-operation, she advocated a new language – not Esperanto but Interlingua. In 1930, she wrote *Save the mothers,* a plea for a national maternity health plan and in 1931, she published *The suffragette movement,* which is partially an autobiography as well as a very personal history of the suffragette movement. The next year she published *The home front,* which detailed her work in the East End during the First World War. Like *The suffragette movement, The home front* is highly personal and semi-autobiographical.

This literary work was, however, overshadowed by another event in her life. In 1927, at the age of 45, she gave birth to her only child. Pankhurst had often expressed a strong desire for a child and in 1926 she confided to her friend Charlotte Drake that she was pregnant. Unfortunately, it was a "ghost pregnancy", but the next year, after a long and difficult pregnancy, labour and delivery, she gave birth to Richard Keir Pethick Pankhurst, named after the most important people in her life – her father, Keir Hardie and the Pethick-Lawrences, who continued to give her money for her personal as well as political endeavours.

Pankhurst's out-of-wedlock baby created a scandal. Christabel visited her, demanding that she marry Corio and give the infant Richard his father's name. That was the last time the sisters met. Pankhurst refused; she and Corio never married. Patricia Romero argues that the shock of an "illegitimate" grandson hastened the death of Emmeline in 1928, but it is more likely that Emmeline Pankhurst's hunger-striking in and out of prisons during the suffragette militancy was the major cause of her declining health. At the time of her death, she was running for Parliament on the Conservative Party ticket.

Pankhurst was ecstatic about the birth of her son. She and Corio were devoted and loving parents. Richard Pankhurst worked with his mother on many of her later projects, shared her interest in feminism and to this day is dedicated to her memory. His book, *William Thompson 1775–1853*, is a biography of the English utopian and feminist. Richard also shared aspects of his mother's pacifism and anti-imperialism. In the 1950s he refused to be inducted into military service, saying he would be willing to help arrest the British colonial secretary but would not use force against Kenyans during the "Mau Mau" rebellion. Today he is a leading scholar of Ethiopian affairs. In 1979 he published a sympathetic account of Pankhurst's work as an artist and also wrote a personal introduction to the 1977 Virago edition of *The suffragette movement*.

Pankhurst resumed political activity in 1932, involving herself in the anti-fascist crusade. She organized the Women's International Matteotti Committee, which publicized the death of the well-known Italian socialist (murdered by Mussolini's troops in 1923) and protected his wife and family. By 1934, she was again publishing political materials – in particular anti-fascist tracts – and speaking at anti-fascist rallies with former comrades such as Norah Smythe and Charlotte Despard. In 1934, she spoke at an anti-fascist rally in Trafalgar Square, demanding the arrest and detention of fascist sympathizers (including a former member of the WSPU, Mary Richardson). In 1937, she returned to the East End, the scene of so many battles with the police, this time to do battle with the British Union of Fascists.

At 55 years of age, she marched to Victoria Park and spoke at a rally called by the Jewish Ex-Servicemen's League, an organization formed to protect Jews from Oswald Moseley's storm troopers. There was a skirmish with the fascists in which Pankhurst's face was scratched and she was hit by a rock.

It was, however, the 1934 Ethiopia crisis that gave Pankhurst a new political direction and a new political idol – Haile Selassie, Elect of God, Conquering Lion of the Tribes of Judah, King of Zion, King of Kings, Emperor of Ethiopia, Chevalier Sans Peur et Sans Reproche and Epitome of True Nobility. How did Sylvia Pankhurst, the socialist and republican, become a starry-eyed defender of an emperor? Part of the explanation lies in her strong anti-imperialist, anti-fascist and anti-racist sympathies. Pankhurst loved to defend the underdog and she saw in Selassie much more a defeated victim of fascism than a reactionary monarch. From 1935 until her death, she basked in Selassie's company as his confidante and political adviser. Perhaps he was another father figure (even though she was much older); whatever the reason, the defence of Ethiopia and Selassie became her total focus.

In 1936, she and Corio began publishing the *New Times and Ethiopia News*. Corio was the printer; Pankhurst the editor and primary writer. As with the *Dreadnought*, she was able to attract a number of skilled writers. The newspaper published reports about Italian atrocities in Ethiopia as well as arguments for the political independence for Ethiopia. During the war, in 1942, Pankhurst made her first trip to Ethiopia, where she denounced British rule.

The paper had some impact in Britain and Italy, for Mussolini approached the Foreign Office demanding its suppression. The Foreign Office prohibited its export to neutral countries, save the Americas, until Britain and Italy were formally at war. The *New Times* was also a leading anti-fascist newspaper and a strong opponent of anti-Semitism. Pankhurst was an ardent supporter of the Republicans during the Spanish Civil War, denouncing British inaction and correctly viewing the events in Spain as the prelude for the Second World War.

By 1939, she held very strong pro-war views, declaring that war was the only way to defeat the fascists. In 1940, a group of Italian London Fascists bombed the offices of the *New Times* and threatened Pankhurst personally. Things had indeed changed: the police, who had formerly harassed and arrested her, now protected her. She received the ultimate anti-fascist accolade; she was put on the Nazi list of people to be killed or interned in the case of a successful German invasion.

Despite her strong anti-fascist sentiments, Pankhurst never made any attempt to rejoin or work with her former comrades in the Communist Party. Shocked and horrified by Stalin, she denounced the 1936 Moscow Trials as a brutal farce. Having known and admired Bukharin in particular, she knew he had been framed by Stalin. In her own mind, Pankhurst remained a socialist; she never commented on the contradictions between her socialism and her devotion to an emperor. In 1948, she joined the Labour Party – the party she had once denounced as cowardly and ineffectual.

In 1954, Corio died. He had always remained in the background, never giving interviews, never upstaging Pankhurst. Her obituary of him did not contain the same level of feeling that she expressed when Hardie died. According to David Mitchell, however, she wept for days. In 1956, Pankhurst stopped publication of the *New Times,* sold her belongings and emigrated to Addis Ababa with her son, to be with her adored emperor. She continued writing and published the *Ethiopia Observer.* On 27 September 1960, at the age of 78, she died of heart failure. She was memorialized in London and in Addis Ababa the lifelong atheist and socialist was given both a state and a Christian funeral.

Towards the end of her life, Pankhurst wrote a letter to Teresa Billington-Greig, a former suffragette, saying that she felt "the victory of Ethiopia has been the most satisfactory achievement I have seen" and denigrating women's suffrage because of "its partial character and the fact that there was not a sufficiently intelligent, progressive and active movement to make it effective as one would have desired".[2] But this assessment of her achievements is not widely shared. Sylvia Pankhurst is known today (in the West, of course) more as a suffragette and socialist feminist than as an apologist for Haile Selassie. She was one of the few women in Britain in the period before the First World War for whom feminism and socialism were linked. Pankhurst was both a feminist and a socialist, however, and her philosophy was rooted more in the nineteenth century than in the twentieth; she always clung to the ideas of her father and of Keir Hardie.

At the heart of her feminism was her concern for women as mothers and housewives. Although she was preoccupied with winning women's suffrage in the early years of militancy, she always believed it was just a tactic in the overall struggle for emancipation. Pankhurst devoted herself to living among and organizing working-class women because they were the most downtrodden and had the most to gain from the struggle.

Pankhurst's initial feminism was deeply rooted in the realities of life in London's abyss. It was far more pragmatic than theoretical: the People's Army would protect women from evictions; the toy factory employed East London mothers; the cost-price restaurants fed working-class mothers and children, freeing them (if only momentarily) from the drudgery of the kitchen; the creches at the Mothers' Arms fed and cared for the children of working mothers.

However, during the period under discussion, Pankhurst changed her position regarding special organizations for women. As a suffragette and during the anti-war agitation, she stressed the importance of women forming their own organizations to fight for equality and liberation. But, as she moved more and more in the direction of revolutionary communism, she argued that the class struggle and not women's special organizations and struggles, would solve the problems of their oppression. Never, though, did she drop her belief that women faced special problems and had special interests. What did change for her was the means by which they would achieve freedom.

In her writings, especially *The suffragette movement*, Pankhurst did exaggerate her role and that of the East London Federation of the Suffragettes in winning the vote. However, the working-class women and men of the East End who mobilized and agitated for the vote have earned their place in history as much as the militants who smashed windows and heckled politicians or the constitutionalists who lobbied Parliament and signed petitions. Whether the working women of the East End could have accomplished more is doubtful, unless of course they had been able somehow to break out of the confines of the East End and to link up with the women of the northern industrial towns. But Pankhurst chose to remain in the East End and other socialist and feminist organizations also chose not to link up with this remarkable woman and her unique organization.

Pankhurst's socialism was as unorthodox as her feminism. It was more utopian than scientific; she had read more Morris than Marx. She clung to the nineteenth-century ideal of collectivism – her father's belief that individuals and communities share a collective responsibility for the welfare of all. This idea carried over through her anti-war activities and her communist agitation. She was not a doctrinaire Marxist; her hallmark was that she was not tied to any particular orthodoxy. This trait, which led her to an isolation of her own choosing, explains why her communism soon came to an end.

Pankhurst tried but unfortunately failed to carry her organization with her as she became more revolutionary. At each crucial juncture in the development of the East London Federation of the Suffragettes, the Workers' Suffrage Federation and the Workers' Socialist Federation, members dropped out. Thus, the militant women of East London did not make a significant impact on the British Communist Party in the 1920s. Furthermore, as Pankhurst became more interested in revolutionary politics – in particular creating a British Communist Party and then later in building a left-wing opposition – the immediate problems and struggles of working-class women occupied less and less of her time. Although she did publish long articles by Alexandra Kollontai, she could do little else. She was one of the few women who could have made a direct feminist contribution to revolutionary politics – to the Communist Party in the early 1920s. That she did not was a tragic defeat for sexual politics in the socialist movement.

The most striking feature about Pankhurst was her fierce and uncompromising independence, her ruthless adherence to principles that she believed to be right regardless of the cost in terms of support. This independence sprang from her personality and family background, from her experience as a militant suffragette and from her work with unorganized women in the East End. Her dissatisfaction with and rejection of existing bodies such as Parliament and the Labour Party were based upon the hard realities of practical politics, *as she saw them,* as much as they were based upon revolutionary theory. Most important was her firm belief that workers' committees or soviets were ultimately the most democratic and practical form of socialist organization. Her commitment to the tiny Communist Workers' Party and the Fourth International was largely an intellectual one. They fitted her theory but had no social base in the working class. Doggedly and unrealistically, she stuck to a principle she held dear while most of her supporters were deserting her.

Sylvia Pankhurst should not be judged too harshly, however, for her inability to build a socialist feminist organization, a larger working-class movement, or a communist party. The tasks she faced were immense and perhaps impossible. For all her shortcomings, she should be remembered as an anti-racist, anti-imperialist and anti-colonialist at a time when very few people shared her ideas. She was one of the few *international* feminists who built a working-class feminist organization that involved thousands of women fighting for their liberation. She stood out not only in her opposition to the First World War but in her attempt to do something about the misery that wartime inflicted on the home front.

Finally, she made a number of contributions to our understanding of socialist feminist theory – in particular, the role of the social soviets and the way in which women would fully participate in the socialist movement. In this respect Pankhurst can be considered an intellectual foremother of today's socialist feminists. Our understanding of the relationship between class and gender, between socialism and feminism, would be far richer today if Sylvia Pankhurst and her work had not been hidden from history.

Notes

Preface

1. Sylvia Pankhurst's Appeal, International Institute of Social History (Amsterdam), Parkhurst Papers [IISH PP] 140, p. 32.
2. George Dangerfield's evocative account of the suffragettes in *The strange death of liberal England* (New York: Capricorn, 1961) is based primarily on Sylvia Pankhurst's *The suffragette movement* (London: Longman, Green & Co., 1931). However, it says little about her work in the East End. The other histories of the women's suffrage movement – *The petticoat rebellion* by Marian Ramelson (London: Lawrence & Wishart, 1967), *Rapiers and battleaxes* by Josephine Kamm (London: Allen & Unwin, 1966), *Women's suffrage and party politics*, by Constance Rover (London: Routledge & Kegan Paul, 1967), *Rise up women!* by Andrew Rosen (London: Routledge & Kegan Paul, 1974), and *The militant suffragettes* by Antonia Raeburn (London: Michael Joseph, 1973) – say little or nothing about Pankhurst. David Mitchell has written condescending journalistic accounts of the Pankhursts in *The fighting Pankhursts* (London: Jonathan Cape, 1966, and *Women on the warpath* (London: Jonathan Cape, 1966). His best-researched book, *Queen Christabel* (London: MacDonald & James, 1977) as the title indicates, is about Christabel but contains some useful material about Pankhurst; unfortunately, this book suffers from Mitchell's homophobia. Pankhurst's son Richard Pankhurst has written an appreciative memoir about his mother entitled *Sylvia Pankhurst: artist and crusader* (London: Paddington Press, 1979); however, it concentrates on her artistic endeavours. In the past 15 years, feminist, social and labour historians have begun to write about the contributions of working-class and socialist women to the struggle for women's suffrage. Sheila Rowbotham, in her two pioneering books, *Women: resistance and revolution* (New York: Pantheon, 1972) and *Hidden from history* (New York: Pantheon, 1973), was the first to recognize Pankhurst's contribution to socialist and feminist history. Jill Liddington and Jill Norris, in *One hand tied behind us*

(London: Virago, 1978), wrote about northern England's working-class women involved in the rebirth of suffrage agitation. These authors believe that, had Pankhurst lived and worked in the northwest of England, "events might conceivably have taken a slightly different turn" (1978:172). Historians of the period of the industrial unrest and the formation of the British Communist Party have also given Pankhurst and both the Workers' Suffrage Federation and the Workers' Socialist Federation short shrift. Orthodox Marxist and communist historians usually dismiss Pankhurst as the womanwho received the blunt edge of Lenin's polemic, *Left wing communism:an infantile disorder* (Moscow: Foreign Language Publications,1920).See, for example, the Communist Party historian James Klugman, *A history of the Communist Party of Great Britain*, vol. 1 (London: Lawrence & Wishart, 1980); K. J. MacFarlane, *The British Communist Party* (London: McGibbon & Kee, 1966). Other historians give Pankhurst more credit – see Walter Kendall, *The revolutionary movement in Britain, 1900–1929* (London: Weidenfield & Nicolson, 1969), and Raymond Challinor, *The origins of British Bolshevism* (London: Croom Helm, Rowman & Littlefield, 1977). Les Garner's *Stepping stones to women's liberty* (London: Heinemann Educational Books, 1984) is an assessment of the feminist ideas in all the women's suffrage organizations, including those organized by Pankhurst. Garner argues that Pankhurst subordinated her feminism to the struggle for communism. In 1987, Yale University Press (New Haven, Connecticut) published Patricia Romero's *E. Sylvia Pankhurst: portrait of a radical*. For a full critique of the book see *Sylvia Pankhurst 1912–1924*, unpublished PhD dissertation by Barbara Winslow, University of Washington, Seattle, Washington, 1990. "Sylvia Pankhurst in perspective: some comments on Patricia Romero's biography, *E. Sylvia Pankhurst: portrait of a radical*" (*Women's Studies International Forum* XI, 1988) by Rita Pankhurst, Pankhurst's daughter-in-law, is a detailed article documenting the numerous factual, textual and other errors in Romero's book. Another review of the interpretation as well as of the numerous factual errors is that of Ian Bullock , "Review of Patricia W. Romero, *Sylvia Pankhurst: portrait of a radical*" in *History Workshop Journal* 26, Autumn 1987, pp. 204–7.

Chapter 1

1. Information about the early life of Sylvia Pankhurst comes from Sylvia Pankhurst, *The suffragette movement*, Rosen, *Rise up women!*, Liddington & Norris, *One hand tied behind us*, and Romero, *E. Sylvia Pankhurst*.
2. Richard Pankhurst, *Sylvia Pankhurst*, p.10.
3. Pankhurst, *The suffragette movement*, pp. 164–8.
4. *Ibid.*, p. 168.

5. Emmeline Pankhurst, *My own story* (London: Eveleigh Nash, 1914), pp. 43.

6. Carolyn Stevens's PhD dissertation (*A suffragette and a man: Sylvia Pankhurst's personal and political relationship with Keir Hardie*, Rochester, New York, 1986) details the sexual politics of Pankhurst's relationship with Hardie. Most of it covers the period before 1912.

7. Two biographies of Keir Hardie are Kenneth Morgan, *Keir Hardie: radical and socialist* (London: Weidenfield & Nicolson, 1975) and Caroline Benn, *Keir Hardie* (London: Hutchinson, 1992).

8. IISH PP 23 12a.

9. Pankhurst, *The suffragette movement*, 85.

10. Pankhurst, "The inheritance", IISH PP 194 10c, pp. 10–11.

11. Pankhurst, *The suffragette movement*, p. 174.

12. Romero, E. *Sylvia Pankhurst*, pp. 34–5.

13. ILP *News*, August 1903, p. 42.

14. George Dangerfield alludes to lesbianism among WSPU militants in *The strange death of liberal England*. He uses it to explain the underlying causes of suffragette violence. David Mitchell also hints at Christabel's lesbianism in *Queen Christabel*, pp. 29–31. His book unfortunately suffers from homophobia, which prevents him from discussing the subject objectively. Here I am discussing the issue of lesbianism among the suffragettes in the context of Blanche Wiesen Cooke's essay "Women alone stir my imagination: lesbianism and the cultural tradition", *Signs* 4, Summer 1979, pp. 718. She argues that lesbianism is more than sexual contact among women. Rather, it is a set of relationships, "the communal and noncompetitive intimacy of the settlement house women, the easy love and support that existed among academic women, and all the variety of women in enduring relationships with each other" that also define the lesbian experience (p. 719). Cooke's discussion of the "world of women's friendships and the crucial role played by female networks of love and support, the sources of strength that enabled independent, creative and active women to function" (p. 720) could also apply to the Pankhursts and the WSPU.

The fact that the suffragettes did not use the words "homosexuality" or "lesbianism" does not mean that they were not erotically involved. As Carroll Smith-Rosenberg asks in a review of Martha Vicinus's *Independent women: work and community for single women, 1850–1920* (Chicago: University of Chicago Press, 1985), "Does their lack of words mean that their passion remained frozen, unable to be expressed – except through the intensity of its own denial?" She goes on to add: "It seems a form of mimetic reductionism to conclude that because the words *we* need to describe the sexual are absent, the sexual was absent as well. We could easily conclude that Edwardian ladies and twentieth century scholars speak radically different sexual languages. These are central theoretical and methodological questions that historians of sexuality, of language and of women must face" (*Signs*, 13, Spring 1988, p. 648).

15. Pankhurst, *The suffragette movement*, p. 221.
16. *Ibid.*
17. Ethel Smythe, *Female pipings in Eden* (London: Peter Davies, 1934), p. 219.
18. Pankhurst, *The suffragette movement*, p. 171.
19. *Ibid.*, p. 217.
20. *Ibid.*, p. 249.
21. *Ibid.*
22. *Ibid.*, p. 189.
23. Vicinus, *Independent women*, p. 251.
24. Pankhurst, *The suffragette movement*, pp. 247–8.
25. *Ibid.*, pp. 215–16.
26. Pankhurst, "Some autobiographical notes", *Yearbook of International Archive of the Women's Movement* 1 (1937), pp. 94–5.
27. Pankhurst, *The suffragette movement*, p. 238.
28. *Ibid.*
29. In his appreciation of his mother, *Sylvia Pankhurst*, Richard Pankhurst says that he has saved and retrieved about half of her artwork. Several portraits are in the National Portrait Gallery in London, and the rest belong to people or their families who were given paintings in lieu of rent during her suffragette and socialist years in the East End. A centennial retrospective of her work was held in 1982 in the East End.
30. I am indebted to Mary Wetzell Gibbons for this insight.
31. Pankhurst, *The suffragette movement*, p. 270.
32. Helen Crawfurd (London: Marx Memorial Library) MS, p. 217.
33. Pankhurst wrote *The suffragette* in 1911 prior to her first trip to America. It is a hurried, uncritical treatment of the WSPU. *The suffragette movement*, published in 1931, is a more detailed autobiographical and historical account of the Pankhurst family and the suffrage movement from 1865 to 1914.
34. Pankhurst, *The suffragette movement*, pp. 263–6.
35. *Ibid.*, p. 269.
36. Emmeline Pankhurst, *Suffrage speeches from the dock* (London: WSPU, 1912), pp. 31.
37. *Ibid.*, p. 30.
38. Christabel Pankhurst, *The great scourge*, in *Suffrage and the Pankhursts*, J. Marcus (ed.), (London: Routledge & Kegan Paul, 1987), p. 188.
39. As quoted in Mitchell, *The fighting Pankhursts*, p. 36.
40. The reasons for advocating women's suffrage changed in the United States as well as in Britain at the beginning of the twentieth century. Class and race privilege, combined with women's superior morality, replaced natural rights. See, for example, Aileen Kraditor, *Up from the pedestal: selected writings in the history of American feminism* (Chicago: Quadrangle Books, 1968).
41. Liddington & Norris, *One hand tied*, pp. 44–6.
42. *Proceedings*, National Women's Trade Union League, USA, 1909, p. 29.

43. *Life and Labour* (July 1911), p. 32.
44. Richard Pankhurst, *Sylvia Pankhurst*, pp. 116–23.
45. For a full treatment of suffragette political art, see Lisa Tickner, *The spectacle of women: imagery of the suffragette campaign 1907–1914* (London: Chatto & Windus, 1987). Writing about Sylvia's work, Tickner remarks, "Curiously, her paintings of rural and urban working women are not reflected in her work for the suffrage movement, except in the WSPU membership card (c.1905–06) and an early banner that has not survived. This may be because the WSPU was already severing its links with the labor movement by 1906, and preferred an imagery which was more neutral in party political terms" (p. 34).
46. Pankhurst, *The suffragette movement*, p. 307.
47. *Ibid.*, p. 316.
48. Pankhurst, "Sylvia Pankhurst", in *Myself when young*, Margot Asquith, Countess of Oxford (ed.)(London: F. Muller, 1938), p. 302.
49. Both her letters to Keir Hardie and newspaper articles about her show 1911 and 1912 dates. IISH PP 63, Letter from Keir Hardie to Pankhurst, 11 March 1911; letter from Pankhurst to Keir Hardie, 5 February 1912; *New York Times*, 13 January 1911; 22 April 1912.
50. *New York Times*, 22 April 1912.
51. Interview with Nellie Rathbone, University of Warwick, Coventry, England 27 June 1972.
52. Pankhurst, *The suffragette movement*, p. 347.
53. E. Gurley Flynn, *Words on fire: the life and writings of Elizabeth Gurley Flynn*, R. Baxandall (ed.)(New Brunswick, New Jersey: Rutgers University Press, 1987), p. 171.
54. Unpublished MS about her trip to America, based on her letters to Keir Hardie, IISH PP 61 4a.
55. *Ibid.*
56. Pankhurst, *The suffragette movement*, pp. 349.
57. *Brooklyn Daily Eagle*, 13 January 1911.
58. *Albany Evening Journal*, 11 January 1911, *Denver Express*, 3 March 1911; *Denver Post*, 3 March 1911.
59. *Columbus Citizen*, 4 February 1911.
60. *Lawrence Daily Journal-World*, 15 March 1911.
61. *Chicago Daily News*, 21 January 1911.
62. *New York Times*, 22 April 1912.
63. Letter to Keir Hardie, IISH PP 60 1d.
64. Unpublished MS about her trip to America, IISH PP 61 4a.
65. Pankhurst to Hardie, IISH PP 591e.
66. Pankhurst, *The suffragette movement*, p. 348; interview with Richard Pankhurst (London, 17 July 1985; "The inheritance", IISH PP 194 10c.
67. Unpublished MS about her trip to America, IISH PP 4e.
68. See, for example, Vron Ware, *Beyond the pale: white women, racism, and history* (London: Verso, 1992).

69. Pankhurst, *The suffragette movement*, pp. 348.
70. IISH PP 61 4a.
71. IISH PP 62 2gd.
72. *Ibid.*
73. *Ibid.*
74. *Ibid.*
75. *Ibid.*
76. Pankhurst, *The suffragette movement*, p. 350.
77. Pankhurst to Hardie, n.d., IISH PP 591e.
78. Hardie to Pankhurst, n.d., IISH PP 63.
79. Pankhurst to Hardie, n.d., IISH PP 591e.
80. *Ibid.*
81. *Ibid.*
82. Romero, E. *Sylvia Pankhurst*, p. 37.

Chapter 2

1. The use of the word "abyss" comes from the title of Jack London's journalistic account of London's East End, *The people of the abyss* (1903; reprinted London: Journeymen Press, 1977).
2. Pankhurst, *The suffragette movement*, p. 416.
3. *Workers' Dreadnought*, 1 December 1917, 1 November 1919.
4. *Workers' Dreadnought*, 1 November 1917.
5. *Ibid.*
6. *Parliamentary Papers* [PP], 1888, 31, *Select Committee On Sweating*, fifth report (London: British Museum), p. lxxiii; PP 1890, 17, *Report on Dock Labour*, p. 505.
7. P. P., 1906, 104, *Unemployed Workmen's Act. Proceedings of the Distress Committee*, p. 507.
8. D. L. Munby, *Industry and planning in Stepney* (Oxford: Oxford University Press, 1951), p. 3.
9. Karl Marx, *Capital*, vol. 1, *A critical analysis of capitalist production* pt. 6, chs. 19, 20, 21 (New York: International Publishers, 1967), pp. 535–58.
10. Munby, *Industry and planning in Stepney*, p. 3.
11. Charles Booth as quoted in Royston Pike, *Human documents of the age of the Forsythes* (London: Allen & Unwin, 1969), p. 299.
12. *Select Committee on Sweating*, PP 1888, vol. 31, p. 569.
13. *Ibid.*
14. P. G. Hall, *The industry of London since 1861*, (London: Hutchinson, 1962), p. 61.
15. *Daily Herald*, 29 October 1912.
16. R. Sinclair, *East London* (London: Robert Hall, 1950), p. 249.
17. Judith Walkowitz, *Prostitution and Victorian society: women, class and the*

state (Cambridge: Cambridge University Press, 1989), pp. 13–22.

18. Pankhurst, *The suffragette movement*, pp. 184.

19. Dora Montefiore, *From a Victorian to a modern* (London: E. Arcer, 1927), p. 51. Montefiore was very critical of Sylvia Pankhurst's description of the early East End work because she had been active doing suffrage work in London before Annie Kenney and Sylvia Pankhurst arrived. She wrote, "The London Committee of the WSPU had been doing good work in London long before Annie Kenney arrived at the scene or Sylvia Pankhurst took the 'scantily furnished sitting room' in Chelsea." Montefiore continued, "Years afterwards, when Sylvia Pankhurst and I were in the advanced ranks of the socialist movement, I asked her one day why she had so willfully distorted facts in her so-called 'History of the Votes for Women Movement' [which appeared in *Votes for Women*, the WSPU newspaper]; and she replied that she was very young at the time and entirely under the influence of her mother, who wished my name to be suppressed; she also added that Mrs. Pethick-Lawrence had also complained to her of mis-statements in the same history." Montefiore was not appeased by Pankhurst's explanation: "Sylvia was neither a school girl nor a bread-and-butter Miss at the time she started her work in the militant movement" (p. 51).

20. Pankhurst, *The suffragette movement*, pp. 197.

21. Minute Book of the Canning Town WSPU, 27 February 1906.

22. *Ibid.*, 31 July 1906.

23. *Ibid.*, 20 January 1907.

24. Christabel Pankhurst, *Unshackled* (London: Hutchinson, 1959), pp. 67–8.

25. Minute Book of the Canning Town WSPU, 10 April 1906, 29 January 1907.

26. Gertrude Conlon to Lucy Baldock, 15 May 1912, Lucy Baldock MS, WSPU Collection (London: London Museum).

27. Letter dated 15 July 1911, Lucy Baldock MS.

28. *Daily Herald*, 14 May 1912.

29. *Ibid.*, 28 July 1912.

30. *Ibid.*

31. Pankhurst, *The suffragette movement*, pp. 416–17.

32. *Madison Democrat*, Sunday, 4 February 1912, p. 24.

33. Emerson to Pankhurst, IISH PP 3d, 1914. In that same letter Emerson wrote the following love poem:
You did not understand and in your eyes
I saw a vague surprise,
As if my voice came from some distant Sphere
Too far for you to hear;
Alas! in other days it was not so
Those days of long ago.
II.
Time was when all my being was thrown wide
All veils were drawn aside
That you might enter anywhere at will.

Now all is hushed and still
Save for a sound recurring more and more
The shutting of a door.

34. Pankhurst, *The suffragette movement*, p. 499.
35. Patricia Romero, *E. Sylvia Pankhurst*, p. 80.
36. Pankhurst, *The suffragette movement*, p. 390.
37. Ellen Spencer to George Lansbury, 26 June 1912, Lansbury Papers (London: British Library of Political and Economic Science).
38. *Daily Herald*, 2 June 1912.
39. W. Andrade to George Lansbury, 26 June 1912, Lansbury Papers.
40. *Daily Herald*, 16 November 1912.
41. *Ibid.*, 18 November 1912.
42. *Ibid.*, 4 November 1913.
43. *The Suffragette*, 15 November 1912.
44. Pankhurst, *The suffragette movement*, p. 425.
45. G. Saunders Jacobs to George Lansbury, 27 November 1912, Lansbury Papers.
46. Pankhurst, *The suffragette movement*, p. 426.
47. *Ibid.*
48. Ramelson, *The petticoat rebellion*, p. 161.
49. Pankhurst, *The suffragette movement*, pp. 423, 424.
50. *Daily Herald*, 27 November 1912.
51. *The Suffragette*, 15 November 1912.
52. *Daily Herald*, 29 October 1912.
53. *Ibid.*, 10 January 1913.

Chapter 3

1. Sylvia Pankhurst, "The woman movement of today and tomorrow", unpublished MS, IISH PP. From 1912 to December 1913, the East London Federation of the Suffragettes was a part of the Women's Social and Political Union. I refer to it in this period as the ELFS/WSPU. After its expulsion from the WSPU, I call it the ELFS.
2. ELFS Executive Minutes, 25 February 1914, IISH PP.
3. Pankhurst to Captain White, 1914, IISH PP.
4. Pankhurst to Mr Lapworth, 19 November 1913, IISH PP, p. 134.
5. Pankhurst, *The suffragette movement*, p. 439.
6. The *Daily Herald* published resolutions protesting against the sentencing. For example, the Haggerstown branch of the Dock, Wharf, Riverside, and General Workers' Union passed a resolution "protesting indignantly the sentence passed and the class bias shown in the case of the suffragists at the Thames Police Court who were charged with breaking windows at Bow

and Bromley. Such savage sentences are derogatory to the dignity of the bench", *Daily Herald*, 1 March 1913.

7. Vicinus, *Independent women*, p. 251.

8. The *Suffragette*, 28 March 1913.

9. Pankhurst to her mother, 18 March 1913, WSPU Collection (London: London Museum).

10. The *Suffragette*, 28 March 1913.

11. *Daily Herald*, 26 May 1913.

12. *Ibid.*

13. A. E. Metcalf, *A woman's effort* (Oxford: Blackwell, 1917), p. 303.

14. "Yearly report", *Woman's Dreadnought*, 2 January 1915.

15. Pankhurst, *The suffragette movement*, p. 466.

16. "Yearly report", *Woman's Dreadnought*, 2 January 1915.

17. Romero, *E. Sylvia Pankhurst*, p. 120.

18. Annie Barnes, *Tough Annie: from suffragette to Stepney councillor* (London: Stepney Books, 1980).

19. *Ibid.*

20. *Daily Herald*, 28 June 1913.

21. *Ibid.*, 14 February 1913.

22. *East London Observer*, 27 December 1913.

23. Barnes, *Tough Annie*, p. 18.

24. Interview with Nellie Rathbone, 1972.

25. As quoted in Dangerfield, *The strange death of liberal England*, p. 205.

26. *Woman's Dreadnought*, 2 January 1915.

27. *Daily Herald*, 24 July 1913.

28. Pankhurst, *The suffragette movement*, p. 482.

29. Kitty Marian MS, WSPU Collection (London: London Museum), p. 256.

30. *Daily Herald*, 29 July 1913.

31. John Cruse to Mrs Lansbury, 28 August 1913, Lansbury Papers, vol. 7, section 1, no. 91.

32. Thomas Attlee to George Lansbury, 31 July 1913, Lansbury Papers, vol. 7, section 1, no. 74.

33. *Daily Herald*, 2 August 1913.

34. *Ibid.*

35. Ben Tillett to George Lansbury, 19 November 1913, Lansbury Papers, vol. 7, section 1, no. 35.

36. Metropolitan Police Records [MEPOL] 2/1556 (London: Public Record Office).

37. The *Suffragette*, 15 August 1913.

38. *Daily Herald*, 27 August 1913.

39. *Woman's Dreadnought*, 2 January 1915.

40. Pankhurst, *The suffragette movement*, p. 478.

41. Mitchell, *The fighting Pankhursts*, p. 44.

42. *Ibid.*

43. *East End News*, 25 November 1913.
44. Pankhurst, *The suffragette movement*, p. 499.
45. The *Suffragette*, 25 July 1913.
46. IISH PP, 121 5, 27 January 1913.
47. *Daily Herald*, 2 February 1914.
48. *East London Observer*, 26 July 1913.
49. *East End News*, 17 October 1913.
50. *East London Observer*, 3 January 1914.
51. Unpublished MS, IISH PP 1992, p. 8.
52. *Ibid.*
53. *Ibid.*
54. Pankhurst, *The suffragette movement*, p. 505.
55. Pankhurst to George Lansbury, 11 November 1913, IISH PP.
56. Pankhurst, *The suffragette movement*, pp. 501; R. Cullen Owens, *Smashing times*, (Dublin: Attic Press, 1984), pp. 87–8.
57. The *Suffragette*, 11 November 1913.
58. *Daily Herald*, 30 May 1913.
59. *London Times*, 20 August 1913.
60. The *Suffragette*, 31 October 1913.
61. *Daily Herald*, 22 November 1913.
62. *Woman's Dreadnought*, 2 January 1915.
63. *East London Advertiser*, 29 November 1913.
64. *Daily Herald*, 29 October 1913.
65. *East End News*, 25 November 1913.
66. *Ibid.*
67. Pankhurst, *The suffragette movement*, p. 528.
68. Metropolitan Borough of Poplar, *Minutes of the Proceedings of the City Council, 1911–1918*, 18 December 1913, pp. 108–9.
69. Pankhurst to the *Daily Herald*, 27 January 1914, IISH PP 1215.
70. *East End News*, 16 December 1913.
71. Metropolitan Borough of Poplar, *Minutes of the Proceedings of the City Council, 1911–1918*, 20 December 1913.
72. Pankhurst to the *Daily Herald*, 9 December 1913, IISH PP 121 3b.
73. Pankhurst, *The suffragette movement*, p. 533.
74. *Ibid.*, p. 534.
75. *Daily Herald*, 21 November 1913.
76. *Ibid.* 5 February 1914.
77. *East End News*, 25 November 1913.
78. Nina Boyle to Pankhurst, 5 January 1913, IISH PP 120.
79. Quoted in Dona Torr, *Tom Mann and his times* (London: Lawrence & Wishart, 1936), p. 297.
80. Dora Montefiore, *From a Victorian to a modern*, p. 158.
81. Pankhurst, *The suffragette movement*, pp. 500–1.
82. *Ibid.*, p. 502.

83. Owens, *Smashing times*, pp. 85–8.
84. *Daily Herald*, 3 November 1913.
85. *Ibid.*
86. From Mabel Tuke, n.d. 1913, IISH PP 3b.
87. Pankhurst to WSPU branches, 19 November 1913, IISH PP 3b.
88. Kenney to WSPU branches, n.d., IISH PP 3b.
89. Christabel to Pankhurst, 11 November 1913, IISH PP 3b.
90. As quoted in Owens, *Smashing times*, p. 88.
91. Christabel to Pankhurst, IISH PP 36.
92. *Ibid.*
93. Theodora Bonwick to Pankhurst, 29 November IISH PP 113.
94. Pankhurst, *The suffragette movement*, p. 517.
95. Minute Book of the East London Federation of the Suffragettes, 27 January 1914, IISH PP 82 Tb.
96. Pankhurst, *The suffragette movement*, p. 517.
97. The *Suffragette*, 13 February 1914.
98. Elsa Dalglish to Pankhurst, 17 February 1914, IISH PP 3b.
99. *Ibid.*
100. Emmeline to Pankhurst, n.d., IISH PP 3b.
101. Pankhurst, *The suffragette movement*, p. 518.
102. Edward Francis, 2 February 1914, IISH PP 168b 22.
103. Barnes, *Tough Annie*, pp. 17–18.
104. *Ibid.* and Pankhurst, *The suffragette movement*, pp. 525–6.
105. *Woman's Dreadnought*, 2 January 1915.
106. *Ibid.*
107. I am particularly indebted to Ken Weller for this information.
108. The *Suffragette*, 24 January 1913.
109. *Daily Herald*, 31 March 1913.
110. Les Garner, *Stepping stones to women's liberty*, p. 82.
111. PP, 1912–13, 67, p. 491.
112. Asquith never explained why he met the deputation. In a letter written to a very close friend, Venetia Stanley, on 18 June 1914, he said: "Another small complication is that Sylvia Pankhurst, whom McK is letting today out of prison – she has been 8 days without food or drink – proposes to continue her 'strike' to the point of suicide, either at her home or perhaps a stretcher in Downing Street, until I receive a deputation of East End suffragists. I don't want, if I can help, to secure her the martyr's crown, but *que faire?*" (M. Brook & E. Brook, eds, *H. H. Asquith, Letters to Venetia Stanley*, Oxford: Oxford University Press, 1982, p. 89). Les Garner argues: "Perhaps it was this threat [the People's Army marching on Parliament], allied to a fear of losing votes to the Labour Party in the General Election scheduled for 1915, that lay behind Asquith's favourable reply to the ELFS deputation" (*Stepping stones*, p. 81). Romero believes the Prime Minister "finally agree[d] through an intermediary to see her deputation" because "Asquith

could not help but remember that, barely two weeks earlier, the suffragette Emily Wilding Davison had died on Derby Day after throwing herself under the King's horse on the race track" (*E. Sylvia Pankhurst*, p. 85).

113. Pankhurst, *The suffragette movement*, pp. 559–61, 580–81.
114. *Ibid.*, p. 472.
115. *Ibid.*, p. 570.
116. *Woman's Dreadnought*, 2 January 1915.
117. Pankhurst, *The suffragette movement*, p. 573.
118. *Ibid.*, p. 576, originally reported in the *Labour Leader*.
119. *Ibid.*, pp. 581–7. In his autobiography, *My life* (London: Constable, 1967), Lansbury said, "We got along very well with Lloyd George, who informed us that Sir Edward Grey, Sir John Simon and himself were willing to give a public pledge that they would decline to enter any government after the next General Election which did not make Women's Suffrage the first plank on its legislative programme" (p. 582). Sandra Stanley Holton's book, *Feminism and democracy: women's suffrage and reform politics in Britain, 1900–1918* (Cambridge: Cambridge University Press, 1986, pp. 124–5), supports Pankhurst's and Lansbury's accounts.
120. The *suffragette*, 24 July 1914.

Chapter 4

1. Pankhurst, *The home front* (London: Hutchinson, 1932), p. 11.
2. Christabel Pankhurst, *Unshackled*, p. 288.
3. Pankhurst, *The home front*, p. 66.
4. *Ibid.*
5. *Ibid.*, p. 67.
6. *Ibid.*, pp. 38, 67.
7. This count is based on the Minute Books of the ELFS/WSF. At no time do they record the specifics of membership.
8. Minute Book of the Bow Branch, 16 October 1917, 17 November, 1917, IISH PP 8211b.
9. ELFS Committee Meeting, 6 March 1915, IISH PP 821c.
10. IISH PP 8211c, 1918.
11. ELFS Committee Meeting, 6 March 1915, IISH PP 821c.
12. Ken Weller, *Don't be a soldier* (London: Journeymen Press, 1985), p. 75.
13. *Ibid.*, p. 74.
14. *Ibid.*, p. 75.
15. Jessie Stephens, "Jessie". Interview with Jessie Stephens by Suzie Fleming and Golden Dallas, in *Spare Rib Reader* (London: Penguin, 1982), pp. 558–9.
16. *Ibid.*
17. *Ibid.*

18. *Ibid.*
19. Weller, *Don't be a soldier*, p. 78.
20. ELFS Executive Committee Minutes, 6 August 1914, IISH PP
21. *Ibid.*
22. Minute Book of the WSF, 6 January 1917, IISH PP 82II 9.
23. *Woman's Dreadnought*, 17 March 1917.
24. *Glasgow Herald*, 29 October 1914.
25. *Labour Leader*, 24 December 1914.
26. Pankhurst, *The home front*, p. 36.
27. *Ibid.*, p. 185.
28. *Workers' Dreadnought*, 13 April, 20 April 1918.
29. Pankhurst, *The home front*, p. 186.
30. *Daily Herald*, August 7 1915.
31. *East London Observer*, 14 August 1915.
32. *Ibid.*, 21 August 1914.
33. Pankhurst, *The home front*, p. 230.
34. Keir Hardie to Pankhurst, 27 May 1915, IISH PP
35. Pankhurst, *The home front*, p. 227.
36. Keir Hardie to Pankhurst, 28 July 1915, IISH PP
34. IISH PP 64 (60).
38. Pankhurst, *The home front*, p. 229.
39. *Woman's Dreadnought*, 1 January 1916.
40. *Ibid.*, 15 January 1915.
41. *East London Observer*, 19 February 1916.
42. *Ibid.*, 3 March 1916.
43. ELFS/WSF Committee Meeting, 6 March 1916, IISH PP 8211b.
44. *Woman's Dreadnought*, 15 April 1916.
45. WSF Minutes, 27 March 1916, IISH PP
46. Annual General Report, 1916, IISH PP
47. *East London Observer*, 8 April 1916.
48. *Ibid.*
49. *Woman's Dreadnought*, 10 June 1916.
50. James Hinton, *The first shop stewards' movement* (London, Allen & Unwin, 1973), p. 44; Arthur Marwick, *The deluge* (London: Bodley Head, 1965), pp. 29–38.
51. *Woman's Dreadnought*, 23 December 1916; WSF Minutes, December 18 1916; IISH P. P. *East London Observer*, 23 December 1916.
52. Pankhurst to George Lansbury, June 1917, Lansbury Papers.
53. *Woman's Dreadnought*, 6 January 1917.
54. *Daily Herald*, 1 September 1917.
55. The *Call*, 8 August 1918.
56. Anne Wiltsher, *Most dangerous women* (London: Pandora, 1985), p. 1; Pankhurst *The home front*, p. 271, refers accusingly to the "WSPU with its women sticking white feathers into the buttonholes of reluctant men,

and brandishing little placards with the slogan, 'intern them all'." This has become accepted as truth. Barbara Castle's popular book *Sylvia and Christabel Pankhurst*, repeats this: "Emmeline Pankhurst toured the country, handing out white feathers to young men in civilian dress. Her battle-cry was an attack on enemy aliens: 'Intern them all'" (p. 134). David Doughey, the archivist at the Fawcett Library, told me in December 1988 that there is no corroboration for the story of the white feathers.

57. Pankhurst, *The home front*, p. 153.
58. Wiltsher, *Most dangerous women*, p. 133.
59. ELFS/WSF Committee Meeting, 18 October 1915, IISH PP 82 IIb.
60. ELFS/WSF Committee Meeting, 20 December 1915, IISH PP 82 IIb.
61. Wiltsher, *Most dangerous women*.
62. ELFS/WSF Committee Meeting, 18 October 1915, IISH PP 821e.
63. Pankhurst, *The home front*, p. 292.
64. *Ibid.*, p. 153.
65. *Daily Herald*, 4 September 1915.
66. Minute Book of General Membership, 18 October 1915, IISH PP 821c.
67. Gretta Cousins to Hannah Sheehy Skeffington, n.d. Skeffington Papers 1915 [National Library, Dublin] 22.672.
68. The *Call*, 6 July 1916.
69. *Woman's Dreadnought*, 19 and 26 May 1917.
70. Minutes of the General Meeting of the WSF, 15 January 1917, IISH PP
71. *Woman's Dreadnought*, 27 January 1917.
72. *Ibid.*, 8 August 1914.
73. Pankhurst to Hannah Sheehy Skeffington, 24 August 1914, NLD MS222, 666(v).
74. *Woman's Dreadnought*, 15 August 1914.
75. Pankhurst, *The home front*, p. 29.
76. *Daily Herald*, 24 August 1914.
77. *Justice*, 5 November 1914.
78. *East London Observer*, 20 February 1915.
79. *Daily Herald*, 17 April 1915,
80. *Woman's Dreadnought*, 17 April 1915.
81. *East London Observer*, 3 June 1915.
82. Pankhurst, *The home front*, pp. 42–3.
83. *Ibid.*
84. *Woman's Dreadnought*, 23 August 1914.
85. ELFS leaflet, 9 November 1914, NLD MS 22, 668.
86. *Daily Herald*, 4 September 1914.
87. *Woman's Dreadnought*, 2 January 1915.
88. *Ibid.*
89. Pankhurst, *The home front*, p. 131.
90. *Ibid.* Nellie Rathbone claims it was she, not Minnie Lansbury, who did all the work for Sylvia Pankhurst in this respect: "She started this thing and I

did all the work. . . . [S]o the soldiers and sailors wives and relatives came to see me and I got such intimate information about their family life . . . . [Y]ou know I spent my time writing to the War Office and goodness knows. . . . [Y]ou see, they were stranded. . . . [T]hey had no money coming through" (interview with Nellie Rathbone, 1972).

91. Pankhurst, *The home front*, p. 132.
92. *Daily Herald*, 17 October 1914.
93. *Woman's Dreadnought*, 2 January 1915.
94. *East London Observer*, 24 October 1914.
95. WSF Finance Committee, 19 January 1918, IISH PP
96. *East London Observer*, 12 June 1915.
97. Metropolitan Borough of Poplar, *Minutes of the proceedings of the council, 1911–1918*, November 1914.
98. *East London Observer*, 25 December 1915.
99. Maud Arncliffe Sennett, *The child* (London: C. W. Daniel, 1938), p. 110.
100. *Ibid.*
101. *Daily Herald*, 9 September 1914.
102. Pankhurst, *The home front*, p. 58.
103. *Woman's Dreadnought*, 2 January 1915.
104. Pankhurst, *The home front*, pp. 142–6.
105. *Ibid*, p. 150.
106. WSF Minute Book 2 November 1917, IISH PP 82IIa.
107. Rowbotham, *Hidden from history*, p. 116.
108. *Daily Herald*, 27 March 1915.
109. *Ibid.*, 24 July 1915.
110. Pankhurst, *The home front*, p. 161.
111. *East London Observer*, 18 March 1916.
112. Sennett, *The child*.
113. The *Call*, 6 July 1916.
114. *Ibid.*, 6 December 1917.
115. ELFS/WSFMinute Book,, 16 April 1917, IISH PP 48.
116. *Woman's Dreadnought*, 22 January 1916.
117. ELFS/WSFMinute Book, 5 May 1917, IISH PP 8211b.
118. *Ibid.*, 19 June 1917.
119. *Ibid.*
120. *Woman's Dreadnought*, 22 January 1916.
121. Pankhurst, *The home front*, p. 322.
122. Challinor, *The origins of British Bolshevism*, p. 169.
123. Patricia Lynch, *Rebel Ireland*, WSF Publication, 1916.
124. Hannah Sheehy Skeffington to Sylvia Pankhurst, 1932, NLD.
125. *Workers' Dreadnought*, 28 July 1917.
126. *The Dreadnought* also encouraged industrial and military sabotage, as well as a peace referendum for the troops. Not surprisingly, the paper was raided by British authorities in 1916 and 1918 WSF Minutes, 12 October

1917, IISH PP; *Woman's Dreadnought*, 31 January 1917.

127. *Solidarity*, July 1917

128. Pankhurst to H. Bryan, 27 March 1918, ILP General Correspondence, vol. 5.5. p.157.

Chapter 5

1. *Womans' Dreadnought*, 2 June 1917.

2. *Workers' Dreadnought*, 1 June 1918.

3. Bow Members, Meeting, 5 May 1919, IISH PP 8211c.

4. This figure was ascertained from the total number of members' names that appear in the WSF Committee Minutes.

5. *Workers' Dreadnought*, 1 February 1919.

6. *Womans' Dreadnought*, 8 January 1916.

7. WSF, Committee Meeting Notebook, 17 February 1916, IISH PP

8. *Workers' Dreadnought*, 9 March 1918. Three issues of the *Record* appeared between October and December 1917. According to Home Office records, the Newspaper Restriction Order of February 1918 suppressed the paper.

9. *Workers' Dreadnought*, 13 July, 20 July 1918.

10. *Ibid.*, 24 August 1918.

11. *Ibid.*, 7 September 1918.

12. *Ibid.*, 18 January 1919.

13. *Ibid.*

14. *Ibid.*, 1 February 1915.

15. Harry Pollitt, *Serving my time* (London: Lawrence & Wishart, 1967), p. 111.

16. *Ibid.*

17. *Workers' Dreadnought*, 15 February, 1919.

18. *Ibid.*

19. *Ibid.*

20. Challinor, *The origins of British Bolshevism*, p. 200.

21. *Workers' Dreadnought*, 22 February 1919.

22. Cabinet Papers 24 GT 6976, 10 April 1919.

23. CAB 24 GT 6916, 2 February 1919.

24. *Solidarity*, September 1919.

25. *Workers' Dreadnought*, 4 October, 1919.

26. Pankhurst "In the red twilight", IISH PP 65. p. 1. Soermus was an active member of the PRIB until he was arrested. Prison officials took away his violin until he hunger-struck. After it was returned, he played for other prisoners and composed the "Song of Sorrows".

27. Interview with Nellie Rathbone, 1972.

28. CAB 24/ GT 5923 7 October 1918.

29. *Ibid.*

30. *Workers' Dreadnought*, 25 January 1919.
31. *Ibid.*; CAB 24/ CP 1355 27 May 1920.
32. *Workers' Dreadnought*, 25 January 1919.
33. Bow Members Meeting, 19 May 1919, IISH PP 8211c.
34. CAB 24/ 84 GT 7790 24 July 1919.
35. *Workers' Dreadnought*, 15 May 1920.
36. Pollitt, *Serving my time*, p. 111.
37. CAB 24 CP/ 455, 2 February 1920.
38. Pollitt, *Serving my time*, p. 111.
39. CAB 24 CP/ 455 2 February 1920.
40. Pollitt, *Serving my time*, p. 110.
41. *Workers' Dreadnought*, 15 May 1920.
42. Pollitt, *Serving my time*, p. 109.
43. Kendall, *The revolutionary movement in Britain*, pp. 188–90.
44. *Workers' Dreadnought*, 9 November, 1918.
45. G. D. H. Cole and Raymond Postgate, *The common people 1746–1946* (London: Methuen, 1971), p. 488.
46. Quoted in Lucia Jones, "The red twilight: Sylvia Pankhurst and the Workers' Socialist Federation, 1918–24" MA thesis, University of Warwick, Coventry, England, 1973, p. 57.
47. CAB 24 GT 6976, 10 April 1919.
48. CAB 24/ CP 2455, 20 May 1920.
49. Ibid.
50. "A survey of revolutionary Movements in Great Britain in the year 1920", CAB 24/ CP 2455, Report for August 1919.
51. *Solidarity*, October 1919.
52. *Solidarity*, May 1919.
53. Noreen Branson, *Poplarism, 1919–1925: George Lansbury and the councillors' revolt* (London: Lawrence & Wishart, 1980), pp. 116–17.
54. CAB 24 3309 15 September 1921.
55. Hannington, *Unemployed struggles 1919–36: my life struggles amongst the unemployed* (London: Lawrence & Wishart, 1977), pp. 151–2.
56. Branson, *Poplarism, 1919–1925*, p. 23.
57. *Ibid.*, pp. 22–8.
58. Cole and Postgate, *The common people*, pp. 216–20.
59. Weller, *Don't be a soldier*, p. 77.
60. Branson, *Poplarism, 1919–1925*, p. 124.
61. *Workers' Dreadnought*, 9 November 1920.
62. *Ibid.*, 16 October 1920.
63. Claude McKay, *A long way from home* (New York: Harvest Books, 1970), p. 74.
64. *Ibid.*, p. 75.
65. I am indebted to Ken Weller for this information.
66. McKay, *A long way from home*, p. 74.
67. *Workers' Dreadnought*, 20 October 1920.

68. Sylvia Pankhurst's Appeal, IISH PP 140, pp.16–17.
69. McKay, *A long way from home*, p. 77.
70. *Ibid.*, p. 85.
71. Pankhurst, "In the red twilight", p. x.
72. *Vanguard*, November 1920.
73. V. I. Lenin, *On Britain* (Moscow: Foreign Language Publications, 1941), p. 496.
74. Sylvia Pankhurst's Appeal, p. 62.
75. *Glasgow Herald*, 31 May 1921.
76. Pankhurst, *Writ on a cold slate* (London: Workers' Dreadnought Publishers, 1921).
77. *Glasgow Herald*, 31 May 1921.

Chapter 6

1. *Woman's Dreadnought*, 30 June 1917.
2. *Communist International*, no. 2, June 1919.
3. *Ibid.*, no. 3, July 1919; no. 4, August 1919.
4. Gwyn Williams, "Proletarian forms", *New Edinburgh Review: Gramsci councils and communism, 1919. A documentary analysis* no. 26 (1974), p. 51.
5. Pankhurst, "In the red twilight".
6. *Ibid.*
7. WSF Minute Book, 19 March 1917, IISH P. P. 82 a & b.
8. *Ibid.*
9. *Woman's Dreadnought* 14 July 1917.
10. *Ibid.*, 31 March 1917.
11. *Ibid.*, 26 December 1914.
12. *Ibid.*, 24 April 1915.
13. *Ibid.*, 18 December 1914.
14. *Ibid.*, 30 June 1917.
15. *Ibid.*, 24 March 1917.
16. *Ibid.*, 2 June 1917.
17. *Worker's Dreadnought*, 28 July 1917.
18. *Ibid.*, 11 August 1917.
19. *Ibid.*, 26 January 1918.
20. *Ibid.*
21. Sylvia Francini, *Sylvia Pankhurst 1912–1924. Dal Suffragismo all Rivoluzione Sociale* (Pisa: ETS Press, 1980), pp. 170–72 (translated for Barbara Winslow by Alex Burgo); *New Times and Ethiopia News*, 23 January 1954.
22. Romero, E. *Sylvia Pankhurst*, pp. 159–60. During Pankhurst's relationship with Corio, she had little contact with Roxanne. In the 1920s, Roxanne

wrote to Pankhurst asking for financial help to study at the London School of Economics (Roxanne to Pankhurst, n.d., IISH P. P.).

23. Francini, *Sylvia Pankhurst*. p. 171.

24. *Ibid.*

25. Interview with Nellie Rathbone, 1972.

26. Mitchell, *The fighting Pankhursts*, p. 314.

27. *New Times and Ethiopia News*. 23 January 1954. In the 1930s, Pankhurst wrote a short story, called "The angel in the house", about the marriage of a couple named Mary and Bill and their son Jim. The marriage has serious difficulties because Mary is the principal breadwinner and Robert does not do his share of work around the house. During the period in question, Pankhurst wrote many short stories that are in part autobiographical, and so it seems that there were conflicts regarding their domestic arrangements (IISH PP 224 32).

28. A cogent analysis and description of Italian revolutionary politics can be found in John Cammett, *Antonio Gramsci and the origins of Italian communism* (Stanford, California: Stanford University Press, 1967).

29. *Ibid.*, p. 69.

30. Quoted in Serrati's *Communismo*, "Impressionnioni sul Congresso di Bologna", 1–15 December 1919, and Andreina de Clemeti, *Amadeo Bordiga* (Turin: Piccola Biblioteca Einaudi, 1971), p. 112. Translations of both were prepared by Alex Burgo.

31. "How Hitler rose to power", *New Times and Ethiopia News*, September 1938.

32. Gwyn Williams, "Proletarian Forms: Antonio Gramsci and the Turin movement of factory councils and the origins of Italian communism", *New Edinburgh Review*, no. 25 (1974), pp. 52–76, and "Proletarian forms: Gramsci's councils and communism, 1919. A documentary analysis", *New Edinburgh Review*, no. 26 (1974), pp. 48–116.

33. *Ibid.*, no. 26, p. 84.

34. *Ibid.*, no. 25, p. 73.

35. *Ibid.*, no. 26, p. 70.

36. *Ibid.* p. 86.

37. *Workers' Dreadnought*, 21 February 1920.

38. Pankhurst, "The inheritance", pt. 2.

39. Pankhurst, "In the red twilight".

40. Pankhurst, "The inheritance".

41. *Ibid.*

42. Pankhurst, "In the red twilight".

43. Pankhurst, "The inheritance".

44. *Ibid.*

45. *Ibid.*

46. *Ibid.*

47. *Ibid.*

48. Walter Kendall, *The revolutionary movement in Britain*. pp. 174–6, and *What happened at Leeds. A report of the Leeds convention* (London: Pelican Press, 1917), edited by Ken Coates for the Archives of Trade Union History and Theory Series No. 4 (no date).

49. "When I sat with the present Prime Minister on the Workers' and Soldiers' Councils", unpublished article, n.d., IISH PP 214.

50. *Woman's Dreadnought*, 9 June 1917.

51 *Workers' Dreadnought*, 21 July 1917.

52. "When I sat with the present Prime Minister on the Workers' and Soldiers' Councils" IISH P.P 214.

53. *Ibid.*

54. *Workers' Dreadnought*, 21 July 1918.

55. *Ibid.*, 26 January 1918.

56. *Ibid.*

57. *Ibid.*, 3 August 1918.

58. Hinton, *The first shop stewards' movement*, pp. 319–20.

59. *Ibid.*, p. 321.

60. CAB/ 24 P 902, 18 March 1920.

61. Hinton, *The first shop stewards' movement*, p. 321.

62. *Workers' Dreadnought*, 20 March 1920; CAB/ 24 OP 960, 25 March 1920.

63. *Workers' Dreadnought*, 27 March 1920.

64. *Ibid.*

65. *East London Advertiser*, 20 March 1920.

66. *Workers' Dreadnought*, 27 March 1920.

67. *Ibid.*, 19 June 1920.

68. *Ibid.*, 27 March 1920.

69. Her personal life did not mirror her writings. According to David Mitchell in *The fighting Pankhursts* (pp. 246–7), Corio did most of the cooking and housework, leaving Pankhurst to earn money writing.

70. *Workers' Dreadnought*, 24 July 1920.

71. Pankhurst, "The inheritance".

72. Sylvia Pankhurst, *Soviet Russia as I saw it* (London: Workers' Dreadnought Publishers, 1921), pp. 36–7.

73. *Ibid.*, p. 41.

74. *Ibid.*

75. Lenin, *On Britain*, p. 201.

76. Challinor, *The origins of British Bolshevism*, p. 216.

77. Lenin, *On Britain*, p. 269.

78. Pankhurst, *Soviet Russia as I saw it*, p. 48.

79. Undated untitled manuscript, a draft for "In the red twilight", IISH PP 126 716.

80. Pankhurst to an unnamed anarchist, n.d. 1921. A copy is in the possession of the author.

81. Alfred Rosmer, *Lenin's Moscow* (London: Pluto Press, 1971), p. 76.

82. Lenin finished *Left wing communism* on 20 April but it was not published in English until July. Extracts were published in the *Call* on 29 July. Harry McShane, a Scottish revolutionary and colleague of John Maclean, was not in agreement with Lenin's pamphlet: "I think that Lenin's *Left wing communism: an infantile disorder* showed an over anxiety to support the BSP against people like Sylvia Pankhurst. Many of the people of the BSP weren't very good" (Joan Smith & Harry McShane, *Harry McShane: no mean fighter* (London: Pluto Press, 1978) p. 120).

83. Pankhurst to an unnamed anarchist, 1921.

84. *Ibid.*

85. Pankhurst, "In the red twilight".

86. Interview with Nellie Rathbone, 1972.

87. *Workers' Dreadnought*, 7 December 1918.

88. WSF General Minutes, January 1917–March 1920, p. 48.

89. WSF Committee Minutes, IISH PP 90.

90. *Ibid.*

91. *Communist International*, September 1919.

92. Pankhurst, *Soviet Russia as I saw it*, p. 46.

93. Minute Book, 26 May 1918, IISH PP 82IIa.

94. WSF Committee Minutes, 9 May 1920, IISH PP

95. Kendall, *The revolutionary movement in Britain*, p. 386, n. 7.

96. Hinton, *The first shop stewards' movement*, pp. 298–9.

97. WSF Minute Book, 26 June 1919, IISH PP 90.

98. *Workers' Dreadnought*, 21 February 1920.

99. The *Call*, 2 February 1920.

100. *Workers' Dreadnought*, 21 February 1920.

101. *Ibid*, 22 May 1920.

102. *Ibid*, 23 September 1922, WSF Minute Book, 14 May 1920, IISH, PP 90.

103. Challinor, *The origins of British Bolshevism*, p. 243.

104. Draft of a letter by Sylvia Pankhurst, 1920, IISH PP

105. Pankhurst to an unnamed anarchist, 1921.

106. Interview with May O'Callaghan (part of Nellie Rathbone interview, 1972).

107. First CP(BSTI) circular to branches, n.d., IISH PP 125.

108. CAB 24/105 CP 1239.

109. CAB 24/118 CP 2429.

110. Challinor, *The origins of British Bolshevism*, p. 246.

111. Sylvia Pankhurst to an unnamed person, n.d., 128 IISH PP 56a.

112. Edgar Whitehead to Pankhurst, 9 December 1920, IISH PP 56a.

113. William Gallacher to Sylvia Pankhurst, n.d., IISH PP 56a.

114. *Workers' Dreadnought*, 27 November 1920.

115. Pankhurst, n.d., IISH PP 56a.

116. Interview with May O'Callaghan (part of Rathbone interview, 1972).

117. Letter and Notes of Joe Thurgood to May O'Callaghan, IISH PP 56a.

118. Edgar Whitehead to Sylvia Pankhurst, 16 January 1921, IISH PP 56a.
119. CAB 24/128 CP 3380.
120. Challinor, *The origins of British Bolshevism*, p. 273.
121. *Ibid.*, p. 250.
122. Pankhurst to unnamed person, n.d. p. 128, IISH PP 56a.
123. *Workers' Dreadnought,* 17 September 1921.
124. *Ibid.*
125. *Ibid.*
126. *Ibid.*
127. *Ibid.*

Chapter 7

1. *Workers' Dreadnought*, 17 September 1921.
2. CAB 24 128.
3. *Workers' Dreadnought*, 24 September 1921.
4. This should not be confused with the Fourth International founded by Leon Trotsky in 1939.
5. Unpublished letter, 1921, IISH PP
6. *Ibid.*
7. *Workers' Dreadnought*, 3 June 1922.
8. *Ibid.*, 1 October 1921.
9. Unpublished letter, 1921, IISH PP
10. *Ibid.*
11. *Workers' Dreadnought*, 31 May 1924.
12. CAB 24 CP/4171, 24 August 1922.
13. *Ibid.*
14. Pankhurst to an unnamed anarchist, n.d., probably 1921.
15. CAB 24 CP 4171, 24 August 1922.
16. CAB 24 CP 4138, 7 September 1922.
17. *Ibid.* According to Home Office reports, a revolutionary named A. B. Dunbar informed Sylvia about the South African comrades who were selling the *Dreadnought* and contributing money to the paper.
18. *Workers' Dreadnought*, 22 October 1921.
19. CAB 24/13 CP 163/ 4302, 13 July 1922.
20. CAB 24/138 CP 165/ 4132 27 July 1922.
21. To John Maclean, no specific date, probably 1923, Maclean Papers, National Library of Scotland, Edinburgh, ACC 4251/51.
22. *Workers' Dreadnought*, 16 July 1921.
23. Quoted in Challinor, *The origins of British Bolshevism*, p. 270.
24. *Workers' Dreadnought*, 16 July 1921.
25. *Ibid.*, 20 July 1921.
26. Jones, "In the red twilight," p. 52.

27. *Workers' Dreadnought*, 4 March 1923.
28. *Ibid.*, 7 July 1923.
29. *Ibid.*
30. *Ibid.*, 28 July 1923.
31. *Ibid.*, 18 August 1923; 4 August 1923.
32. *Ibid.*, 1 September 1923.
33. *Ibid.*, 29 September 1923.
34. Branson, *Popularism, 1919–1925*, p. 192.
35. *Workers' Dreadnought*, 6 October 1923.
36. *Ibid.*
37. *Ibid.*, 19 January 1923.
38. *Ibid.*, 6 October 1923.
39. *Ibid.*, 13 October 1923.
40. Nan Milton, *John Maclean* (Pluto Press, 1973), p. 300.
41. Branson, *Poplarism, 1919–1925*, p. 193.
42. *Workers' Dreadnought*, 9 January 1924.
43. *Ibid.*, 19 January 1924
44. *Ibid.*, 13 August, 1921.
45. *Ibid.*, 18 February, 1921.
46. Thanks to Paul Avrich for this information.
47. *Workers' Dreadnought*, 22 September 1923.
48. *Ibid.*, 19 August 1922.
49. *Ibid.*, 17 March 1924; 24 March 1923; 26 May 1923; 4 November 1923; 11 November 1923.
50. *Workers' Dreadnought*, 31 March 1923; 26 May 1923.
51. Mitchell, *The fighting Pankhursts*, p. 109.
52. Pankhurst "In the days of my youth," n.d., IISH PP 30.

Chapter 8

1. The four sources used for this brief synopsis of Sylvia Pankhurst's life after 1924 are Romero, *E. Sylvia Pankhurst*; David Mitchell, *The fighting Pankhursts*; Richard Pankhurst, introduction to *The suffragette movement* (London: Virago, 1977); and Richard Pankhurst, *Sylvia Pankhurst*.
2. Pankhurst to Teresa Billington-Greig, n.d. (London: Fawcett Library).

Bibliography

Personal papers

Crawfurd, Helen. MS. (Marx Memorial Library, London).
Independent Labour Party General Correspondence (British Library of Political and Economic Science, London).
Lansbury, George. Papers (British Library of Political and Economic Science, London).
Maclean, John. Papers (National Library of Scotland, Edinburgh).
National American Women's Suffrage Association. Papers (Library of Congress, Washington D.C.).
Pankhurst, Christabel, Emmeline, and Sylvia. Miscellaneous letters (Fawcett Library, London).
Pankhurst, Sylvia. Papers (International Institute for Social History, Amsterdam).
Skeffington, Hannah Sheehy. Papers (National Library, Dublin).
WSPU Collection (London Museum, London).
WSPU Collection (People's Palace, Glasgow).

Government publications

Cabinet Papers. CAB 24/57 – CAB 24/140 *Reports on revolutionary organisations in the United Kingdom.*
Home Office Papers. HO 45/331.366; HO 45/356.800; HO 45/432.652; HO 45/ 236.973 (London: Public Record Office).
Metropolitan Police Records. MEPOL 2/1488; 2/1526; 2/1551; 2/1556; 2/560; 2/1571; 2/1568; 2/1016; 2/1956; 2/1957; 2/1962; 2/1963 (London: Public Record Office).
Parliamentary Papers (British Museum).
PP 1912–1913, 111–113, 1913, 75–80, *General report and return of the census of England and Wales (1911).*
PP 1890, 17, *Report on dock labour.*

PP 1908, 92 (483), *Report to the President of the Local Board on dock labour in relation to poor relief.*

PP 1911, 62 (679), *Return showing with regard to each parliamentary constituency in the United Kingdom the total number, and, as far as possible, the number in each class of electors on the Register for the year 1911.*

PP 1912-13, 67, *Return showing to each parliamentary constituency in the United Kingdon the total number of electors on the register now in force, and also shaping the population of each constituency.*

PP 1919, 40 (242), *Return showing the numbers of parliamentary and local government electors on the register of electors for the United Kingdom which came into force on the 15th Day of October 1919.*

PP 1888, vol 31, *Select Committee on Sweating.*

PP 1906, 104, *Unemployed Workmen's Act, Proceedings of the Distress Committee.*

Other reports

British Socialist Party. *Report of the annual conference of the British Socialist Party.* (London: Marx Memorial Library, 1912, 1913, 1914, 1918) .

Deputation of the Unemployed to the Right Honorable A. J. Balfour, MP. *Proceedings* (London: Twentieth Century Press, 1905).

Dock, Wharf, Riverside, and General Workers' Union. *Annual reports.* (London: Trades Union Congress House, 1911, 1912, 1913).

Independent Labour Party. *Report of annual conference* (London: Marx Memorial Library, 1911, 1914)

Metropolitan Borough of Poplar. *Annual report of the year 1901 on the sanitary conditions of Poplar.*

Metropolitan Borough of Poplar. *Annual report for the year 1903.*

Metropolitan Borough of Poplar. *Minutes of the proceedings of the council 1911-1918.*

Minute Book of the Canning Town WSPU, 1906-07 (London: London Museum).

National Women's Trade Union League, USA. *Proceedings.* 1909.

Poplar Borough Municipal Alliance. *The breakdown of local government: The story of Poplar, 1922.*

United Kingdom. War Office, *Women's War Work* (London: His Majesty's Stationary Office, 1916).

What Happened at Leeds: A Report of the Leeds Convention, 3 June, 1917 (London: Pelican Press, 1917). Edited by Ken Coates for the Archives of Trade Union History and Theory Series No. 4 (n.d.).

Women's Industrial Council, *Women's Work.* (London: TUC House, 1911, 1914, 1915).

Women's Labour League, *Annual Report* (London: TUC House, 1911, 1914, 1915).

Women's Trade Union League, *Minutes of the Proceedings of the Executive Committee* (TUC House, 1912–14).

Newspapers

Albany Evening Journal, 1911
Big Stick, 1920
British Socialist, 1915
Brooklyn Daily Eagle 1911
Call, 1916–18
Chicago Daily News, 1911
Clarion, 1912–18
Columbus Citizen, 1911
The Communist, 1918–22
The Communist International
Daily Herald, 1912–18
Denver Express, 1911
Denver Post, 1911
East End News, 1912–18
East End Advertiser, 1913
East London Observer, 1912–18
Germinal, 1924
Glasgow Herald, 1915–21
ILP News, 1903
Justice, 1912–17
Labour Leader, 1912–13
Lawrence Daily Journal-World, 1911–12
Life and Labour, 1910–14
Link, 1912–13
Madison Democrat, 1911
Manchester Guardian, 1912–24
New Statesman, 1914–20
New Times and Ethiopia News, 1936–54
New York Times, 1911, 1912
Out of Work, 1921
Pall Mall Gazette, 1909
Socialist, 1918–21
Solidarity, 1917–21
Suffragette, 1912–14
The Times, 1905–24
Votes for Women, 1912
Votes, 1912–14
Woman's Dreadnought, 1914–28 July 1917

Workers' Dreadnought, 28 July 1917–24
Vanguard, 1918
Young Socialist, 1912–18

Interviews

Pankhurst, Richard. Interview with author (London, 17 July 1985).
Rathbone, Nellie. Interview, University of Warwick, Coventry, (England, 27 June 1972).

Unpublished manuscripts

Jones, Lucia. *The red twilight: Sylvia Pankhurst and the Workers' Socialist Federation, 1918–1924* (MA thesis, University of Warwick, 1973).
Stevens, Carolyn. *A suffragette and a man: Sylvia Pankhurst's personal and political relationship with Kier Hardie, 1892–1915* (PhD dissertation, University of Rochester, New York, 1986).
Winslow, Barbara. *Sylvia Pankhurst and the East London Federation of the Suffragettes, 1912–1914* (MA thesis, University of Warwick, 1971).
—, *Sylvia Pankhurst in the East End of London, 1912–1924* (PhD dissertation, University of Washington, 1990)

Secondary sources

Alberti, J. *Beyond suffrage: feminists in war and peace* (New York: St Martin's Press, 1898).
Andrews, I. & Hobbs, M. *Economic effects of the war upon women and children in Great Britain* (New York: Oxford University Press, 1918).
Barnes, A. (in conversation with Kate Harding and Caroline Gibbs). *Tough Annie: from suffragette to Stepney councillor* (London: Stepney Books, 1980).
Benn, C. *Keir Hardie* (London, Hutchinson, 1992).
Billington-Greig, T. *The militant suffragette movement* (London: Frank Palmer, 1911).
Blewitt, N. The franchise in the United Kingdom. *Past and Present* 32 (December 1965), pp. 27–56.
Branson, N. *Poplarism, 1918–1925: George Lansbury and the councillors' revolt* (London: Lawrence & Wishart, 1980).
Briggs, A. & Saville, J. *Essays in labour history, 1886–1923* (London: Macmillan, 1971).
Brock, M. & E. Brock (eds). *H. H. Asquith. Letters to Venetia Stanley* (Oxford:

Oxford University Press, 1982).

Broodbank, Sir Joseph. *History of the port of London* (London:Daniel O' Connor, 1921).

Bullock, I. Review of Patricia W. Romero, *Sylvia Pankhurst: portrait of a radical*. *History Workshop Journal* 26 (Autumn 1988), pp. 204–7.

Cammett, J. *Antonio Gramsci and the origins of Italian communism* (Stanford, California: Stanford University Press, 1967).

Castle, B. *Sylvia and Christabel Pankhurst* (London: Penguin Books, Lives of Modern Women Series, 1987).

Challinor, R. *The origins of British Bolshevism* (London: Croom Helm, Rowman & Littlefield, 1977).

Cole, G. D. H. & R. Postgate, *The common people, 1746–1946* (London: Methuen, 1971).

Cooke, Blanche Wiesen. Women alone stir my imagination: lesbianism and the cultural tradition. *Signs* 4 (1979), pp. 718–39.

Dangerfield, G. *The strange death of liberal England* (New York: Capricorn, 1961).

Dodd, K. *A Sylvia Pankhurst reader* (Manchester: Manchester University Press, 1993).

Drake, B. *Women and trade unions* (London: Labour Research Department, 1921).

Edmondson, L. Sylvia Pankhurst: suffragist, feminist or socialist? In *European women on the left: socialism, feminism and the problems faced by political women, 1880 to the present*, Jane Slaughter & Robert Kern (eds) (Westport, Connecticut: Greenwood Press, 1981).

Fawcett, M. *The women's victory and after* (London: Sidgewick & Jackson, 1920).

Flynn, E. Gurley. *Words on fire: the life and writings of Elizabeth Gurley Flynn*, Rosalyn Baxandall (ed.) (New Brunswick, N.J.: Rutgers University Press, 1987).

Francini, S. *Sylvia Pankhurst – 1912–1924, Dal Suffragismo alla Rivoluzione Sociale* (Pisa, Italy: ETS Press, 1980).

Freid, A. & R. Elman, *Charles Booth's London* (New York: Pantheon Books, 1968).

Gallacher, W. *Revolt on the Clyde* (London: Lawrence & Wishart, 1936).

Garner, L. *Stepping stones to women's liberty: Feminist ideas in the women's suffrage movement 1900–1918* (London: Heinemann Educational Books, 1984).

Graubard, S. R. *British labour and the Russian revolution, 1917–1924* (Oxford: Oxford University Press, 1956).

Graves, P. *Labour women: women in British working-class politics, 1918–1939* (Cambridge: Cambridge University Press, 1994).

Graves, R. *Goodbye to all that* (Harmondsworth: Pelican, 1966).

Hall, P. G. *The industry of London since 1861* (London: Hutchinson, 1962).

Hannam, J. *Isabella Ford* (New York: Basil Blackwell, 1989).

Hannington, W. *Unemployed struggles 1919–36: my life struggles amongst the unemployed* (London: Lawrence & Wishart, 1977)

—. *The first shop stewards' movement* (London: Allen & Unwin, 1973).

Hinton, J. *Labour and socialism: a history of the British labour movement, 1867–1974* (London: Wheatsheaf Books, 1983).

Holton, S. Stanley. *Feminism and democracy: women's suffrage and reform politics in Britain, 1900–1918* (Cambridge: Cambridge University Press, 1986).

Howart, E. G. & M. Wilson, *West Ham: a study in social and industrial problems* (Outer London Inquiry Committee, 1907).

Jones, G. Stedman. *Outcast London* (Oxford: Oxford University Press, 1971).

Kamm, J. *Rapiers and battleaxes* (London: Allen & Unwin, 1966).

Kapp, Y. *Eleanor Marx*, 2 vols (New York: Pantheon, 1972).

Kendall, W. *The revolutionary movement in Britain 1900–1929* (London: Weidenfeld & Nicolson, 1969).

Kenney, A. *Memories of a militant* (London: Edward Arnold, 1924).

King, E. *The Scottish woman's suffrage movement* (Glasgow: The People's Palace Museum, 1978).

Klugman, J. *Formation and early years, 1919–1924*, vol. 1, *A history of the Communist Party of Great Britain* (London: Lawrence & Wishart, 1988).

—. *The general strike, 1925–19*, vol. 2, *A history of the Communist Party of Great Britain* (London: Lawrence & Wishart, 1988).

Kraditor, A. *Up from the pedestal; selected writings in the history of American feminism* (Chicago: Quadrangle Books, 1968).

Lansbury, G. *My life* (London: Constable 1967).

Lenin, V. I. *On Britain* (Moscow: Foreign Language Publications, 1941).

—. *Left wing communism: an infantile disorder* (Moscow: Foreign Language Publications, 1920).

Liddington, J. *The life and times of a respectable rebel: Selena Cooper* (London: Virago, 1984).

—. The Women's Peace Crusade. In *Over our dead bodies: women against the bomb* (London: Virago, 1983).

Liddington, J. & J. Norris. *One hand tied behind us: the rise of the women's suffrage movement* (London: Virago, 1978).

Lipman, V. D. *Social history of the Jews in England, 1850–1950* (London: Watts 1954).

London, J. *The people of the abyss* (London: Journeymen Press, 1977).

MacFarlane, L. J. *The British Communist Party* (London: MacGibbon & Kee, 1966).

McKay, C. *A long way from home* (New York: Harvest Books, 1970).

Maclean, J. *In the rapids of revolution*, Nan Milton (ed.) (London: Allison & Busby, 1978).

Marcus, J. (ed.) *Suffrage and the Pankhursts* (London: Routledge & Kegan Paul, 1987).

Marwick, A. *The deluge* (London: Bodley Head, 1965).

Marx, K. *A critical analysis of capitalist production*, vol. 1 of *Capital* (New York: International Publishers, 1967).

Metcalfe, A. E. *A woman's effort* (Oxford: Blackwell, 1917).

Milton, N. *John Maclean* (London: Pluto Press, 1973).

Mitchell, D. *The fighting Pankhursts* (London: Jonathan Cape, 1966).

—. *Women on the warpath* (London: Jonathan Cape, 1966).

—. *Queen Christabel* (London: MacDonald & James, 1977).

Mitchell, H. *The hard way up: the autobiography of Hannah Mitchell* (London: Virago, 1977).

Montefiore, D. *From a Victorian to a modern* (London: E. Arcer, 1927).

Morgan, K. *Keir Hardie: radical and socialist* (London: Weidenfeld & Nicolson, 1975).

Munby, D. L. *Industry and planning in Stepney* (Oxford: Oxford University Press, 1951).

Murphey, J. T. *Preparing for power* (London: Pluto Press, 1972).

—. *The worker's committee: an outline of its principle and structure* (London: Pluto Press, 1972).

Owens, Rosemary Cullen. *Smashing times, a history of the Irish woman's suffrage movement, 1889–1922* (Dublin Attic Press, 1984).

Pankhurst, C. *Unshackled* (London: Hutchinson, 1959).

Pankhurst, E. *My own story* (London: Eveleigh Nash, 1914).

—. *Suffrage speeches from the dock* (London: WSPU 1912).

Pankhurst, E. Sylvia. *The suffragette* (London: Gay & Hancock, 1911).

—. *The birth rate* (London: Workers' Dreadnought Publishers, 1921).

—. *Soviet Russia as I saw it* (London: Workers' Dreadnought Publishers, 1921).

—. *Writ on a cold slate* (London: Workers' Dreadnought Publishers, 1921).

—. *India and the earthly paradise* (Bombay: Sunshine Publishing, 1926).

—. *Delphos, or the future of international language* (London: Kegan Paul, 1927)

—. *Save the mothers* (New York: Alfred A. Knopf, 1930).

—. *The suffragette movement* (London: Longmans, Green, 1931).

—. *The home front* (London: Hutchinson, 1932).

—. *The life of Emmeline Pankhurst* (London: T. Werner Laurie, 1935).

—. Some autobigraphical notes, in vol. 1 of *Yearbook international archives of the women's movement*, pp. 89–98 (Leiden: E. J. Brill, 1937).

—. Sylvia Pankhurst. In *Myself when young*, Margot Asquith, Countess of Oxford (ed.) (London: F. Muller, 1938).

Pankhurst, R. *Sylvia Pankhurst: artist and crusader* (London: Paddington Press Ltd., 1979).

Pelling, H. *Social geography of British elections, 1885–1910* (New York: St Martins Press, 1967).

Pethick-Lawrence, E. *My part in a changing world* (London: Victor Gollancz, 1938).

Pike, R. *Human documents of the age of the Forsytes* (London: Allen & Unwin, 1969).

Pollitt, H. *Serving my time* (London: Lawrence & Wishart, 1967).

Postgate, R. *The life of George Lansbury* (London: Longman, Green, 1951).

Potter, B. *Beatrice Webb's diaries, 1912–1924* (London: Longmans, Green, 1952).

Pribicevic, B. *The shop stewards' movement and workers' control, 1910–1922* (Oxford: Blackwell, 1959).

Raeburn, A. *The militant suffragettes* (London: Michael Joseph, 1973).

Ramelson, M. *The petticoat rebellion* (London: Lawrence & Wishart, 1967).

Reed, J. *Ten days that shook the world* (New York: Vintage, 1960).

Rendall, J. (ed.) *Equal or different: women's politics 1800–1914* (Oxford: Basil Blackwell, 1987).

Richardson, M. *Laugh a defiance* (London: Weidenfeld & Nicolson, 1953).

Romero, P. E. *Sylvia Pankhurst: a portrait of a radical* (New Haven, Connecticut: Yale University Press, 1986).

Rose, M. *The East End of London* (London: The Grosset Press, 1951).

Rosen, A. *Rise up women! The militant campaign of the women's social and political union, 1903–1914* (London: Routledge & Kegan Paul, 1974).

Rosmer, A. *Lenin's Moscow* (London: Pluto Press, 1971).

Rover, C. *Women's suffrage and party politics in Britain, 1866–1914* (London: Routledge & Kegan Paul, 1967).

Rowbotham, S. *Women resistance and revolution* (New York: Pantheon, 1972).

—. *Hidden from history* (New York: Pantheon, 1973).

—. *Friends of Alice Wheeldon* (London: Pluto Press, 1986).

Rowbotham, S. & J. Weeks. *Socialism and the new life: the personal and sexual politics of Edward Carpenter and Havelock Ellis* (London: Pluto Press, 1977).

Sennett, Maud Arncliffe. *The child* (London: C. W. Daniel, 1938).

Sinclair, R. *East London* (London: Robert Hall, 1950).

Sirianni, C. *Workers' control and soviet democracy: the soviet experience* (London: New Left Books, 1982).

Smith, Herbert Llwellyn. *The new survey of London life and labour* (London: P. S. King & Son, 1930).

Smith J. & H. McShane. *Harry McShane: no mean fighter* (London: Pluto Press, 1978).

Smith-Rosenberg, C. The female world of love and ritual: relations between women in nineteenth century America. *Signs* 1 (Autumn 1975), pp. 1–30.

—. Review of Martha Vicinus, "Independent women: work and community for single women", 1820–1920. *Signs* 13 (Spring 1988) pp. 644–9.

Smythe, E. *Female pipings in Eden* (London: Peter Davies, 1934).

Stephens, J. Jessie. Interview with Jessie Stephens by Suzie Fleming and Gloden Dallas. In *Spare Rib Reader* (London: Penguin, 1982).

Stockham, A. *Karezza: ethics of marriage* (New York: Diehl, Landau & Pettit, 1886).

Tate, G. K. *London Trades Council 1860–1950* (London: Lawrence & Wishart, 1950).

Thompson, P. *Socialists, Liberals and Labour* (London: Routledge & Kegan Paul, 1967).

Tickner, T. *The Spectacle of Women: Imagery of the suffrage campaign 1907–1914* (London: Chatto & Windus, 1987).

Torr, D. *Tom Mann and his times* (London: Lawrence & Wishart, 1936).

Trades Union Congress. *The history of the* TUC (London: Trades Union Congress, 1968).

Van Voris, J. *Constance de Markievicz: in the cause of Ireland* (Amherst: University of Massachusetts Press, 1967).

Vicinus, M. *Independent women: work and community for single women, 1850–1920* (Chicago: University of Chicago Press, 1985).

Walkowitz, J. R. *Prostitution and Victorian society: women, class and the state* (Cambridge: Cambridge University Press, 1989).

Ware, V. *Beyond the pale: white women, racism and history* (London & New York: Verso, 1992).

Weller, K. *Don't be a soldier: the radical anti-war movement in North London, 1914–1918* (London: Journeymen Press, 1985).

Williams, G. Proletarian Forms: Antonio Gramsci and the Turin movement of factory councils and the origins of Italian communism. *New Edinburgh Review*, no. 25 (1974), pp. 52–76.

—. Proletarian forms: Gramsci councils and communism, 1919. A documentary analysis. *New Edinburgh Review* no. 26 (1974), pp. 48–116.

Wiltsher, A. *Most dangerous women: feminist peace campaigners of the Great War* (London: Pandora, 1985).

Wood, N. *Communism and British intellectuals* (New York: Columbia University Press, 1959).

Young, J. *Women and popular struggles: a history of Scottish and English working-class women, 1500–1984* (Edinburgh: Mainstream, 1985).

Index